HORIZON®
ANCIENT
ROME

ROBERT PAYNE

ibooks

new york

www.ibooksinc.com

An Original Publication of ibooks, inc.

CONTENTS

A TIMELESS PORTRAIT

Fifteen centuries after its fall, the Roman Empire still has the power to fascinate. The crumbling ruins and rutted roads in the lands where its mighty empire once held sway are testament to the vast scope of its greatness and a reminder of the mortality of glory.

When the first edition of the *Horizon Book of Ancient Rome* appeared in 1966, it set the standard as an introduction to this great empire, and today, it continues to be a magnificent guide-book to a civilization that had endured for more than a thousand years and left to us a bequest both timeless and dynamic.

Since the book's publication, there have been exciting discoveries and fresh interpretations that have deepened our understanding of the Roman world. Numerous archaeological excavations have found evidence of Roman architecture and communities throughout the Mediterranean and have revealed such precious jewels as the Vindolanda Tablets (a marvelous collection of private letters from Roman soldiers stationed at the Empire's lonely outpost in northern England). Increasingly sophisticated techniques in excavation have revealed entire Roman cities in northern Africa, and in the heart of Rome itself, the great Imperial markets have been unearthed and reconstructed. The Emperor Nero's palace, the *Domus Aurea,* also has been meticulously restored and opened to the public for the first time since the fall of Rome. Roman coin discoveries (the Hoxne Hoard being only one) and their display on dozens of accessible Internet sites have made it as easy to own and study a genuine piece of Roman history as it was formerly to read about it.

Along with archaeologists, historians continue to make progress uncovering the Roman world. Pioneering studies since the 1970s have given a voice to Roman women and places them squarely in the forefront of Rome's development. Ethnographers now try to map Rome's diverse racial and religious populations, and anthropological studies attempt to understand more about statistics, food supplies, common cultural and religious beliefs, often using computer technology to process vast amounts of information—an asset not yet realized when this book was originally published. Further scholarly interest has focused on the political and sociological consequences of the gaps between rich and poor, the abandonment of the individual farm, the consequences of technologies (in Rome's case, slave technologies) that resulted in unemployment, homelessness, and want. These difficult issues are as real to us today as they were in the time of the Caesars.

Popular culture has also rediscovered Rome. The success of the mini-series *I, Claudius* on PBS reflected the appeal of the ever-fascinating personalities of the Empire. A new major film epic, Ridley Scott's *Gladiator,* has made Rome a lively subject for millions who never learned a word of Latin. A new theme park near Rome is currently under construction; it will house facsimiles of the buildings from the ancient City—the Coliseum, Forum, Circus Maximus—for those who wish to sample its imagined wonders.

In the 1990s, the proliferation of personal computers and the World Wide Web brought with it a new medium through which a wider audience can gain access to the past. Internet search engines routinely return thousands of entries on a vast array of Roman subjects. The advent of web sites and computer games is evidence of a new generation of ancient history savants. Graphic designers can now try to recreate the Roman Forum as it stood in the age of Augustus with unprecedented skill and realism (as exemplified in the selection of computer-generated images that follow).

This volume uncovers the splendid panorama of the Roman world, with details on Roman statecraft, commerce, provinces, domestic life, warfare, amusements, and social customs, which all help recreate the flavor and vitality of life in that faraway age.

–Suzanne Cross and
John Altemueller
February, 2001

SWORD AND SPIRIT

Rome. It has a resonance like a deep bronze bell. It clangs like a heavy shield struck by a heavy sword. It is the keynote of a noble theme in which other names are overtones: Caesar, triumph, legion, forum, senate, emperor, pope. The majestic word has rung through twenty-seven centuries. It is one of the greatest utterances of mankind: it is heard all round the world and will not soon be silenced.

It means, first of all, Power. The appellation Rome was a mystery to the Romans themselves: they did not know what meanings were concealed within it; perhaps originally it was no more than the name of a noble Etruscan family. But in Greek there was a noun rome, meaning "strength," "vigor," "might." As the Greeks watched the little Italian city making itself into the head of a league of neighboring cities, and then dominating other Italian peoples, and fighting off foreign invaders of Italy, and conquering the whole peninsula, and extending its strength and its laws and its roads and its tax system and its language and its morality farther and farther outward from the Capitol, they came to believe that the name expressed the nature of the city and its people. Power.

And that was the center of the Roman achievement. Starting from almost nothing, a city of a few thousand citizens built up the greatest structure of political power that the western world has yet seen. It was greatest in extent, for at its widest it covered most of the known world, from Scotland to Arabia and from the Straits of Gibraltar to the Black Sea. It was greatest in durability, for it survived, in the area commanded by Constantinople and still designated the Roman empire, until the fifteenth century of our era, to fall only a generation or so before Columbus discovered the new continent. Or, looked at in another way, the Roman empire, which started from Romulus and fell before the barbarians in the fifth century of the Christian dispensation, did not die, but continued to exist for another thousand years in the Holy Roman Empire, and still exists, transformed and spiritualized, in the Holy Roman Catholic Church, whose language is Latin and whose central seat is Rome.

Roman power was more constructive than destructive. All power systems destroy those who resist them and strive to eliminate those who compete with them; so did Rome. But it rebuilt. It did not glory in building pyramids of heads as did the Assyrians or leaving mighty cities in ruins as did the Mongols. Where it conquered, it made roads and bridges and aqueducts, market places and meeting halls. In many, now desolate, regions of Turkey and North Africa and Spain and Yugoslavia, one still finds those ruined fragments of its civilizing structures that the peasants used to point to and say: "Giants made these."

Rome's power sprang from some spiritual source. What that source was, the Romans themselves did not surely know. Nor do we. Their greatest poet Vergil, gave a simple, lofty explanation of it. The dominion of Rome, he said, was willed by almighty God in order to bring peace to the warring world. Christian interpreters have often thought that, although born a pagan, Vergil was a "naturally Christian soul," and foresaw something of God's purpose in making Rome the capital of the Prince of Peace. There were others, in Vergil's day and earlier, who had a harsher explanation. These men were cultured Greeks, who saw their little city-states losing identity in the vast power system of Rome, who watched helplessly as massive wars between Romans and foreign foes or Romans and Romans devastated whole countrysides and swept through their fields and streets in a bloody avalanche, and who saw their intellectuals demoralized and their art treasures removed by rich and tasteless Roman collectors. They said that the power of Rome had no rational cause whatever and sprang from no comprehensible source. It was merely a disaster for civilization—as we ourselves should think if a race of giant apes were to emerge with irresistible weapons and dominate mankind. It proved, they held, that the world was ruled not by God but by Chance, not by Fate but by Fortune: capricious, silly, and cruel. For such men the triumph of Rome made life a "tale told by an idiot, full of sound and fury, signifying nothing." Such a conclusion was a shallow and spiteful answer to the problem. Vergil wrote his Aeneid largely in order to propose a nobler explanation that would harmonize with the willing acceptance of Roman majesty and might by many half-barbarous peoples and with the selflessness of many great Romans.

Other thoughtful men, both Roman and Greek, believed that the explanation must be that the Romans had painfully acquired, through centuries of historical struggle, a particularly strong and sensitive talent for communal effort. In the second century B.C., a well-educated and intelligent Greek called Polybius was deported to Rome as a political prisoner. He met the cultivated Roman statesmen and generals such as Scipio, the final conqueror of Carthage; traveled with them on their expeditions; watched them in their staff conferences and political meetings; and concluded that the Romans possessed a real genius for administration and for corporate achievement, which they transmitted by advice and example from one generation to the next; this was the source of their strength.

One of the principles thus transmitted was the subordination, not the sanctity, of the individual. They were keen, greedy, energetic, ambitious people, and so they devised a check on themselves. A man was unimportant in comparison with his family: it was his duty to make the family great or to maintain its greatness. A citizen was unimportant in comparison with the whole body of the citizens: he could live only through them, and if he must die for them, his death was good. A magistrate was important only during his term of office and within the limits of his authority: he had power, and majesty, and honor only because he was the embodiment of the whole community past and present.

For five hundred years the Romans governed themselves through elected magistrates. This was their main period of growth. The chief authority lay in the hands, not of one man, but of two; and not for life, but for one year, during which time the consuls were watched for any sign of personal ambition. On lower levels the other magistrates served as checks and balances on one another's power; a dictator; when an emergency compelled the state to appoint one, held his authority only for the duration of the crisis and was then forced to surrender it; and the highest power of all was not single but dual—the Senate and the Roman people.

Eventually this magnificent system was corrupted from inside by the destructive disease that it was created in order to control: personal ambition and the selfish competition of families and factions. There had been a number of dictators in the five hundred years of the republic, and many men had held absolute power for a time; but when Julius Caesar became perpetual dictator, and later when his adoptive son Augustus founded a dynasty so that power should no longer be held and transmitted by the Senate and the Roman people, but by one individual and his immediate family and kinsmen, then a noble historical enterprise came to an end. The republic fell. The empire was created on its ruins. The republic had been debilitated by personal ambitions, class enmities, and civil wars. Julius Caesar gave it the deathblow. His barely disguised monarchy lasted for four years until he was struck down by lovers of the republic in 44 B.C. Then, after enormous effort and a war that exhausted the Mediterranean world, his monarchy was re-established under tactful concealment by the brave, kindly, far-sighted, generous, surely almost godlike Gaius Julius Caesar Octavianus, who became Augustus. Less than seventy years later, his descendant Gaius Julius Caesar Germanicus, the emperor Caligula, was challenging almighty Jupiter to wrestle, and insisting that his statue be put in the Temple at Jerusalem. Not long after him came Nero.

How did Rome survive, first the early struggles against foreign enemies, and then the tyranny of crazy individualist rulers? Through another of the principles in which its growth was rooted—adaptability. The Romans never claimed to be original. They borrowed nearly everything from others and amalgamated their borrowings into their system. Yet at the same time they were scrupulously conservative. So, when Julius and then Augustus made themselves monarchs in fact, they did not abolish the Senate. They and their successors, even the lunatics and criminals, often sat in it and often held the rank of consul. Thus, the Senate survived for many centuries more and was a counterweight, however light and mobile, to the power concentrated in a single emperor.

Adaptability was not only the secret of survival for Rome. It was the secret of its civilizing mission. From the Greeks it

learned poetry, philosophy, the fine arts: it resisted them for
some time, but then assimilated them, producing poetry, philosophy, and art of its own, based on Greek form and imagination
but changed by Roman strength and Italian fancy into something new, equally viable, often equally noble. From the Greeks
it borrowed gods who could embody the impersonal numinous
presences of its own religion: it made them into its own pantheon with its own names for them. So the faceless divinity
named Grace acquired the heavenly smile and bewitching body
of the Hellenic Aphrodite, and is now, as lady Venus, better
known to the world than her Greek model. When a new conception of deity was born in Judaea its representatives came to
Rome. They were resisted by some, welcomed by others; they
struggled, and suffered, and proved themselves, and in due
course they made their way into the Senate and the emperor's
palace, and their message was at last accepted; and now, across
the Tiber, rises the mighty Roman dome of St. Peter's crowned
by the cross.

One of the most difficult things for a modern western man is
to understand the three roots of our civilization: Greece, and
Rome, and Judaea. Each of the three cultures is so complex that
it is a lifetime's work to appreciate it fully. And it is hard to do
justice to one without downgrading the others. Anyone intoxi-
cated by the clarity of Greek art and Greek philosophy, anyone
dominated by the overpowering Jewish-Christian vision of man
as a grain of dust in the Creator's hand, is tempted to dismiss
Rome as the supreme assertion of materialism. Marching armies
as efficient and cruel as the ancient Assyrians or the modern
Germans, massive buildings as graceless and senseless as the
Egyptian pyramids or the American skyscrapers, the world plundered to enrich a single city when the city's favorite amusement
was to watch men hunting animals or men in pairs killing each
other—surely it can scarcely be called a civilization except in the

external sense, wealth and vulgar pleasure, a titanic body without a heart. That would be true indeed, except for the fact that the body as it grew acquired a heart and a soul. We can hear the beating of the heart and share in the soul's strivings when we read the *Dream of Scipio,* which is Cicero's loftiest work, his assertion of the pettiness of this world and the grandeur of the cosmos and the law of duty linking the two; when we study Vergil's epic poem, hearing behind every line an echo of Homer or of Greek tragedy, seeing in the entire structure an adaptation of a Greek symphonic plan, and yet realizing as the whole wealth of its music and meaning sweep through us that there is something here which is Greek but different from Greece, which is Roman but higher than Rome itself. For noble thoughts, these men and others molded, out of a crude and narrow dialect, a masterful and subtle language in which great thoughts could be expressed. And later, when the classical speech was hardening into polite rigidity, such men as Tertullian and Saint Augustine took it over and stretched it and strained it and simplified it and strengthened it once again to carry the new message of Christianity. At first little more than the power of the sword carried Rome forward; but as it grew, it acquired the power of thought, the power of the law, and the power of religious and poetic vision. These are the spiritual powers, which it bequeathed to its heirs, the modern nations of the western world.

Gilbert Highet

At the time at which this introduction was originally written, Gilbert Highet was the Chairman of the Department of Greek and Latin at Columbia University and one of the foremost classical scholars of his day.

Some five hundred years elapsed from the date of Rome's presumed founding to the time, in the third century B.C., when it won control of Italy. Yet within another century or two it was fated (in the words that Shakespeare applied to Julius Caesar) to "bestride the world like a colossus." This map shows four stages in the building of the empire, tracing

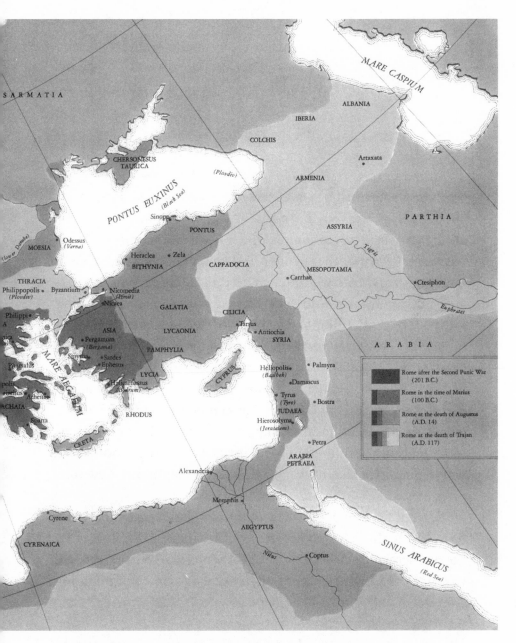

SARMATIA

MARE CASPIUM

ALBANIA

IBERIA

COLCHIS

CHERSONESUS
TAURICA

(Plovdiv)

Artaxata

ARMENIA

PONTUS EUXINUS
(Black Sea)

PARTHIA

Sinope

Odessus
(Varna)

PONTUS

ASSYRIA

Ctesiphon

MOESIA

(lower Danube)

Heraclea • Zela

Tigris

THRACIA

BITHYNIA

CAPPADOCIA

MESOPOTAMIA

Philippopolis • Byzantium

• Carrhae

(Plovdiv)

Nicomedia
(Izmit)

Euphrates

Nicaea

Philippi •

GALATIA

CILICIA

A

ASIA

LYCAONIA

Tarsus

• Pergamum

• Antiochia

ARABIA

(Bergama)

SYRIA

PAMPHYLIA

• Sardes

Pharsalus

• Ephesus

Heliopolis •

• Palmyra

MARE AEGAEUM

LYCIA

CYPRUS

(Baalbek)

• Damascus

polis

Halicarnassus

(Bodrum)

• Tyrus

• Bostra

• Athens

(Tyre)

ACHAIA

RHODUS

JUDAEA

• Sparta

Hierosolyma

(Jerusalem)

CRETA

• Petra

ARABIA
PETRAEA

Alexandria •

CYRENE

Memphis •

SINUS ARABICUS

AEGYPTUS

(Red Sea)

CYRENAICA

Nilus

• Coptus

Rome after the Second Punic War
(201 B.C.)

Rome in the time of Marius
(100 B.C.)

Rome at the death of Augustus
(A.D. 14)

Rome at the death of Trajan
(A.D. 117)

its growth from the time of Rome's victory in its desperate war for survival against Hannibal of Carthage, to the time, little more than three hundred years later, when one of its greatest emperors, Trajan, extended Roman power to its outermost geographical limits.

RECONSTRUCTED ANCIENT ROME

For well over a thousand years, artists and illustrators have portrayed the ruins of imperial Rome, using the city as a metaphor for *sic transit gloria mundi* ("thus passes the glory of the world"). Today, technology has made it possible to recreate the ancient city in 3-D computer-generated images, allowing us to visualize what the city may have looked like in its full glory nearly 2,000 years ago. Such technology was used to create the following pictures of the Forum Romanum.

Bustling with political, religious, business, and social activity, the Forum Romanum was the center of Rome's civic life during both Republic and Empire. While the Forum evolved over the centuries, the following images depict the Forum as it would have looked in A.D. 205, during Septimius Severus's rule.

Created by a team of architectural scholars, these images are based on both archeological discoveries and historical sources: the numerous excavations of the Forum, as well as the full resources of Columbia University's Avery Architectural Library with its architectural documents, maps, folio drawings, and plans of major archeological excavations. Utilizing ancient sources, contemporary scholarship, and today's computer technology, these scholar-artists have recreated the Forum's ancient grandeur—a testament to the ageless magnificence of Rome.

In the background of this aerial view of the west end of Forum Romanum, the Temple of Jupiter rests on Capitoline Hill. The smallest of the seven hills of Rome, the Capitoline was part of a strategic landscape that provided a natural fortress to keep the city safe from enemies.

The Forum, originally constructed as a public square around 600 B.C., stretches through the valley between Rome's Capitoline and Palatine hills. At its peak—during the Republic and the Empire—the Forum housed the city's main public buildings, temples, basilicas, shops, colonnades, triumphal arches, and statues.

Public speeches were often delivered from the Forum's Rostra, center, a platform initially decorated by the prows of enemy ships
captured in battle. Directly behind it stands a distinctive green
cone, the umbilicus urbis, or the navel of the city of Rome, marking the center of the city. (Documentation is inconclusive whether

the object was marble or copper, but it is known to have been green and cone-shaped.) At left is the Basilica Julia, and at right stands the Arch of Septimius Severus, which was built to commemorate the emperor's victories in the Parthian campaign in A.D. 198–202.

The rectanglar shape of the Forum was defined by the large
Basilica Aemilia, at left, and the Basilica Julia, at right, with the
Temple of the deified Julius (Caesar), center. The triumphal

columns lining the quad are topped with statues of Roman heroes; precisely which historical figures were represented is not known, but they were likely famous generals and statesmen.

This panoramic view details the layout of the Forum's northeast corner, from left to right: the Temple of the deified Julius, the Temple of
Castor and Pollux, Basilica Julia, the Tabularium (in background), and
the Basilica Aemilia. Octavian built the temple of Caesar in 29 B.C. to

honor his great uncle, Gaius Julius Caesar, who was assassinated in 44 B.C. Today, the temple's remains include only a portion of its foundation. Castor and Pollux were the divine twin sons of Jupiter and considered to be protectors of the Roman people.

These side-by-side models are based on the temple dedicated to the emperor Vespasian and the Basilica Aemilia, which in real life were separated by several hundred feet. The Basilica Aemilia was built in 179 B.C. by two censors, Marcus Aemilius Lepidus and Marcus Fulvius Nobilior. In the fifth century, the Visigoths sacked the basilica and burnt it to the ground. Traces of the destruction still remain in the form of green-spots on its marbled floor—remnants of copper coins that had melted into the marble.

A panoramic view atop the Arch of Severus, one of the best preserved monuments of the Forum, displays the tight cluster of
three temples (from left to right): the Temples of Saturn, Vespasian, and Concord. The Temple of Saturn, rebuilt many times

after its original dedication around 500 B.C., has eight surviving
Ionic columns from the temple façade, which were restored in A.D.
320. The temple was one of the most respected religious monuments of ancient Rome; it also housed the Roman treasury.

A panoramic view sweeps west along the Via Sacra, or the Sacred Way, toward the Arch of Severus. The wide road was the earliest street through the Forum. It served as a route for both solemn and triumphal

processions leading to the capitol. It was later paved, and during the reign of Nero, lined with colonnades. At right is the Basilica Aemilia, and in front of it stands the equestrian statue of Emperor Domitian.

Only three columns of the Temple of Vespasian still stand today, but this rendering suggests its original splendor. The structure was built by Domitian in A.D. 81, in honor of his father, Vespasian, and his brother, Titus.

The large building behind and to the right of the temple is the Tabularium (78 B.C.), or Hall of Records, which housed the state archives. Its arcaded façade, framed by pilasters, was a style popular by the first century B.C. The original structure survives only to first floor level, but in the sixteenth century, three new stories were built, and today, the building is used as a city hall. On the left are columns of the Temple of Saturn, and in the distance between the two temples is the Temple of Jupiter, high on Capitoline Hill.

The Basilica Julia was the largest basilica of the Forum. Its façade—approximately 110 yards long—occupied the entire side of the Forum. The basilica, begun by Caesar in 54 B.C. and completed by Augustus, was one of the great judicial buildings of the capital; it housed the civil court of the centumviri. Only the foundation remains today.

I

THE ETRUSCAN MYSTERY

The sum of things is ever being replenished, and mortals live one and all by give and take. Some races wax and others wane, and in a short space the tribes of the living are changed, and like runners hand on the torch of life.

—Lucretius, *On the Nature of Things*

Italy is a stern and rugged land that makes hard demands upon its people. There are not very many places where the earth is fertile; only the Po Valley, the lowlands of Latium around Rome, and the volcanic regions of the Campania to the south produce a natural abundance. The mountains ride the land hard; there are few rivers, few harbors, few plains. The Apennines form a spiny ridge down the whole length of the country, dividing it in two, making it difficult in ancient times to form a united people. The land was always an enemy to be conquered, and it bred tough, resourceful men. Even today it offers them backbreaking labor and few rewards.

We think of Italy as a boot poised delicately over the Mediterranean, but to the Italians themselves it resembles a muscular and thickly veined arm plunging out of Europe into a dangerous sea. We remember the calm sunlight and the ripening fruits, but the Italian peasant is more inclined to remember the bitterness of winter. The gaunt mountains, the remote valleys, and the lack of communications fostered the growth of isolated communities of farmers, shepherds, and woodsmen living out primitive lives in secluded hamlets, maintaining themselves with difficulty, and living in fear of the next hamlet over the hill. Yet this narrow arm of Europe, forbidding in many respects, was inviting in others. It offered temperate climate, good pasturage, ample timber, and a strategic position with eventual promise of raid or trade.

When we see Italy first in the interval between the darkness of prehistory and the dawn of the first, large, settled communities, the original inhabitants are being pushed deeper and deeper into their remote fastnesses by invaders who have come down from central Europe over the Alpine passes or from the Balkans by way of the bend of the Adriatic. The invaders came in wave upon wave, and just as the aboriginal inhabitants were pushed back into more desolate regions, so they in turn were dispossessed and forced to occupy less desirable lands. It was the time of the great folk wanderings that marked the end of the Bronze Age and that set the whole Mediterranean area astir with new blood. Men known as Dorians were moving down into Greece, superseding the ancient cultures of Mycenae and Crete. In Italy nameless tribes moved like shadows over the land, leaving scarcely any trace of themselves. At the beginning of the last millennium before Christ we cannot yet speak of a civilized presence there. Most of the peninsula, however, had been occupied by Indo-European tribes speaking related dialects. They raised horses, sheep, and cattle, lived in round huts made of mud-daubed wattle, and farmed their lands with the same primitive instruments they had employed before they entered Italy. They were not a nation, but formed independent tribal communities. One last wave of these Indo-European tribesmen, known as the Latins, entered Italy in the ninth or eighth century B.C. and established itself among the dark crater lakes and high cone-shaped mountains of the Alban hills: these were to become the Romans.

The boundaries of the tribes were unstable and continually

changing. We know that the Veneti occupied the territory at the head of the Adriatic, the Piceni occupied the central Adriatic coast, the Samnites were in the hill country east of Campania; the Sabines, Aequi, and Volscians were in the regions northeast, east, and south of the Latins. There were also countless sub-tribes, each with its local loyalties and local gods. Here and there small pockets of the original neolithic inhabitants remained, but they too were falling under the sway of the invaders.

About this time there began to appear on the western coast of Italy a new tribe that challenged the settled habits of the invaders and radically changed the fortunes of Italy. They were a hard, warlike people determined to carve out new settlements. These were the Etruscans, whose origins remain cloaked in mystery, but who were to stride forth as the first civilized folk in Italy, immensely gifted and original in art and governance. They were to contribute to the making of Rome a vast store of skill, from the use of the arch and the organization of a town to the ceremonials of majesty, the first structure of civil polity, and the rituals of augury and respect for the gods. As they expanded from their coastal settlements, near the Tyrrhenian Sea, they became Italy's first city builders and men of money, at a time when the Latin tribes to the south of them were still lit-tle more than unlettered peasants bent on local feud and har-vest. Any chronicle of Rome must begin with these extraordinary settlers of Etruria, who both awakened and for a time ruled the future capital. Their influence upon the Romans was to remain profound over the centuries, matched in later years by that of Greece, to which the Etruscans themselves had also become beholden. The composite civilization we know as Roman owed immense debts to both.

There are so many mysteries about the origin of the Etr-uscans that scholars despair of a solution. In the fifth century B.C. the Greek historian Herodotus declared that they came from

Lydia in Anatolian Asia Minor. He tells how the Lydians, suffering from famine, quietly reconciled themselves to their fate and for eighteen years amused themselves by playing dice, knucklebones, and ball. However, when conditions did not change King Atys decided that half the population should be sent away to colonize a more fruitful land. At Smyrna (the present Izmir) they built a fleet, put their household objects on board, and set sail under the command of Tyrrhenus, the king's son. It was evidently a long voyage, for we are told that they skirted many lands. When they settled in Italy they no longer called themselves Lydians, but adopted the name of Tyrrhenoi after their princely leader. (It should perhaps be noted here that the hellenized term *Tyrrhenoi*, meaning the "Etruscans," has also been thought by modern scholars to derive from the word *Tyrra*, which was the name of a locality in Lydia.)

According to Herodotus, the Lydians were a charming and resourceful people who enjoyed pleasure and the wealth that flowed down to them in the gold-bearing streams of Mount Tmolus. Herodotus believed that they were the first people to engage in retail trade and the first to mint gold and silver coins. He describes, too, how the Lydians built a tomb in Sardes to honor the father of King Croesus with five columns bearing inscriptions showing who had contributed to the work, and notes that the prostitutes had contributed more than the merchants and the artisans. Herodotus, who saw the tomb, described it as one of the wonders of the world, comparable to the pyramids and the works of the Babylonians.

Herodotus is not, of course, an infallible guide, but since he is often surprisingly accurate when he seems to be telling old wives' tales, he deserves to be read sympathetically. He is quite certain that the Lydians settled in Etruria, and he was not alone in this belief. Among the Roman historians it was generally believed that the Etruscans originally came from Lydia, and

Vergil, Horace, and Ovid often call the Etruscans Lydians in their poems.

Four centuries after Herodotus, the Greek historian Dionysius of Halicarnassus rejected the theory of an oriental origin for the Etruscans. He said they were an indigenous people who had inhabited Italy from time immemorial, and he pointed out that they neither spoke the Lydian language nor worshiped the Lydian gods. He wrote that "they cannot be said to preserve any trait which may be considered to derive from their supposed homeland" and dismissed all those chroniclers who thought otherwise as pure fantasists.

Living in the age of Augustus, Dionysius of Halicarnassus had advantages over modern scholars. He was living at a time when the Etruscan language was still being spoken and their sacred books and traditional histories were still in existence. As late as Cicero's time we hear of Roman aristocrats sending their sons to Tarquinii, the old Etruscan capital, to learn the language and to study the sacred lore, and in the first century A.D. we find the emperor Claudius writing a history of the Etruscans in twenty volumes, which are now lost. A vast amount of written information about them was available. Still, Dionysius was not wholly dependable, if only because he was composing a history designed to prove that Rome's founders were in reality Greeks.

Today scholars are still divided: there are those who hold that Etruscans were indigenous to Italy and those who follow Herodotus and accept an Asiatic origin. In any event, there are resemblances between the arts of the Etruscans and those of the Lydians. Vaulted tombs with painted frescoes found in Lydia are remarkably similar to the painted tombs of the Etruscans. Etruscan names like Tarchon, Tarquinii, and Tages are common in Asia Minor, where Tarkhuni was the name of a storm god. Though we know comparatively little about the language of the Etruscans, we know that they employed the genitive case ending *-al*, which is also found in Asia Minor. In 1885 there was discovered on the island of Lemnos, in the Aegean, a seventh-century B.C. funerary stele bearing the portrait of a warrior grasping a spear with two inscriptions in Greek characters, though the language was not Greek. Scholars pointed to an apparent similarity between these words and others found in Etruria. A similar stele, with a design of a warrior grasping a two-bladed axe, was subsequently discovered in Vetulonia, in Etruria. For the first time a link between the ancient cultures of Lydia and Etruria seemed to have been established. Yet, though Etruscan art suggests Asiatic influences, it was also rooted in the earthy vigor of the Italian soil.

Wherever these mysterious people came from, they were a people with a highly developed civilization far superior to that of the earlier Indo-European invaders. They were not only farmers and fishermen, but merchants and adventurers, with a taste for grandeur and ostentatious luxury, proud of their artistic skills. Determined colonizers, they were soon spread out from Tuscany to Umbria and Latium, building their fortified cities on hilltops. Their fleets sailed out into the Tyrrhenian and Ionian seas. They appear to have established colonies in Corsica and to have traded with Sardinia (then under Carthaginian influence) and with the Balearic Islands, possibly setting up posts there as well. During the seventh and sixth centuries B.C. they were carving out a small empire of their own, reaching up the Po Valley in the north and toward the Greek settlements clustered in southern Italy and Sicily. They were a people on the march.

The presence of Greeks on the peninsula was also a result of great stir and movement throughout the Mediterranean area. Dorian and Ionian invaders had descended upon mainland Greece before the start of the millennium. Then they had spread over the Aegean islands and the Asia Minor coast, founding local colonies or city-states as they advanced. The next step, beginning in the eighth century B.C., saw these individual settlements engaging in colonization efforts of their own as they grew and as the eyes of many of their citizens turned westward in search for ampler space. A highly imaginative technique was worked out by Greeks and specifically by those of Euboea and Corinth and Ephesus: it was that of encouraging citizen groups to sail forth and found daughter-cities that would be bound to the parent city by ties of blood, interest, and worship of common local gods, but that would be politically almost autonomous. Thus, colonists from Euboea (the long island that flanks and hugs the seaward site of Attica) in about 750 B.C. established a western offshoot at Cumae, on the Campanian shore of Italy, from which the city of Naples was to emerge. Further south, Megara and Croton (the latter to become the seat of the philosopher Pythagoras) also came into being. Sicily saw the founding of the Greek outposts of Syracuse and Acragas, well selected by colonizers and sailors for their harbors and commanding coastal positions. The thrust of the Greeks led them to found colonies or trading stations as far west as Marseilles and along the Spanish coast.

The western Greeks, as historians have called them, were adventurous men, profoundly tied by ancestry and culture to the emerging life of the Greek mainland. From at least the seventh century B.C. on, they were a major civilizing influence in the central and western Mediterranean. They carried over into western Europe the skills and fine craftsmanship they had learned in the East. They came as colonizers, not conquerors.

While the western Greeks were diffusing their culture in the central Mediterranean, the Carthaginians were exerting formidable naval power from their bases along the North African coast. The trade routes and spheres of influence of the three contending peoples—Greeks, Etruscans, and Carthaginians—

were continually crossing, and conflicts were inevitable. In the West the advantages lay with Carthage and Etruria, which set about forming an uneasy alliance against the Greeks.

In this struggle for domination the Etruscans possessed one great advantage denied to their adversaries: the rich and extensive iron deposits on the island of Elba. In addition they made good use of the deposits of lead, copper, and iron at Volaterrae, Vetulonia, and Populonia, on the mainland. Iron gave them armor, battle-axes, grappling hooks, the sharp prows of their ships. The Greeks credited them with the invention of the iron anchor (though scholars since have disputed this). Iron, indeed, appears to have been the basis of their economy and their power.

One would scarcely guess how great a part iron played in their culture by looking at their ruined towns and surviving works of art. Iron rusts and crumbles away, and few of their pots and pans, sometimes shown in charming relief on the walls of their funeral chambers, have survived. A good deal of their wealth may have come from the export of everyday kitchen hardware. That they were indeed wealthy is shown by the gold ornaments—bracelets, necklaces, and pectorals of exquisite delicacy—found in their tombs.

Unlike most of the Indo-European invaders of Italy, the Etruscans possessed a body of laws, believed to have been transmitted to earth by the gods. Cicero in the first century B.C. tells the legend of a plowman at Tarquinii who was once working his field when his plow turned up from a furrow the god Tages, who had the appearance of a child and the wisdom of an old man. The plowman cried out in surprise and wonder, and soon a crowd assembled to see the prodigy who had risen from the earth. Tages then revealed to the assembled Etruscans the laws for interpreting omens. According to another story, a nymph named Vegoia appeared to them and revealed the divine laws governing ritual and even the principles of measurement. Codes were established, governing the study of thunder and lightning and the entrails of beasts for purposes of divination. The Etruscans became adept in the arts of augury.

These arts were well known in ancient Babylon, where examination of entrails and the study of storms were practiced assiduously. The Babylonians, like the Etruscans, interpreted the meaning of a peal of thunder according to the particular day or month. The Etruscan augurs, facing southward, divided the sky into sixteen segments—eight on their left, eight on their right—and sought to foretell the future by observing the direction from which a bolt of lightning fell, and by the brilliance and color of its light. Lightning on the left promised good fortune; on the right, evil tidings. The lightning of the supreme god Tinia was always blood red, whereas the other gods wrote across the sky in other colors. In this way the gods spoke to the people, sometimes promising abundance of crops, sometimes foretelling a coming drought or a future victory. The Etruscans also examined the entrails of the animals they sacrificed, and they were especially concerned to examine the liver, which they thought of as representing the seat of life.

The entire doctrine of divination was later taken over by the Romans, who translated the original texts. Plutarch wrote in the first century A.D. that when Romulus founded Rome he called upon Etruscan priests to superintend the foundation rites. They consulted their laws, ordered a circular trench to be dug, and filled it with offerings and first fruits. The trench was called *mundus*, a word which the Etruscans used both for the circle of a city and for the circle of the heavens. In time the Romans used the word to mean the "world." And many other strange customs of the early Romans were probably inherited from the Etruscans.

Yet it would be a mistake to suggest that the Etruscans were

a solemn people burdened with mysteries. Magic and divination
were the commonplaces of the ancient world, and the Greeks in
the age of Socrates often practiced strange rites of divination,
summoning up the dead and holding converse with the moon.
Such practices were an essential part of ordinary living. The
men of Etruria, who dug tunnels through hills, drained lakes,
diverted rivers, built furnaces, and sailed into the Atlantic,
combined their dependence on omens with bold adventure.

They were a people who lived in the open and enjoyed
dancing, horse racing, and gladiatorial contests. They especially
relished the theatre, and Livy credited them with the invention
of satirical drama. Their women possessed remarkable sexual
freedom. The Greek historian Theopompus, writing in the middle of the fourth century B.C., tells how Etruscan women were
shared "in common"; Herodotus describes them as exercising in
the nude with men and mentions that they attended banquets
not with their husbands but in the company of the men who
pleased them. Herodotus may have been exaggerating, but the
Roman comic poet Plautus, writing a century later, reproached
the Etruscan girls for being inveterate wantons. Few children, it
was said, knew their fathers. Sexual relations were conducted
openly, without shame. Men enjoyed the same liberty as
women, and Theopompus observes that "though the men
approached the women with great pleasure, they derived as
much pleasure from the company of adolescents and boys."
Aristotle noted that Etruscan men and women dined together
on the same couch with a common mantle over them.

Both the Romans and the Greeks somewhat wistfully
regarded the Etruscans as devotees of sexual freedom, lovers of
luxurious living, gaily indifferent to the moral codes. The early
Romans were especially shocked by the freedom given to the
women of Etruria, since they themselves kept their wives subordinate and permitted them no voice in government or civil

affairs. Unlike early Roman women, Etruscan women spoke their mind in public and regarded themselves as men's equals. Theopompus tells us that their women were unusually beautiful, and the paintings in funeral chambers and terra-cotta images confirm this. The charge of profligacy may not be generally applicable, for there are countless paintings and funerary statues showing husband and wife reclining on the same couch, embracing with exquisite tenderness.

But if the private lives of the Etruscans were free, their public lives were severely disciplined by their aristocratic rulers, one for each of the twelve city-states that formed the Etruscan confederacy. The people worked hard, there were continual wars, and there can have been few prolonged periods of rest. They were building ships, mining iron, spreading across north-

The wall painting, above, of a couple provides an example of how these civilized Etruscans left brilliant, if silent, testimony to their life in the form of art.

ern Italy, and reaching toward the Adriatic, where they founded the naval port of Spina, now silted over, but once a place of great power and wealth. The bronze statues of their warriors show lean, hard-muscled men armed with spears or short stabbing swords; they have the look of conquerors.

Power belonged to the local prince, the *lucumon*, who appears to have combined the roles of magistrate and high priest. His person was surrounded with brilliant panoply, and it was deliberately intended that he should live in a world so remote from the common people that he would have the appearance of a god. He presided over audiences once a week, but it would appear that only the nobility attended. One of the *lucumones* was chosen to act as king of the confederacy, but in practice the powers of the local prince were probably autonomous. The confederacy consisted of a loose linking of independent states, all of which had a common culture and a common purpose.

The emblems and privileges of the *lucumones* were worked out with special care. When the *lucumon* appeared in public everything about him glittered. He wore a gold diadem, a toga patterned with palms, or with the images of the gods. He sat on an ivory folding stool decorated with plaques of ivory and carried an ivory scepter and took part in processional triumphs in a gilded, four-horse chariot with gold horse trappings. In front of him marched the lictors bearing the emblem of sovereignty, a bundle of elm rods tied with a scarlet strap and enclosing an axe, the head of which jutted above the rods. These emblematic weapons, known as fasces, symbolized the prince's absolute authority over life and limb. The historian Diodorus Siculus wrote that the Etruscans were "the authors of that dignity which surrounds rulers." The Romans, vividly aware of the impression created by the dazzling appearance of an Etruscan prince, wore the entire panoply, and their consuls and magistrates unashamedly borrowed the same clothing and carried the same insignia as the *lucumones*. The military standard topped with a bronze eagle was originally Etruscan; so, too, was the scarlet military cloak worn by a Roman general in the field and the purple-bordered toga of the nobility.

The Etruscans handed down to the Romans a multitude of forms, traditions, and observances, which were assimilated into the body of Roman customs. And while panoply and divination were among the greatest gifts transmitted to the Romans, there were also smaller gifts. Etruscan words entered the Roman vocabulary, and some of them have survived into our own language. *Antenna, histrio, persona, magister, atrium, sacer, caerimonia* were all originally Etruscan words. *Antenna* was originally a yard-arm, *histrio* comes from *hister*, the Etruscan word for an actor, *persona* appears to be derived from the Etruscan word *phersu*, denoting a mask. Scholars are still attempting to find out how many other Etruscan words are concealed in Latin vocabularies, and what effect Etruscan grammar may have had on Latin grammar in its formative stages. Though philologists have worked for decades, they are still far from solving these problems, because the Etruscan language has proved curiously difficult to translate. Some ten thousand inscriptions, usually very brief, have survived, but only about one hundred root words can be translated with accuracy. A few are surprisingly close to modern English. The Etruscan *cupe* means "cup," *nefis* means "nephew" or "grandson," and the Etruscan *mi* means "me."

But it was in the realm of religion that Etruscan influence on Rome went deepest. "In the West, in antiquity, there was no people more given to rites of all sorts than the Etruscans," writes the modern authority Raymond Bloch, adding that "this constant attitude of anxiety vis-a-vis the divine powers who regulate the life of man is undoubtedly one of the characteristic traits of this extraordinary nation." Ancient writers, as Bloch observes, also noticed this. Thus the Roman historian Livy remarked that they were a people all the more devoted to religious rites because they excelled in the art of performing them. The body of revelation gathered in the sacred books known as the *disciplina Etrusca*, set forth complex codes of ritual and behavior—so complex that only the Etruscan college of priests could interpret them. The priests presented themselves as the sole interpreters of the divine will; and the *lucumon*, moving in a divine radiance and acting as the supreme pontiff, would interpret the will of the gods with regard to important matters of state.

The Etruscan gods who ruled the earth from their abodes in the high heavens are generally depicted with a quiet and kindly gravity. Tinia, the lord of the skies, was the most powerful, for he was granted three thunderbolts, whereas the other gods were granted one. He was not the absolute master of heaven, but the chairman of the board who looked for advice to the other gods. He was permitted to hurl one thunderbolt at his pleasure; he could hurl the second only after he received the approval of the rest; and the terrible third bolt could only be hurled when all the gods in concert demanded it. Tinia was usually flanked by his wife Uni and his virgin daughter Menerva. There was a god of fire called Sethlans, who was especially worshiped in the iron-smelting centers, and a goddess of female beauty and enchantment called Turan (Venus), which may mean the "lady" or simply the "goddess." Maris was the god of war and Turms was the god of trade. As contacts with the Greeks increased we find the Greek gods entering the Etruscan pantheon. Under the names of Apulu and Artumes we find the familiar figures of Apollo and Artemis. The Etruscan Hercle is of course Heracles. These gods were taken over bodily and no attempt was made to disguise their origin; and with the gods came their legends.

While the Etruscans entertained a deep affection for the

Greek gods, they did not follow the Greeks in their form of worship, nor did they copy the shape of the Greek temple. They had their own way of venerating the gods, with a direct and concentrated approach to divinity. Whereas the Greek temple was designed to be beautiful on all four sides and to radiate its presence in all directions, the Etruscan temple was designed to be beautiful only from the front. There were usually two entrances to the Greek temple, on the east and west; there was only one entrance to the Etruscan temple, which backed against the wall of the sacred enclosure. The temple was approached by a high stairway reaching to a platform with a colonnaded portico opening on three chambers, the larger chamber being occupied by a powerful god while the side chambers were occupied by his divine attendants. All over ancient Etruria we find traces of such temples. When they built the great temple to Jupiter on the Capitoline hill, the Romans imitated the Etruscans by building a high stairway, a portico, and three chambers—one for Jupiter, one for Juno, and one for Minerva. They probably employed Etruscan architects, and it is known from historical records that they employed an Etruscan sculptor to make the terra-cotta images of the gods.

Among the Romans there was a tradition that during the first one hundred seventy years following the foundation of Rome there were no statues of deities at all. The gods were mysterious presences, having neither form nor features; they were felt rather than seen. Sometimes the gods took up their abodes in trees or stones, and sometimes altars were raised to them; here they were placated with offerings and sacrifices. From the beginning the Etruscans made their gods in the images of men. Like the Greeks, they rejoiced in their gods in human form and saw no reason to worship the invisible presences.

They fashioned their gods nobly, and many statues of them have survived. In the Museum of the Villa Giulia, in Rome, there stands the Apollo with a hole in his back and one leg half destroyed, found in 1916 among the ruins of Veii; but the springing energy in the warm life-sized terra-cotta figure remains undiminished by time. The Apollo dates from the end of the sixth century B.C., a time when, according to Livy, the influence of Etruria extended over the whole of Italy, from the Alps to the Straits of Messina. It is Apollo in all his majesty, superbly in command. He leans slightly forward, the curve of his body forming a benediction, an archaic smile hovering on his lips. Although he betrays his Greek origin, he is fashioned with purely Etruscan feeling. This warmth of feeling, combined with a suggestion of Hellenic influences, is also present in the terra-cotta figure of an enthroned woman with child, which has been thought by some to represent the Mother Goddess. Her strong hands hold the child in its swaddling clothes with an exquisite tenderness; and there is about that statue, now lost in one of the dark corners of the museum, a quiet and brooding monumentality. In looking at a photograph of it you would hardly guess that it is only three feet high.

But it is in the painted tomb chambers and funerary sculptures that we come closest to the religious and human feeling of the Etruscans. Terra-cotta statues show husband and wife reclining together in death on a couch, the sculptor suggesting their continuing affection for one another, their silent enjoyment of each other's presence. These are people who gaze on death calmly, looking out on the world as though they had just awakened from a refreshing sleep. In the painted tomb chambers in the hills above Tarquinii there is a sense of spaciousness and airy lightness, as though another sun were shining in the underworld. The colors are apple green, sky blue, red, orange, yellow, the colors of spring; in one painting we see musicians and dancers, wrestlers and jugglers, youths on their high-stepping horses, lovers caught in an eternal embrace. There are

One of the most famous Etruscan works of art, the Apollo of Veii, above, was created at the end of the sixth century B.C. Apollo was one of the many gods adopted by the Etruscans directly from the Greeks. Apparently even his functions as god of order and reason and artistic inspiration were not changed by the move.

chariot races and bullfights. Always there is the sense of movement, of life's pleasures continuing after death. Only rarely are
there moments of solemnity as in the Tomb of Augurs, where
among hovering birds we see professional mourners standing
before blood-red gates that symbolize the barrier between the
living and the kingdom of death. Sometimes, too, we encounter
the demons of hell with their bright blue faces and serpentine
hair; yet their presence is rare. Far more frequent are scenes of
banqueting. For the function of these paintings was more than
a decorative one; it had a magical intent, designed to re-create
for the dead man in his tomb the surroundings of his earthly
life and to prolong by means of pictures his relationship with
the living.

Etruscan art suggests a people charged with energy, vividly
alive, sinewy and alert, delighting in color and the joys of the
flesh, but capable of enduring the hardships of war. They were
not, one would have thought, a people who would vanish from
the earth, and in fact they did not vanish entirely. The Romans
destroyed the confederacy of the twelve city-states, but the Etruscans remained in Umbria, Tuscany, and Latium, giving their
features and their gifts to their descendants. As a people they
survived until 82 B.C. when Sulla ordered a general massacre.
Then, at last, they lost the remnants of their independence. By
the second century A.D. there was scarcely anyone alive who
could speak Etruscan or read the sacred books. Yet as late as the
fifth century A.D. a few Etruscan priests could be found among
the entourage of the emperor Julian.

The mystery is how so great a culture could have perished. A
strange silence surrounds them. We have the paintings, the
sculptures, the jewelry, a host of stone inscriptions, but the living voice is absent. If all the books written by the Greeks had
perished, and we knew them only by their works in the world's
museums, we would conclude that they had reached marvelous

heights in artistic expression, but we would know little about their thoughts. We do not know just what was said in the long-lost sacred books of Etruscan ritual and divination, and we might not comprehend them even if we found them. Most of what we know about the Etruscans comes down through Roman legends. We would know more about the Etruscans, and per-haps more about their language, if the history of the Etruscans written by the emperor Claudius had survived. No Etruscan grammar or dictionary by Roman scholars has been found. A recent discovery at San Severo, near the site of the ancient sea-

This sarcophagus showing an affectionate married couple reclining on a couch was fashioned in the sixth century B.C. The Etruscans believed that if the soul was properly supplied with the necessities of life as well as some of its luxuries, it would stay in the houselike tomb that had been prepared for it. The relatives of the deceased had dual motives for taking good care of the dead; naturally they wanted the soul to live happily ever after, but they also believed that if the spirit became discontent it would leave its abode to return to haunt the living.

port of Caere, of three thin gold plates inscribed in Punic and Etruscan to record the dedication of a temple to the Carthaginian goddess Astarte, may have provided a clue in the form of a parallel text, and scholars of Punic may be able to solve a problem which has baffled scholars of Etruscan for centuries. Meanwhile the Etruscan enigma remains. All we know is that there arose in early Italy a brilliant and charming people whose influence fed into the mainstream of Italian culture and helped to shape the destinies of Rome.

II

THE SEVEN HILLS

The fates were resolved, I believe, upon the founding of this great city and the beginning of the mightiest of empires, next after that of heaven.

—Livy, *A History of Rome*

According to a pleasant Roman fiction Rome was founded by a chieftain named Romulus on April 21, 753 B.C. at about eight o'clock in the morning.

This story appears in Plutarch. Archaeologists and historians, however, have long looked upon the tale as unsubstantiated and outside the realm of record. They are inclined to doubt whether the city's foundation took place as early as the eighth century. They are not sure that anyone called Romulus ruled over the Romans. So many layers of legend have accumulated over the figure of Romulus that if there ever was such a man, he has all but vanished beneath their weight. At various times before the dawn of history many chieftains and many tribes must have contended for those hills that rose strategically out of the marshes to dominate the Tiber. But Rome's actual origins remain dark. There is a sense in which the small, precarious settlement was less the result of the work of men's hands than of the marriage of the river and the hills.

When we first become aware of these hills in early time, they are occupied by various tribes fighting for the control of river crossings that offered passage between the south and what was to become Etruria, and perhaps also to the salt flats near the river's mouth. There were many tribes and each had its own totems, its own gods, its own customs. Though most of them shared a common Indo-European heritage, they showed no particular love for one another, each tribe being jealous of its own power and its own divinities. The tribesmen were shepherds, hunters, farmers, cattle thieves, occasional merchants and lived in small huts crowding the wooded heights. The hut poles were planted firmly in the soft volcanic tufa; there was a hearth or earthenware furnace in the center of the hut and a roof hole to draw off smoke. Such primitive dwellings, often round in shape, are found even today in the Campania, south of Rome, and their design has scarcely changed over the centuries.

No names can be attached to the first settlers. They represent various Iron Age cultures. We know that some buried their dead in hollowed-out oak trees; others cremated them and stored the ashes in votive jars. These remains have been unearthed in the Roman Forum, about five acres of land between the Palatine and Capitoline hills that were to become the center of a vast empire. In early days the Forum was nothing more than a marsh, fed by springs, with here and there a few dry knolls rising above it. In the rainy season it became a lake. Yet this marshland had a special importance, for the pathways from the south and the east met there, whereas beyond the river were those to the north. The word *forum* means "the place outside the door." It was the area outside the little hill settlements of the early tribesmen, where they could meet and exchange goods without trespassing on one another's land. Even as Rome grew, *forum* always kept its dual meaning—"meeting place" and "market."

Gradually, as time passes, we are able to recognize some of the tribes on the hills. The Sabines, congregating from the mountain valleys in central Italy, which their Indo-European

ancestors had settled, were entrenched on the Quirinal, worshiping the sun and moon and the god Quirinus, whose name
was thought to mean the "lance bearer." Generally they were a
rather phlegmatic people, but they were ferocious in battle and
famous for their long shields. Some Greek influence had
touched them, and there was a vague tradition that they came
originally from Sparta.

On the Palatine there lived a Latin tribe formed of refugees
from Alba Longa, a settlement on the shores of the Alban Lake,
about a dozen miles southwest of Rome. The Latins' presence
was explained by early chroniclers in the tale of Romulus and
Remus. According to the myth, Romulus and Remus were the
twin sons of Rhea Silvia of the royal house of Alba Longa. She
was a vestal virgin, who had made a vow of perpetual chastity.
When she produced children her uncle, who had usurped the
throne, imprisoned her and ordered the babies to be drowned,
even though she claimed she had been raped by the god Mars.
The men who were ordered to drown the babies, instead, left
them on the banks of the flooded Tiber, where they were suckled by a wolf and fed by a woodpecker, which made its home in
the shelter of a sacred fig tree. The wolf, the woodpecker, and
the fig tree were probably tribal totems arranged to lend a kind
of sanctity to the children of Rhea Silvia. A shepherd, Faustulus, found them at last and carried them home to be brought up
by his wife. The brothers grew up to be robbers who shared
their spoils with Faustulus. One day Remus was caught and
taken before the king of Alba Longa. Romulus came to help his
brother, and together they killed the monarch. After they had
restored the rightful king to the throne, they left their native
town, but they took with them a small band of landless and
masterless men.

Romulus took possession of the Palatine hill and founded a
new principality, marking out its limits by plowing the bound-

aries of a special area on the hill and sanctifying them by sacrifice. He was a man of daemonic energy and a forceful diplo-
mat. Romulus and Remus soon became rivals, however, for
Remus declared that he in turn would build his own settlement
on the Aventine hill nearby. As the city walls of Romulus were
rising, the rivalry grew intense. Remus jumped over his
brother's wall in a symbolic gesture that was part jest, part
challenge, and Romulus killed him. It was a senseless crime that
could never be expunged. At intervals throughout their history,
the Romans felt the spell of this original bloodguilt and acted
out the myth with monotonous frequency in their fratricidal
civil wars and palace murders.

Romulus does not appear to have confined his realm to the
Palatine alone. He is said to have swelled the ranks of his followers by appealing to the heterogeneous and fugitive elements—the young, the landless, the murderers. He offered them
land, booty, and a lawless life, and prepared for them a retreat
on the Capitoline hill which was called the *asylum inter duos
lucos* (that is, a place of refuge between the two wooded heights
of the Capitoline). Dimly discernible behind the legend is the
familiar image of the bandit chieftain, the resourceful man of
war and stratagems, towering above his band of followers
because he possesses an indomitable spirit of violence.

The attentive reader of legends soon learns to look for
chains of logic concealed among the fairy tales, and sometimes
the most improbable legends contain their own logic. Even in
fable Romulus seems to be acting out a consistent role. The stories told about him have a ring of truth; those of his origins are
such as a bandit might deliberately invent in order to impress
his followers. It is said that when he died he was carried up to
heaven in a thundercloud, and this too is the kind of legend
that might be invented about a war chief venerated by his followers. A loftier tale, immortalized by Vergil, set forth the idea

Rome, which was to become the jealous guardian of an empire, had as its emblem a bronze likeness of a she-wolf, the animal that suckled Romulus and Remus in the legend of the city's founding. The ancient Etruscan statue, above, was discovered on the Capitoline; the twins were added during the Renaissance.

that the primordial father of Rome was Aeneas, the Trojan chieftain who survived his city's fall at the hand of the Greeks and brought his followers to a promised land, where he sired the breed that produced Romulus. The Aeneas legend was surely splendid poetic invention; yet the Romulus of the myths has the appearance of being the memory of an actual man.

The famous story of the rape of the Sabine women is plausible, given the character that legend assigns to the followers of Romulus. A lack of wives to share the beds of the outcasts and fugitives and to produce offspring may have provoked this first Roman assault upon neighbors. The Roman stratagem was a simple one. Romulus announced that somewhere in his territory

an altar to the god Consus had been found buried in the earth.
Then, as now, buried objects possessed magical significance in
the Mediterranean world, and people would travel a great distance to see them. According to legend, the neighboring tribesmen (most of whom were of Sabine stock) were invited to attend
the ceremonies in honor of the newly discovered altar and to
bring their womenfolk. They came willingly and they were
unarmed. Romulus and his followers, who were armed, had no
difficulty in capturing the women and speeding off with them.
According to the Mauretanian king Juba II, who became one of
the most learned antiquarians of the Augustan age, 683 women
were captured. Another tradition states that only 30 women
were seized. Whatever the number, Romulus had acquired a
useful addition to the population and had shown that he was
perfectly capable of defying the gods by breaking the sacred
truce. Though few in number, his followers had administered a
psychological shock to the Sabines, who were unlikely to
recover without winning a full-scale war against Rome.

Yet curiously we hear of no war, only of a series of retalia-
tory campaigns that met with little success. The long truce that
appears to have followed had enduring consequences, for it laid
the foundations for the dual government which was to be characteristic of Rome in later years. Since neither side had won, an
agreement was made that the seven hills should be governed
jointly by Romulus and by Titus Tatius, the chieftain who ruled
over the Sabines. This system of joint rule was to be revived at
intervals throughout Roman history. When Rome was ruled by
consuls, they were generally appointed in pairs; nearly all the
important officers of state also worked in pairs, each checking
the activities of the other. The Romans were proud of this safeguard against tyrannical rule, and in later years it pleased them
to remember that they had brought reason and intelligence into
the art of government.

Far from being the conqueror of all the hills of Rome, Romulus appears to have been merely the chieftain who finally accepted a life of amity with the neighboring Sabines. Following his death they are said to have taken possession of the Palatine, and the small principality founded by Romulus was joined to the far larger community of the Sabines.

In time more and more legends accumulated around the memory of Romulus, "the son of the she-wolf." He was credited with the capture of Alba Longa, the original seat of his royal house, and with a great but unlikely victory over Veii, an almost impregnable Etruscan citadel some twelve miles north of Rome. He was remembered as the founder-father, the shaper of destinies, the stern lawgiver, and the great harasser of the countryside; and his memory was kept alive by his followers. Primitive ceremonies arose about him, many to survive for a thousand years. At the festival of Lupercalia, youths sacrificed goats in the cave where the wolf had suckled Romulus and Remus, below the western slope of the Palatine, and then ran around the hill wearing loincloths; they carried strips of goatskin with which they struck women to promote fertility. The Sabines paid tribute to Romulus in their own way by calling him Quirinus after their own god of war, with the result that the Romans eventually adopted Quirinus as a second war god, to rule with Mars. It was as though the dual system of government extended even to the deities.

The legendary Romulus remains a mysterious figure. He left no dynasty, no body of doctrine, no tables of law. Yet some emanation of dynamic purpose was believed to flow from him after his death. In Romulus, the Romans found the symbol of an all-powerful king. In the Forum there survives a part of a four-sided column, which may represent the cenotaph of Romulus, bearing in archaic lettering an inscription intended perhaps as a proclamation of divine vengeance against those who would

pollute a place that was sacred to a king. We can read only a
few words: *sakros, recei, kalatorem, iouxmenta*—"sacred," "for
the king," "attendant," "beasts of burden." This broken stone—
the city's oldest surviving document—suggests the awe surrounding the kingship.

The immediate successor of Romulus was the Sabine king
Numa Pompilius, whose long reign was devoted, if we can trust
the chroniclers, to the pursuit of peace. Tradition ascribed to
him the kingly virtue of benevolence. He inaugurated many
rites that were to endure with little change until the advent of
Christianity, and he was especially remembered as the king who
installed the pontiffs in their office. The word *pontiff* comes
from the Latin *pons*, a "bridge," and has been a problem for
generations of commentators, who have wondered why a priest
should have anything to do with bridges. One explanation may
be that the bridges across the Tiber were regarded as having
special sanctity, since the command of the river crossings gave
Rome its power and prestige in the ancient world; but it is just
as possible that the word was used in an abstract sense. Among
the Jains of India the greatest saints bear the title *tirthankara*,
meaning "the maker of the river crossings." So we may imagine
the pontiffs building their sky bridges to the gods.

The college of pontiffs, presided over by the *pontifex maximus*, the chief bridgebuilder, preserved the sacred books,
superintended all public religious ceremonies, and drew up the
calendar of festivities. We hear of other priestly colleges instituted by Numa, so many that he seems to be the inventor of all
the rituals that the Romans practiced assiduously, long after
their original meaning had been forgotten. They thought of him
almost as the personification of ritual, strangely detached from
affairs of everyday life: the story was told that when a messenger came running to him to say that the enemy was approaching, Numa replied, "Hush, I am worshiping." Above all, Numa

stands against Romulus in the Roman saga as the peacekeeper
and the embodiment of a lost golden age when no wolves
attacked the flocks and no armies breached the walls. Romans
were told, too, that he had built the small temple to the god
Janus, ordering the doors to be closed in peace and kept open in
war. After his benevolent reign they were rarely closed.

Under his successor, Tullus Hostilius, whose very name
sounds warlike, the doors flew wide open. The new king
appears to have been a throwback to Romulus, fiery and energetic. After long and difficult campaigns, he destroyed the city
of Alba Longa, which, according to legend, had been founded
by the son of Aeneas and had been the birthplace of Romulus
and Remus. (Castel Gandolfo, the summer residence of the pope,
stands on the site of the ancient city.) This ruthless act helped to
give Rome the primacy among the Latin tribes and cities.

Next in the legendary line of kings came Ancus Marcius,
who was credited with re-establishing the traditional Sabine
reign of peace, with founding a colony at the Tiber's mouth,
and with encouraging agriculture and trade. It may well have
been that he built a bridge across the Tiber, thereby promoting
commerce between Etruscan merchants, who were then pushing southward across the Latin plain, and Greek settlements in
the south.

The next king, however, was neither Sabine nor Roman. He
was half Etruscan and half Greek, and with him—or at least in
his time—the configuration of Rome changed profoundly. Like
Romulus and Numa, Tarquinius Priscus left his enduring
imprint on the Roman mind. According to tradition, he was the
son of a rich Corinthian immigrant named Demaratus, who had
settled in Etruscan Tarquinii. Being considered a half-breed he
moved to Rome and established himself there, becoming the
adviser to Ancus Marcius. Upon the latter's death, Tarquinius
led a bloodless revolution which bore him to the throne. Pre-

sumably this took place just before the end of the seventh century B.C., and Tarquinius became the master of the primitive hill town, seeking to convert it into an Etruscan metropolis.

Roman historians were inclined to view Tarquinius Priscus in the same magical light in which they viewed Romulus and Numa. It was said that when he first drove up to the gates of Rome in an open cart with his Etruscan wife Tanaquil, an eagle swooped out of the sky, lifted Tarquinius' cap, and then set it down on his head. Tarquinius was heaven-sent and therefore above reproach. The chroniclers omit all reference to the southward march of Etruscan power. They regard him as a Roman king, Greek by accident of birth, wed to an Etruscan woman. In fact he—or someone like him at that time—began the process of Rome's advancement by introducing the half-barbarous people to the cultivated habits of Etruria. The several lakes in the Forum were drained and channeled to the Tiber through the Cloaca Maxima, a sewer which survives to this day as a testimony to the engineering skill of the Etruscans. Hills were fortified with stone walls, and foundations were laid on the Capitoline for the great temple to the Etruscan deities Tinia, Uni, and Menerva. In time Tinia became identified with the god Jupiter, and the goddesses Uni and Menerva, their names only slightly changed to Juno and Minerva, were retained in the Roman pantheon. Tarquinius is thought to have either built or greatly enlarged the Circus Maximus, the race course below the steep cliff of the Palatine where games and contests were held. Etruscan words, ideas, techniques, and customs poured into Rome. As the Romulus of story gave the Romans a taste for conquest, and Numa gave them a deep-seated affection for ritual, Tarquinius gave them a delight in luxury, in vast buildings, and in civilized comforts. The Romans were presented with the evidence of the Etruscan splendor and succumbed avidly to the temptations offered by their conqueror.

In a hundred different ways Etruscan influence penetrated the minds and hearts of the Romans. It was felt particularly in the arts, in ceremony, and in divination, and perhaps most of all in a sense of spaciousness, as the Romans absorbed the characteristics of the Etruscans and moved on to conquests of their own. The colorful emblems of Etruscan rule were taken over, and Roman historians preserved for posterity a record of the insignia and titles of the royal Tarquins.

With the Etruscans came aristocratic rule, formality, a taste for elegance, a superb sense of style, and though the Romans later condemned aristocratic elegance, they were rarely to free themselves from it. The Etruscan influence took deep root, and in their private lives the rich retained the imprint of Etruscan ways long after Etruria had vanished into the limbo of the past. Etruscan influence, however, also had its dangers, for by introducing a method of government that was tyrannical and hierarchic, its kings brought about an inevitable conflict between classes, and particularly between themselves and men of landed property. And on that rock the power of the Etruscans was eventually broken.

Greek influence, too, was being felt in Rome. It was the age of luxury-loving Pisistratus, ruler of Athens. The expanding Greek colonies in Sicily and southern Italy were increasing in wealth and splendor. Direct traffic between Rome and such Greek settlements as Syracuse and Acragas, however, was still in its infancy, so that Greek influence filtered into Rome chiefly through Etruria. We hear of Greek artisans working near the ancient Etruscan city of Caere. Greek pottery was used and adapted in Tarquinian Rome.

Under the Tarquinian rule Rome made war on its Latin neighbors, starting with the conquest of the city of Apiolae; and the returning soldiers brought so much booty that the Romans were able to indulge their new taste for luxury. Tarquinius offered elaborate games with race horses and boxers imported from Etruria. Dancers and musicians were also brought in, and the Etruscan ceremonial dances and modes of music were imitated by the Romans. Rome was becoming a large and prosperous city adorned with monumental architecture. By 500 B.C. it may have had a population of twenty or twenty-five thousand spread over the seven hills. Moreover, by seizing neighboring villages in the Latin plain and by extending its domain from the Tiber's mouth into the Alban hills and beyond, it was growing into a nation that may then have numbered a few hundred thousand. One modern authority holds that even before the year 500 Rome had won control of some three hundred fifty square miles in just one advance.

The rule of the Tarquins lasted, according to tradition, from 616 B.C. to 509 B.C. Modern scholars, while prepared to accept these dates and to regard Tarquinius as an Etruscan conqueror, are puzzled by his successor Servius Tullius, whose origins are as obscure as the events of his reign. Romans said he was the good king who built the first stone wall around Rome—portions of the Servian Wall still exist—and who signed a treaty with the Latin League, a confederacy of villages and tribesmen dedicated to joint worship of Jupiter on the Alban Mount. He is said to have built a temple to the goddess Diana on the Aventine as a sanctuary for the Latin people, thus showing his sympathy for the Latin communities, who regarded Diana with special veneration. Roman records make the claim that he was a Roman or a Latin and describe him as a man of peace. Yet the antiquarian Emperor Claudius, who made a prolonged study of Etruscan history identified Servius Tullius with Mastarna, an Etruscan soldier of fortune.

The tyrannical majesty of the first Tarquinius was equaled only by Tarquinius Superbus, who was perhaps the son of the man reputed to have brought Etruscan civilization to Rome. The name Superbus seems to have been given him by an admiring people; it could mean "the proud," but is more likely to have meant "the magnificent." He is said to have completed the works begun by Tarquinius Priscus, employing the artist Vulca from Veii to adorn the temple of Jupiter, Juno, and Minerva on the Capitoline, and he seems to have made war chiefly to acquire slaves to build the great monuments intended to immortalize his fame. Livy says that he led his army into the territory of the Hernici and the Volsci, despoiled their lands, and established armed camps among them. He abolished the civic rights bestowed on the people by Servius Tullius and brought Rome to a position of dominance as the head of the Latin League. He was more powerful than any king of Rome before him, and he reveled in his power.

The temple he built to the trio of gods on the Capitoline was to be his most lasting memorial and the first major monument in Rome. The historian Dionysius of Halicarnassus tells us that "it stood on a high base and was 800 feet in circuit, each side measuring close to 200 feet." (The Periclean Parthenon at Athens, built nearly half a century later, is only 228 feet in length and 101 feet in width.) The temple appears to have been a structure in the Etruscan style, its figures of gods no larger than life-sized. Later, under the republic, it was to be peopled with towering statues reaching to its lofty roof. Gilt shields were to ornament its pediment, trophies to adorn its interior; stucco facings and floor mosaics were also to appear. In 83 B.C. it burned down, to be replaced by a second temple of the same size but of greater magnificence. Pillared with marble and roofed with gilded bronze, this was to be the shrine which the poet Horace called *Capitolium fulgens*, the shining Capitol. There was a tradition that when the foundations of the first

temple were being laid, a human head (*caput*) was found buried
in the earth. Soothsayers interpreted this as meaning that Rome
was to become the head of all Italy, and indeed the words *capital* and *capitol* both mean "the head place." The Romans always
regarded this sanctuary as the most sacred of all: it was the true
habitation of Jupiter, the most powerful of the gods, and the
place where the supreme offerings were made. Within the
walled enclosure that surrounded it, stood the altar at which
sacrifices were offered at the start of each year and in celebration of triumphs. Today only its foundations and some fragments of its marble columns survive.

The temple was still unfinished in 509 B.C. when (again,
according to tradition) a palace revolt, led by the king's nephew
Lucius Junius Brutus, brought about the fall and expulsion of
Tarquinius Superbus. The historical basis of such an uprising
remains obscure; and though Brutus himself may be legendary,
there is no doubt that at about this time the Romans threw off
Etruscan overlordship as well as the institution of kingship as a
whole, replacing it by a republic. It is known that under the
kings a strong class of nobles had arisen to challenge their
power. These men were patricians, landholders who claimed
descent from the leading families of Rome's earliest times. A
council of elders, or a *senatus*, had come into existence, composed of persons selected by the king from among the patricians. It held only advisory powers, but upon the death of the
king it had the very important function of choosing one or
more viceroys, or *interreges*, who in turn would nominate the
next king for the Senate's approval. A tribal assembly of all citizens, known as the Comitia Curiata, had also come into being
to witness and vote on certain acts—another early step toward
representative government. Even though the plebeians, or folk
without patrician lineage or property, were regarded as citizens,
they appear to have had little political power as against the

A powerful bronze bust dating from the third century B.C., above, exhibits lingering traces of the Etruscan style, but contains more than a promise of what was to be one of Rome's greatest contributions to world art—its mastery of uncompromising portraiture. The head may be that of Lucius Junius Brutus, who expelled the Tarquins.

clans of the nobles. The time of the plebs lay ahead; what occurred at the end of the sixth century was undoubtedly an uprising of the "best" families.

In Roman history Lucius Junius Brutus was depicted as a popular leader, the personification of liberty, the stern lawgiver who gave direction and purpose to the republic he supposedly founded. But this was a legend invented to give substance to the claim that the expulsion of the kings came about as the result of a popular movement. Some chronicles also have it that Brutus, the revolutionary aristocrat, soon proclaimed himself dictator, thereby merely exchanging one form of tyranny for another. Plutarch described him as "a man like steel of too hard a temper, who never had his character softened by thought or study." His portrait, or what is believed to be his portrait, shows him as a person with deep-set eyes and powerful features half hidden by a thick and unruly beard. In the imagination of the Romans he was a man so loyal to the state and so remote from pity that he could watch unmoved when his two sons, arrested as traitors, were executed before his eyes. To Brutus was given the credit of founding the republic and shaping it in accordance with his own vigorous and puritanical character.

There seems to be no doubt that someone like Brutus lived and played an important role in the expulsion of the Tarquins. What is in doubt is whether he actually founded the republic. We learn that his dictatorship was short-lived, and that he was soon compelled to accept as co-ruler a certain Lucius Tarquinius Collatinus, evidently another member of the royal family. Then both were overthrown and the last vestiges of Etruscan rule were extinguished. When the Etruscans departed, Rome came under the personal rule of Publius Valerius, a man descended from an ancient family reputed to have taken part in the promotion of peace between the Sabines and the Romans.

With Publius Valerius we may emerge from legend into fact—though his historicity has been doubted. Kindly in peace, generous to his enemies in war, ruthless in his determination to win for Rome its place in the sun, he gives the impression of a man with a carefully-thought-out political philosophy. His first test came, according to Livy, when the Etruscans massed their forces, demanding the subjugation of the city that had dared to expel them. Under Lars Porsenna of Clusium, wave upon wave of Etruscan cavalry was thrown against Rome; but a Roman soldier, Horatius, heroically defended the Tiber's bridge. For a time the invaders held the Janiculum hill; they also occupied large areas of the city. Publius Valerius was compelled to come to terms with the common people, exasperated by more than a century of aristocratic rule and in no mood to fight for its prolongation.

According to classical sources it was at this time that Valerius issued a series of extraordinary enactments giving to the people powers which they had never previously enjoyed. He set about creating a popular army. He introduced the death penalty for anyone who attempted to make himself a tyrant against the will of the people. The same penalty was reserved for anyone who attempted to usurp a public office. He gave the right of appeal to citizens sentenced to death. He ordered the treasury to be removed from the keeping of the chief magistrates known as consuls, and it was entrusted to civil servants called quaestors, who became the chief financial agents of the republic with offices of their own in the temple of Saturn. He inaugurated the custom whereby a consul on entering the assembly must part the axes and the rods of his ceremonial fasces and lower them before the people. The story is told by Plutarch that when Publius Valerius heard the people murmuring against the splendor of his mansion on the Velia, he simply ordered the house and everything in it to be destroyed and then went about asking for lodgings in a friend's house. A grateful populace gave him the name Poplicola, meaning "the friend of the people." Probably it was he who was the father of the republic that was to endure for nearly five hundred years.

Meanwhile there were wars to be fought, not only against the Etruscans but also against those Latin tribes which saw advantages in destroying Rome and allying themselves with the powerful princes of Etruria. These savage wars at times reduced Rome to the size of a small provincial town cut off from foreign trade, impoverished, with pestilence running through the streets. But it was characteristic of Rome to be most resolute when it was weakest. It fought back. Thirteen years after the expulsion of the Tarquins, Rome won a resounding victory over the Latins at Lake Regillus. Then at last there was peace with the Latins and no longer any real fear of the Etruscans. Rome had shown its mettle.

The text of the treaty of peace with the Latin tribes has survived. It says: "There shall be place between the Romans and all the communities of Latins as long as heaven and earth endure. They shall not wage war with each other, nor summon enemies into the land, nor grant passage to enemies; and when any community is attacked, they shall render help in concert, and whatever is won in joint warfare shall be equally distributed." The treaty was signed in 493 B.C. In the previous year a popular revolt even to the creation of a new government office which was to have even more enduring consequences, for in that year the first tribune of the people was elected.

By granting new powers to the people, by which he meant the middle classes, Publius Valerius Poplicola had set in motion a process that could be stopped only with the greatest difficulty. Liberty once given inevitably attracts more liberties to itself. The poor—the peasants, the farm workers, the artisans, the small landholders—demanded their own liberties, and when these were refused they marched out of Rome in a body, encamped on the Sacred Mount on the river Anio, three miles from the city, and refused to return until their demands were met. What they wanted above all was freedom from arbitrary punishment and from the abuses of power; they would return only if the Senate—the governing body made up largely of rich landowners, aristocrats, and leaders of the army—agreed to protect their rights by giving full powers to their representatives. A class war had begun.

Because all the ordinary work and life of the city as well as of the farms had come to a halt, the Senate was compelled to accept the demands of the plebs. It was agreed that a magistrate or tribune representing the plebs should enjoy full powers of veto against the decisions of the senators. His person was to be inviolate, and the entire body of the Roman citizenry was to be under his protective care. From time to time the number of tribunes changed: there were never less than two, sometimes there were as many as ten. In the slow and laborious history of the development of the democratic process the tribunes of the people occupy a special place. Even Athens, fount of the idea of popular government, had not gone so far as this.

With the establishment of the tribunate came a proliferation of Roman law, for although the tribunes were in theory armed only with the power of veto, in fact they sometimes became the lawmakers, and the decisions of the plebeian assembly, expressed through the tribunes, were regarded as binding once the Senate confirmed them. In effect the plebeian assembly which came into existence in 471 B.C. and comprised the greater part of the population, had become a powerful political force determined, if possible, to wrest power from the patrician rulers or at least to hold them in check. There was now a system of government by different representative groups and a growing body of enactments, rules, customs, and covenants which eventually was to produce the magnificent Roman legal structure, with its many safeguards and checks and balances.

The machine, so carefully contrived to put an end to acts of tyranny, was far from perfect. It often creaked badly and sometimes came to a standstill. The inviolate tribunes were sometimes murdered, or they were bribed, or they themselves became tyrannical. In times of crisis dictators emerged and made a mockery of the laws. But the tribunate survived until the last days of the republic, and even when the republic was finally overthrown the emperors took the proud title of *tribunus plebis*. Then, at last, the title lost all meaning.

In the fifth and fourth centuries B.C., however, the wars in central Italy went on like brush fires that could not be put out. Every year there was a new campaign or a drawn-out war against the neighboring towns; the Latin League split up and the various fragments fought against one another. From these wars Rome emerged as an increasingly strong power, driving itself dangerously close to exhaustion and suffering periodically from famine and plagues which the chroniclers record with the air of men recording events as inevitable as sunrise and sunset.

There was nothing yet to suggest that Roman power would soon extend over large areas of Italy. Rome dominated little more than the plains on both sides of the Tiber, and the endless border wars were little more than skirmishes. There had been no prodigious gains of territory, and indeed there was very little to show for the wars. Yet the period between the expulsion of the Tarquins and the great upheaval at the hand of the Gauls which was to reduce the Romans temporarily to impotence—those decades which saw the rise of the plebeians to a position of importance in government—showed that an intellectual expansion was taking place. It was not only that new forms of government were being hammered into shape, new offices were being created, and new aspects of rule were being explored, but the Romans were demonstrating a passionate concern for a just society, a more mature way of living. Those years left an enduring heritage, and in later days when the republic was destroyed by the revival of autocratic government, the Romans would look back on that period with a sense of longing. They recognized that during that embattled century they had laid the foundations of their greatness.

These tough-minded hill people had come far. They had built a workable civilization, absorbed the arts of the Etruscans, shown themselves to be possessed of a ferocious spirit of independence, and could look forward to increasing their influence. Then quite suddenly in a single day they lost the gains of centuries.

Unknown to the Romans, a power much greater than the combined ones of all the Latin states and principalities was massing in the north. The Gauls were on the march. They were herdsmen who had drifted westward from the plains of central Europe, and for a century they had been pouring along the valley of the Danube River into France and Spain. They were tall, large-limbed, and fair-haired; they fought from chariots with long swords and spears. They struck at Etruria, which never completely recovered from their assaults. In 390 B.C. they met the Roman army on the banks of the river Allia, eleven miles north of Rome. The battle was soon over, as the Romans fled in the direction of Veii, recently conquered by Marcus Furius Camillus, the most resourceful of Rome's generals. Three days later the Gauls marched into Rome to find only the temple on the Capitoline defended; they plundered the city at their leisure and left most of it a smoking ruin. There is a legend that they found the senators sitting tranquilly on ivory thrones in their homes near the Forum, and massacred them. For seven months the Gauls are said to have ruled over the city, abandoning it only when they were offered a ransom to withdraw. According to Plutarch, the amount was to be a "thousand weight" of gold; but the Gauls were discovered cheating in the weighing of it, upon which their chieftain Brennus contemptuously threw his own sword and belt upon the scales, crying, "*Vae victis* (Woe to the defeated)!" Whatever the truth of the stories, the Romans never forgot they had been beaten to their knees.

Rome all but perished, only to rise again. Within a hundred years it grew into a power that threatened the entire Mediterranean world. Then the Romans, not the Gauls, carried the message "*Vae victis!*" Coming from them, it had a more ominous import. Although it could still mean death or slavery to a defeated warrior, it could also doom his nation to centuries of Roman rule or even to annihilation.

III

FAITH AND THE STATE

Parent of Rome! by gods and men beloved,
Benignant Venus! thou, the sail-clad main
And fruitful earth, as round the seasons roll,
With life who swellest, for by thee all live,
And, living, hail the cheerful light of day . . .

—Lucretius, "Invocation to Venus,"
On the Nature of Things

The first herdsmen and farmers who settled in Rome brought with them the beliefs they had nourished for generations in the countryside. They were men with a brooding love of the earth and its fruits, and they saw no reason to change their beliefs when they became town dwellers. The gods of the woodland and the harvest, of storm and clear skies, of budding leaf and warming flame accompanied them from their hamlets into Rome, and even after the Romans had conquered most of the known world seven or more centuries later, these gods were still being worshiped. Some of the early deities grew old and died and were replaced by others with names borrowed from different tribes encountered during the long wars, but always at the heart of the Roman religion there were the gods and spirits of the hearth and countryside.

When the Romans were still an unlettered, agricultural folk, their first or chief god appears to have been Janus, at various times thought of as the sun god, the sky, the thunderer, and the governor of all beginnings and entrances. He was also associated with the door, or *ianua*, of a house. Doorways were invested with magical or numinous significance; Janus, present in every household, exerted great power over the household's undertakings. In some way he was connected with the goddess Diana, who evolved from a wood spirit with some governance over the cycles of the moon and of women into the goddess of fertility, of the woodland and protectress of huntsmen. Diana was to retain her power over the Roman imagination through the ages; but at some very early period in Roman history all-powerful Janus was superseded by other gods, led by Jupiter. The reasons for this remain obscure, though the explanation has been set forth that the Romans, becoming more mature and literate, felt a need for godheads more advanced than Janus. Yet the Romans never completely forgot his former eminence, and the god was invoked before any other god, even before Jupiter, at the beginning of any important undertaking. The memory of his ancient, warlike powers was preserved in his small temple located in the Forum and dedicated to military prowess; the temple gates being thrown open in times of war and closed in times of peace.

When we first see Jupiter, who was eventually to preside over the entire pantheon, he is the god of the oak forest, the thunder and the rain, and the maintainer of peace who presides over tribal loyalties and the making of oaths. His shrine is a grove of oaks; and his presence is revealed in the trembling of leaves that announce a storm. Originally he was perhaps simply the power of the sky, manifesting itself in various ways: as Jupiter Lapis, his image was a meteorite or a stone; as Jupiter Pluvius, he gave rain to the land; as Jupiter Fulminator, he was the hurler of lightning; as Jupiter Tonans, he was the thunderer.

From those earliest days, only Diana and Vesta survived unchanged. Vesta was the goddess of the hearth-flame, which was kept burning continually. The flame symbolized communal life, the continuity of the family and its welfare; it cooked the meats, kept the wild beasts at bay, and dispelled the horrors of the night. To this ever-burning flame the Romans paid tribute by instituting ritual offerings in each household, while each tribe had its own public hearth-fire, tended only by maidens known as vestal virgins, who offered special prayers in its honor. When Rome became master of a great and powerful empire the vestal virgins, living in the Forum in a round temple evidently shaped to resemble the ancient wattle huts, continued to tend the flame with quiet decorum. Their persons were sacrosanct, and according to Plutarch, if they passed a condemned criminal, the criminal was freed. Some mysterious power was believed to reside in the maidens as long as they remained virgin. The worship of the flame was one of the most ancient and most enduring of all surviving Roman rituals, for the flame continued to burn long after Rome was ruled by a Christian emperor, being extinguished only in A.D. 382 during the reign of Emperor Gratian.

Roman household worship took forms different from the emerging state religion, though both relied on consultation of omens and auspices, and on propitiatory rituals. The state cult, too, was to adopt many festivals from home observances. The high priest of the household was the paterfamilias—father of the family, breadwinner, preceptor, and judge—and he was to be regarded with awe and reverence. He possessed powers of life and death, his word was law, and through him the gods and the spirits influenced the household. He was the guardian of the family; a long-lived patriarch might rule despotically over the lives of his grandsons and great-grandsons. His daughters, however, once they were married, could pass out of the orbit of his command. Originally *pitir* or *pater* seems to have meant "power" or "authority" rather than a man who had begotten children.

As high priest of the family the paterfamilias superintended the household rites. He made offerings to the lares and penates, guardian spirits of the home. The lares were originally the spirits who presided over the land outside the house, and the penates protected the food in the store cupboards and the grain in the bins. They were familiar, friendly spirits, grateful for small offerings. They were depicted on household altars, and offerings were placed before them—myrtle wreaths, honeycakes, cups of wine. They fostered gaiety and good living, and were especially remembered when the family sat at table. For the Romans there was always something holy about sitting together at a meal, under the presiding eyes of the lares and penates. These spirits, too, survived the pagan empire, and the Christian emperor Theodosius was compelled to issue an edict against those who offered burnt sacrifices to the lares and perfumes to the penates. Even today some traces of the worship of the household gods are to be found in villages in Italy.

Beyond the realm of the paterfamilias lay the world of nature, where he had little or no authority. In this world the gods of harvest, rain, and lightning wielded their powers, and the entire community would take part in prayer and offerings. They were the gods of the fields and the woods, and the nymphs who hovered over springs and lakes. There were hundreds of these minor gods, some of them scarcely more than sprites. There was sweet-tempered Faunus, a god of the woodlands; Pomona, the goddess of orchards, who was especially fond of apple trees; Silvanus, who presided over timber lots and saw that the boundary stones were kept in place; Pales, who guarded shepherds from danger. Not all the little gods were kindly: Robigus was a malevolent deity who would place a blight on the crops unless he was properly propitiated with offerings of wine and the sacrifice of dogs. The lemures and larvae were even more intractable deities; they were ghosts of the dead, mysterious specters who hovered invisibly in the air, to be propitiated by the head of the household, who would fill his mouth with beans and then spit them out saying, "I throw away these beans, and with them I redeem myself and mine."

We do not have any complete account of the ancient rituals practiced by the Romans. We hear of magic spells and incantations that were derived from the distant past and were still being used in republican times. The Romans, aware that many of the gods were nameless, sometimes addressed their prayers to an unknown deity, *sive deo sive deae* ("whether god or goddess"). Beyond the known gods was an infinite number of unknown ones, who also had to be placated and given offerings. Sometimes the ritual took the form of a re-enactment of an ancient legend, illustrated by the fact that the claimant for the priesthood of the goddess Diana at Nemi obtained his office only by killing his predecessor; often it took the form of a sacred dance performed to the accompaniment of music. An early surviving fragment of a hymn that was addressed to Mars in the days when he was still a god of fecundity and husbandry reads:

> *Enos Lases iuvate.*
> *Neve lue rue Marmar sins incurrere in pleores.*
> *Satur fu, fere Mars: limen sali, sta berber.*
> *Semunis alternei advocapit conctos.*
> *Enos Marmor iuvato.*
> *Triumpe, triumpe, triumpe, triumpe, triumpe!*

> *Come, help us, O lares.*
> *Let neither blight nor ruin hasten upon the people.*
> *Be satiated, fierce Mars: leap the threshold, stay the scourge.*
> *Summon in turn the gods of the harvest.*
> *Come, help us, O Mars.*
> *Triumph, triumph, triumph, triumph!*

In this way, with a fierce flourish of excitement and with the clang of resounding drums, the Roman peasants leaped to imitate the growing grain and called to the earth to feed them. There was a directness in their approach to the gods in the primitive times, the village community gathering together to give commands to the gods during high holidays. In later times an intricate priesthood would come between the public worshipers and the gods; but in the villages the ancient hymns with their direct summons to the gods survived, and they were still being sung long after the advent of Christianity.

Then there were the great gods, who held the destiny of the country in their hands; they were massive and spectacular, accumulating power by virtue of some extraordinary process of accretion, restlessly seeking to spread their dominion wider. These were the gods of the state cult, remote from the lives of the peasants. Their origins were often lowly: Mars, the god of the ripening grain, became god of war; and Jupiter, who once dwelt in the oak trees, presided over the heavens and the earth. Many of the great gods were simply borrowed and reshaped to serve Roman needs. In pre-Roman times Jupiter appears to have been worshiped particularly in Alba Longa as a sky god of magical powers. When his cult was brought to Rome it lost its strength and became relatively stable only when he took on some of the characteristics of Tinia, the sky god of the Etruscans, and of Zeus, worshiped by the Greek settlers in southern Italy with whom the Romans came into early contact. Under the Etruscan kings he was conceived of as the protector of the city and the people, the supreme legislator of their destinies, at the same time retaining his empire over the heavens and the works of nature. As the divine king with all the radiance of majesty he became Jupiter Optimus Maximus—the best and greatest of all gods—honored by a temple on the steep rock of the Capitoline overlooking the Forum. The Etruscan sculptor Vulca of Veii may have been the first to fashion his image; in 385 B.C. a terra-cotta statue of the god was placed in the temple. Jupiter came to Rome in the company of Uni and Menerva. Uni became Juno and Menerva became Minerva, retaining the name even when she was linked with the Greek goddess Athena.

Jupiter was derived from several gods. Not only Tinia and Zeus went into his making, but he took over many of the powers of the fallen Janus. He became the guardian of the Roman state, the loftiest representative of Roman power; but he was divided into many shapes and functions, and bore many titles. He was a complex, restless figure, though outwardly he appeared to have an unnerving calm and to possess a simple, single-minded purpose. He presided over the seasons, but so did Anna Perenna. He decided battles, but so did Mars and Quirinus. He helped the grapes to ripen, but so did Bacchus and Liber. He was worshiped at the beginning of the harvest, but so was Janus. He was the light bringer, but so was Apollo. Though called the best and the greatest, he was never, like Zeus, the supreme arbiter of the universe and the governor of the world. Zeus reigned from the heights of Mount Olympus, Jupiter from a low and easily accessible hill. Zeus belonged to the shining space of the air, while Jupiter, as represented by the Romans, belonged as much to the earth as to the sky. Zeus was free, Jupiter was rigid. When we compare the two gods, we find we are comparing the imagination of the Greeks to the imagination of the Romans; they had almost nothing in common.

Under the empire Jupiter was represented in the form of Olympian Zeus, heavily bearded and curly-haired, with a look of wisdom and calm maturity. All that was known of his legendary life was borrowed from the Greeks. It was difficult to imagine him smiling (though he does so on two occasions in the *Aeneid*) or plunged into deep gloom. Duty, dignity, inflexibility, oath, power—these are the words that seemed to come from his impersonal lips. Though earthbound, he was remote; and though physically present, he was curiously inaccessible. He was concerned above all with law and morality; he watched over justice and truth. Though he blessed the vineyards, brought down the rain when it was required, permitted the sacrifice of white cattle in his honor, and sometimes indulged in prophecies, revealing the future and showing his approval or disapproval of contemplated undertakings by the Roman state, these were all minor activities which he could perform using only a small part of his available power. Where he excelled in the eyes of the Romans was in the divine personification of authority. He represented the archetypal image of the paterfamilias, ruling gravely over his enormous family of Romans.

It is necessary to understand the stern, austere Jupiter, because in a sense he is the *only* god of the Romans. As Jupiter Optimus Maximus, he was the god from whom most was expected, the one whose favor was most desired and whose blessings were most efficacious. The other great gods—Saturn, Ceres, Venus, Neptune, Mercury, and the rest—served as decorations for his throne, deriving their powers from him. Jupiter was almost an abstraction, but one with hard outlines. In his temple on the Capitoline was kept a flint stone or meteorite, and when men swore oaths in his name, they sometimes spoke of him as Jupiter Lapis—Jupiter the Stone. Stonelike he loomed over Rome.

For those who wielded power over the Romans and their rapidly expanding empire, the state cult of Jupiter served a useful function. The ceremonies and rituals in his temple were unexampled in magnificence, and his temple was the largest and most imposing of all. His high priest, the *flamen Dialis*, was traditionally granted extraordinary powers and hedged with equally extraordinary taboos. He was never allowed to perform any physical labor or to see others at work; a herald preceded him to warn the people to stop working in his presence. He must wear nothing binding, not even a ring, nor touch anything that was binding, like the tendrils of a vine hanging from a trellis. He must never mount a horse or see a dead man or come in sight of a funeral. He must not touch iron. Insofar as it was possible, he must live in perfect freedom and detachment as did the god he served. He wore the purple-edged toga of the magistrate and sat on a curule chair. The *flamen Dialis* was the earthly representative of Jupiter; and to maintain the cult he was assisted by a flock of priests whose powers and taboos were equally strange, derived from customs so old that no one could remember their origins. In the name of Jupiter the Romans went to war, and when the conquering general returned to receive a triumph, the procession followed the Sacred Way and then mounted the Capitoline hill to reach the temple of Jupiter. There the general made a sacrifice to the god and laid his laurel wreath on the god's lap.

The temple on the Capitoline, then, was the focus of the state religion, the place from which divine power was believed to radiate. There the pontiffs, who supervised all sacred observances under the *pontifex maximus*, and the augurs, who examined the entrails of sacrificial victims or the play of lightning to foretell the will of the gods, had their priestly colleges and pronounced their verdicts. Originally there were three pontiffs and three augurs, all elected from the patrician families, but their numbers were continually changing: there were sixteen pontiffs and sixteen augurs in the time of Julius Caesar. The first college was entrusted with guardianship of the divine law, or *ius divinum*, and the calendar; the second with the power to read omens, or *auspicia;* the result was an extraordinary exercise of priestly power within the state. While Greeks turned to the Delphic oracle on the distant heights, Romans turned to well-connected interpreters within the walls. Here, too, the texts of the sacred books were kept, to be consulted at times of grave emergency, and there they remained until the time of Augustus, who, in his special reverence for Apollo, removed the books to a vault in the new temple to the god he had had erected on the Palatine.

Apollo was only one of many Greek gods who successfully invaded the Roman pantheon. Mercury was the Greek god Hermes, Venus was Aphrodite, Neptune was Poseidon, Ceres was Demeter. They came to Rome wearing the Greek dress and were given high positions among the gods. But sometimes the mythologies of Roman gods were incorporated with those of the Greek gods; the result was that some gods were encrusted with layer upon layer of mythology. On the other hand Ceres, an ancient Roman goddess of agriculture, took on all the legends connected with Demeter and shed her Roman past almost completely. In Rome the service of the goddess was performed in Greek by women of Greek extraction in a temple built on the Greek model. Such tributes to Greek origins were rare.

Venus, originally perhaps a goddess of the flowers, became a love goddess when Aphrodite was grafted onto her. From a love goddess she was changed into the queen of fecundity, rivaling Ceres, but this was only the beginning of her transformations. She became the generative force of the universe and the goddess who presided over the destinies of Rome. The philosopher-poet Lucretius, living in the first half of the first century B.C., described her as the fountain of all blessings and the divine mistress of Rome, greater than Jupiter because she governed all created things:

> O guardian Mother of Rome, joy of gods and mortals,
> Venus, who beneath the march of the swimming stars
> Dost make the many-voyaged ocean teem with fish
> And the earth with fruit, through thee alone

All living things owe their conception,
And through thee alone they rise toward the Sun.

Even as Lucretius was writing, the goddess was in the process of transformation. Under Julius Caesar, who claimed descent from her, she was to become the goddess who guided the destinies of his imperial family. When he became the unquestioned ruler of Rome, he built in the Forum a shrine in her honor, which was also a temple to his own glory.

Venus continued to rule in Rome, growing in power and influence long after Julius Caesar was dead. She became almost indistinguishable from the civic goddess Roma, and under the emperor Hadrian, a strange, new, double temple was built where Venus and Roma sat back to back. It was as though Hadrian had come to the conclusion that the equation Venus equals Rome could be solved satisfactorily only by placing them under a single roof. In the imperial age Venus became the symbol of the beauty of conquest, the serene embodiment of the Roman world empire. That the humble goddess of flowers should have grown in power and acquired so many virtues only demonstrates the changing nature of Roman mythology, which became amazingly intricate and almost unmanageable.

Since the beginning of their history the Romans had been accustomed to borrowing the gods of other tribes and nations. The result was that they accumulated more gods than they needed and more festivals and games than any single person could attend. Nearly every day there was a local feast honoring some god, with prayers and sacrifices and gifts to be given to the priests. The Roman religious calendar, perhaps established in the days of Numa Pompilius, was overflowing with names of gods and holy days. Some were so ancient that no one any longer remembered their precise significance or understood the meaning of the prayers spoken in an archaic language by priests who themselves had forgotten what the prayers meant.

What purpose was served by the multiplicity of gods? The Romans would have answered that they could see no harm in numbers. No god must be left without the proper sacrifices and prayers for fear that he might take umbrage, punish those who had rejected him, and perhaps even visit punishment on rival gods who were receiving too much worship. Above all, it was necessary to maintain peaceful relations with the gods by scrupulously observing the proper amenities and by addressing them in the way that was most pleasing to them. When the Romans spoke of *pax deorum* ("the peace of the gods") they were speaking of a state of affairs that resembled peaceful relations between neighboring states. To preserve the peace and to draw favor from the gods was the duty of every Roman. It was one of his many obligations, like fighting for his country, paying taxes, and raising a family, and perhaps it was neither more nor less important than any of these.

The sense of duty, or *pietas*, was inculcated in the Roman from his youngest years. The stern, grave expression that appears on Roman portraits reflects their sense of *gravitas*—the conscious acceptance of burdens or the disposition to take things seriously. They saw themselves as a people dedicated to the gods, and the religious ceremonies were far more formal and ritualistic than those of the Greeks, who were often light-hearted in their devotions. The Greeks told amusing stories about their gods and were on familiar terms with them; they laughed and sorrowed with them, and they liked to imagine the gods' lives as being very similar to their own. They approached their gods openly, without knocking on the doors, and they would never have thought to veil themselves in the presence of the deities as the Romans did, drawing their togas over their heads.

The word *religion* comes from *religare*, "to bind." Basically Roman religion was a contract between men and divinities, who offered service in exchange for gifts given. It provided favors and accommodation, but little in the way of what we would call a moral code. It filled the people's lives more with holidays than with meaning, and in time it was doubted or rejected by intelligent men. The very oaths uttered to the gods were composed in legalistic language. *Do ut des* ("I give so that you may give") was one of the principles of worship, though it was not the only one. Especially in the countryside, worship

An undated floor mosaic, above, depicts Neptune, originally a god of fresh water, driving a sea chariot.

provided an excuse for communal gaiety, and the contractual obligations to the gods were forgotten in merrymaking, in which the gods themselves were assumed to take part. The Romans enjoyed the great processions and games held in the honor of the gods, and some were also dedicated to the little, familiar gods of the household, the fields, and the orchards.

The gods provided so many holidays that these seriously interfered with the normal conduct of affairs. The Roman year opened in March with the ceremonial rededication of the vestal flame and the lively clanging of the sacred shields removed from the temple of Mars. The twelve Salii, or dancers and leapers who clanged the shields, wore armor and conical caps, which may have represented the thrusting of seeds. For many days the Salii danced in procession through the streets, halting at all the temples and shrines, feasting every night, then continuing their wild processional dance the next morning to the accompaniment of piercing trumpet blasts. March was a noisy month, for there was also the festival of the Liberalia in honor of the ancient god Liber, who demanded unrestrained merriment. April was crowded with festivals. There were festivals for Tellus, mother of the earth; for Ceres, bringer of fruitfulness; and for Jupiter, in whose honor the wine of the previous year had been broached. At the end of the month came the Floralia in honor of the goddess Flora, when men decked themselves and their animals in flowers, and women set aside the staid costumes they had worn during the winter and put on colorful dresses. With May came solemn ceremonies, as though to atone for the gaiety and license of April. Despite the Roman spring, it was a time of danger, doubt, and foreboding, of offerings to the dead and fearful pleas to the gods to permit the crops to grow. Then in June came the great celebrations connected with the ripening of the harvest.

So it was throughout the year, the rhythm of the festivals

following the rhythm of the seasons, and sometimes there were strange alterations of mood as the people withdrew into themselves and gave in to their fears, only to burst out joyfully again a few weeks later. December and January were months of wild festivity, February was a month of gloom.

The Romans found a deep satisfaction in these festivals. Worship was entertainment as well as duty, release from toil as well as the fulfillment of an obligation. Significantly there were no important underworld divinities, and the Romans themselves felt no great dread of death. Although their religion was not a very exalted one, it permitted them to live fully and colorfully, without a gnawing sense of inadequacy and with the certainty that the gods, however malevolent and unruly on occasion, would fight for them to the end. It was a religion that had grown almost casually over the centuries, with no obvious plan, no body of doctrine, no contours. We speak sometimes of the Roman religion as though it possessed a firm basis, but in fact it was constantly changing, the gods melting away and being replaced by others. Although such continual flux was at times disconcerting—nothing comparable to this had existed among the ancient Greeks—it must be interpreted as a sign of health.

Ultimately the religion failed to satisfy all the needs of the Romans. The divine machinery often creaked, and if the restless borrowing of gods was sometimes a sign of imagination and strength, it was also a sign of weakness. Too many questions were left unanswered. The religion said little about death and afterlife; it was sternly masculine and therefore had comparatively little to say to women; it derived its sanctions from ancient legends and therefore it had little to say about the present. By the end of the republic, educated men regarded state religion as a survival from an archaic past. They preserved an antiquarian interest in the gods, discussing them endlessly, but they were beginning to wonder whether their worship served any useful purpose. Although Cicero proclaimed his belief in the supreme gods and professed to regard divination as the proper vehicle by which the gods communicated with men, it is clear that he shared the skepticism of the Stoics and Epicureans,

An ancient bust, above, portrays Cicero as a mature, distinguished sena-tor in about 50 B.C.

who regarded the gods as uncertain and scarcely probable
denizens of an uncertain and scarcely probable heaven.
Pythagoras of Samos had spoken of the one god who ruled the
universe without the aid of any divine servants. Varro, the great
encyclopedist of the late republic, wrote of time when all the
minor gods would be swept away, leaving Jupiter in sole command. He would abolish the worship of the images, pointing
out that in the early days the Romans had neither altars nor
temples nor statues, and the gods were numinous presences.
What was the purpose in dressing them in the shapes of men?
He would permit the country festivals to continue because the
countryfolk delighted in them, but he would put an end to the
offering of sacrifices. Did Jupiter really derive pleasure from the
sight of slaughtered bulls and sheep at his altar? But Varro
admitted that Roman religion, with all its faults and inconsis-
tencies, had served a great purpose. It had trained men to be
pious and obedient to the demands made by the state.

Cicero, too, felt that the state cult was necessary for the survival of the empire. He had only a distant and troubled affection for the gods and was not quite sure whether they existed,
but he was certain that the people needed them. "We must persuade our citizens that the gods are the lords and rulers of all
things and what is done, is done by their will and authority;
and they are great benefactors of men, and know who everyone
is, and what he does, and what sins he commits, and what he
intends to do, and with what piety he fulfills his religious
duties." But this was a counsel of despair, for he was simply
restoring the gods to their high places because they were useful
to government; he was offering no justification for their existence. Lucretius, however, went further. Though he opened his
great poem *De rerum natura* (*On the Nature of Things*) with an
invocation to Venus as the supreme goddess of all blessings, his
purpose was to remove from men the fear of the gods and to

show them how little justification there was for the existence of
the deities, even for the ones who were officially encouraged by
the state. If Lucretius and Cicero could come to directly contrary opinions regarding the gods, clearly the status of the gods
was in jeopardy.

In the first century B.C. strange, exotic cults were emerging
in Rome itself to satisfy a people thirsting not only for novelty
but more importantly for spiritual fulfillment. Isis, Mithra, and
a host of minor deities from Egypt and Asia Minor were being
worshiped in Rome by sects that had abandoned the formal
state religion for far more colorful religions that grew up on the
eastern shores of the Mediterranean. These religions spoke of
the promise of immortality, provided complex and exciting rituals, and were directed at the most intimate hopes and fears of
the worshipers; they celebrated the individual, not the state.
The white-robed Egyptian priests waving their softly tinkling
sistrums were poles removed from the harsh-voiced priests of
Mithra, who bathed their converts in the blood of freshly killed
bulls; but both promised a continuing life after death and
painted its glories. Mithraism, which derived from Persia,
became the favored cult of the Roman army, and Mithraic temples have been found in all the regions of the Roman empire.
(Recently, the remains of a Mithraic temple were discovered in
the heart of London.) Neither Isis nor Mithra succeeded in
entering the Roman pantheon. Unlike the Greek gods they
could not be assimilated into the state cult, and therefore they
were kept a little apart in a kind of annex reserved for strange
gods whose powers were still unexplored and whose presence
was disturbing. Efforts were made to ban them; laws were
passed against them; Varro prayed for the day when foreign
cults would perish from the earth; but they remained. The more
the devotees were punished, the more they flourished.

Isis and Mithra opened the way for Christianity, with its

demand for a revolutionary reversal of values. Instead of *grav-itas* there was to be a quiet joy; instead of brute strength there were to be meekness and gentleness; instead of a pious venera-tion of the state there was to be indifference to the state. Ten years after the Crucifixion there were Christians in Rome, rejoicing in something so foreign to Roman beliefs—the immi-nent Second Coming of Jesus of Nazareth and the end of the world—that it is understandable that the Romans found them incomprehensible. Like Mithra and Isis, Jesus was excluded from the Roman pantheon, and although a pagan emperor might worship a statue of Jesus in private, Christianity remained obstinately remote from the state cult. Christ and Jupiter belonged to different worlds, and there could be no peace between them.

The triumph of Christianity in Rome was to have prodigious consequences—not the least of these was that Christianity itself was colored by Roman religious practices. The robes of Christ-ian priests, the shape of Christian churches, the order of serv-ices, the offerings at the altars, the title of the supreme pontiff, and the very language of Christian ceremonial were derived from the Romans. For a thousand years a hard, stubborn, earthy people had built a pragmatic edifice of belief, and though it was to be superseded by a far loftier one, many of its foundation stones survived.

IV

THE THRUST OF POWER

Moribus antiquis res stat Romana virisque.
*"It is through the ways of old and through the heroes of old
that Rome stands fast."*

—Ennius

In the year 390 B.C. the Romans were at the lowest ebb of their fortunes, their city sacked and looted by the Gauls, their power reaching no farther than to a few neighboring villages. But before the close of the century Rome, risen from the ashes, was beginning to be a major Mediterranean power. By the end of the third century B.C., it had broken the power of Carthage and was well on the way to becoming the mistress of all the lands bordering the sea. In this phenomenal revival and masterly assertion of strength, all its resources of character and energy were made manifest.

When the Romans returned to their city after the withdrawal of the Gauls, they found no gods to console them for their defeats—all the religious statues and sacred objects had either been buried by the priests or removed to Caere for safekeeping—and only a few houses were left standing. Here and there they came upon a palatial residence formerly occupied by a Gallic chieftain or some storerooms that the Gauls had not troubled to fire, but among the deserts of rubble they had difficulty in making out the shapes of the streets or even the sites of the temples. February had come; the cold winds blew over the Tiber; there was no shelter among the ruins. So little of Rome had survived that many Romans thought it would be best simply to uproot themselves and abandon the city; they would march to the former Etruscan citadel of Veii and settle there, leaving Rome to its ghosts.

This is as Plutarch and Livy tell the story. Modern scholars have come to doubt whether the destruction was as general as ancient chroniclers claim, writing as they did with dramatic and heroic intent. The episode of the proposed migration to Veii may be fictional. But the figure who now moves to center stage—the veteran general Marcus Furius Camillus—appears to be historical, though his exploits may have been greatly embellished by writers anxious to enlarge the saga. They said he had been in exile at the time of the battle against the Gauls on the river Allia; thus, he was one of the few surviving generals who bore no responsibility for the defeat. He was a stern taskmaster, a brilliant organizer, a fearless general, who won so many battles that legend credits him with driving the Gauls from Rome. But the Gauls were not driven from the city; they abandoned it in their own good time after removing everything of value and making it uninhabitable; and Camillus was confronted with the task of building a new city on the rubble.

He went about this with extraordinary intelligence and cunning. First, he ordered a ritual purification of the city. He sent the priests probing among the ashes and the broken walls in search of foundation stones and sacred relics, and drew a map indicating the sites of temples. He needed their protection, but he also needed the protection of Romulus, and so it came about the priests in charge of recovering the sacred sites found the lituus, or augural staff, of Romulus hidden deep below the ashes in the burnt-out temple of Mars. A lituus was an object of special potency because it was used by diviners to quarter the heavens; and Romulus, according to a long-established tradition, had made use of the staff on the day of the foundation of Rome. When Camillus heard that people were discussing abandoning the city, he argued with them. There was a long silence after he had finished speaking; in the silence was heard the loud voice of a centurion who accompanied a standard-bearer: "Halt! Fix the standard! Here is the place to stay!" Stay they did; and almost singlehandedly Camillus assumed the responsibility for rebuilding the city. An awed and grateful people was to call him the second founder of the city.

Camillus belongs to a type that recurs frequently in Roman legend and history. He appears at a time when Rome is given over to anarchy and the edifice is crumbling; he restores order by his commanding presence and the energy of his personality; in alliance with the aristocracy and the military leaders, he presents himself as the savior of his country; and having stamped Rome with his own image, he spends his last days in a melancholy quarrel with the people. The theme of the dictator as savior was to be repeated not only under the republic but during the empire and through the Middle Ages and the Renaissance into our own day.

Whatever his precise nature, Camillus is the first Roman general with a credible history and a recognizable program of action who can be seen in three dimensions. As he grew older, he grew increasingly stern and authoritarian. Conservative to the core, he was impatient with the popular demand for a greater voice in government and a better share of economic reward. In bringing forth the institution of the people's tribunes in the fifth century B.C., the republic had seen a marked advance in plebeian power; the tribunes held the right to veto any enactment by the aristocratic Senate that ran against the interests of the organized plebs or any individual member of it. But this much power only whetted the appetite for more. Since the Gallic invasion the economic situation of the plebs—urban arti-

sans, traders, free peasants, and immigrants—had deteriorated
seriously. Their chief grievances concerned the gathering of
land into great estates and the harsh laws against those who
failed to pay their debts. Roman seizures and colonization had
indeed brought in considerable tracts of public land, which
were widely assigned to private holders, thereby easing the land
hunger of a fast-growing populace. While large holdings generally were profitable, small ones were uneconomical. Moreover,
the small holder in need of cash could not raise a mortgage on
his property, he had to do so on his own person, which made
him a bondsman of his creditor. Failure to work off his debt,
often made at usurious rates, could lead to his imprisonment,
sometimes for life, or sale into slavery.

In about 367 B.C. the plebs, struggling under the poverty of
postinvasion years, made three demands that were to usher in a
crisis of classes in Rome. They called for drastic reform of the
debt laws and for remission of interest; for restrictions on the
amount of land held by any one owner (many plebeians had
sold their holdings to wealthy creditors in lieu of debt service);
and thirdly, for re-establishment of the consulship (suspended
under Camillus' dictatorship), with the provision that one of the
two consuls be chosen from the plebs.

When Camillus heard that these revolutionary demands
were being seriously presented, he was outraged. He immediately ordered that the Forum, which had become the place of
public debate and the seat of the government, be cleared by the
lictors, and the characteristically threatened to administer the
oath of service to all men of military age and to lead them out
of the city. His aim was to stifle all opposition; the aim of the
tribunes was to silence him. They had power to impose fines
and decided on the sum of fifty thousand drachmas if he continued to obstruct the popular will. Camillus was in his seven-
ties. He had no stomach for further quarrels with the Romans

and soon retired, pleading ill-health—though he was recalled to repel another incursion of the Gauls. He had served his country well and had no desire to see himself banished from Rome nor to have his legend destroyed, his wealth confiscated, his power shattered. Meanwhile, under the tribunes Sextius and Licinius, a new law was promulgated requiring that one of the consuls be chosen from the plebs. It was a notable victory for the majority. Camillus had vowed to build a temple to Concord if ever there was an end to the struggle between the orders, and in about 367 B.C. the temple was built, or at least begun, at the northwestern corner of the Forum, as a perpetual reminder of the new relationship existing between the aristocracy and the people. We are told that the temple was originally constructed of wood and ornamented with terra-cotta plaques in the Etruscan manner, so deeply was Etruscan influence felt long after the expulsion of the kings.

The temple to Concord, though often rebuilt, survived through the centuries. Camillus, we are told, presided over its dedication. It was his last official act; he died of the plague two years later. In time the Etruscan ornaments vanished, and the wooden columns were replaced by marble ones. Today little remains except the concrete base and the marble threshold beside the winding road leading to the Capitoline; but in the history of democracy this temple has a special place, for it was built to celebrate the day the plebs gained equal rights with the aristocracy to elect from among their number the highest magistrates of the republic.

The break-through by the plebs was to lead to a whole series of laws limiting the privileges of the aristocracy. The promised agrarian reforms were carried out, some debts were remitted, and new measures were passed making it an offense to hold a debtor in slavery; his goods could be placed under bond, but not his person. By the beginning of the third century B.C. the plebs, economically strengthened, were entering the priestly colleges and exercising the functions previously reserved for the aristocracy—with the result that a new class of rich plebeians emerged to ally themselves with their former enemies. The struggle for democracy therefore had to be renewed, and with the Lex Hortensia, passed in 287 B.C., a further victory was won through its provision that resolutions of the plebeian assembly should be binding upon all Romans—patrician no less than commoner. The growing machinery of public administration had already involved the creation of many new offices, many of them held by plebeians: there were praetors (or magistrates) and aediles (roughly equivalent to mayors), who together with the censors (tax and census officials and drafters of senatorial lists) divided many powers previously held by the consuls. Therefore the essential elements of a working democracy were in existence when the Romans set out to create an empire in about the middle of the first century B.C.

Into the creation of the empire went a singular belief of the Romans in the benefits they brought to the people they conquered. Not the least of these was the system of government, which they had hammered out in the fourth century B.C., with its scheme of two consular magistrates, a senate, and a popular assembly. Roman imperialism was the product of Roman democracy, but it was also to a far greater extent the product of a particular kind of mind that takes grave comfort from disaster and pleasure from risk. The Romans were a people who were always drawing strength from their wounds. They were hard and unyielding, thrifty, cautious, and simple in their tastes in spite of the overlay of Etruscan splendor. In every family absolute and unquestioning obedience was owed to the paterfamilias, who had power of life and death over his wife and children. In much the same way as conquerors, they imposed themselves on their subjects, laying a heavy hand on them, yet at the same time admitting them step by step to the rewards of membership in the Roman family. The subjects were regarded by the Romans somewhat in the manner of children over whom the state should cast its protection, raising them in due time—if they behaved—to full citizenship. So Vergil placed in the mouth of Anchises, father of Aeneas, legendary ancestor of Rome, a prophecy of world empire and a warning to administer the empire according to law:

> *Remember, Roman, to guide the nations with authority.*
> *Let these be your arts: impose the laws of peace,*
> *And spare the humbled and lay low the proud.*

Long before Vergil the Romans were aware of their heritage.

They had scarcely recovered from the destruction of their city by the Gauls when they embarked on the long, arduous, and dangerous adventure that was to lead to world empire. The Latin tribes, with whom the Romans had blood ties and with whom they had long ago struck up alliances against the Etruscans, had taken the occasion of Rome's disaster to break away from the city's leadership of the Latin League and to enlarge themselves before Rome did. Calls for independence were made; a fear of Roman hegemony was in the air—a justified fear, it turned out, for the Romans in their treaty with Carthage in 348 B.C. asserted the right to speak for the towns of the Latin coast. Revolts, border wars, raids, and counterraids marked several decades, resulting in 338 in Rome's subjection of almost all the Latin tribes around it, and of the troublesome Volscians of the Latin hills in particular. Town after town surrendered and gave up its independence and its property in exchange for a promissory note of leniency and participation in the rising Roman state. The Latin League was dissolved, to be succeeded by a federation of Latin colonies owing loyalty to the

Romans. Each colony had a Roman garrison, which kept the peace and watched over municipal officers and saw to it that people obeyed Rome's laws. However, with each conquest, Rome made a particular settlement, leaving some people with a modicum of independence and incorporating others into the Roman system. The result of this carefully graduated scheme of submission, occasional freedom, and participation in rewards overcame further rebellion and attached great numbers of people to Rome. The success of this policy became manifest when Rome, in the collision with Carthage across the sea, far from finding another revolt by Latins on its hands, found them to be friendly or at least quiescent.

The Latins enjoyed many rights of citizenship; in theory they remained free, in practice they were subordinate to the whims of the local garrison commander. If they intermarried with the Romans, their children acquired Roman citizenship. In Roman eyes this was a supreme privilege granted to them only because they were regarded as natural allies of the same stock. Two towns, Tibur (Tivoli) and Praeneste (Palestrina), were permitted independence because they possessed ancient historical ties with Rome; but they were the exceptions that proved the rule that Rome permitted no independent authority anywhere in its domains. Tibur and Praeneste were both near Rome and could still be watched closely.

Already in the fourth century B.C. the Romans were working out their laws of conquest. Like the Israelites, they saw themselves as divinely inspired missionaries serving a divine purpose and regarded war as a religious vocation not to be undertaken without suitable rituals, prayers, and sacrifices. Strange magical rites were practiced in order to induce the gods of a besieged city to abandon it and defect to Rome. The enemy city would be consecrated to the infernal gods, and the general in command would sometimes offer himself as a willing sacrifice. Such a *devotio* was pronounced by the consul Publius Decius Mus during one of the wars with the Latins. The Roman army was about to be overwhelmed when Decius covered his head with his toga and communed with the gods, urging them to visit the enemy with fear, shuddering, and death. It was not enough that they should die; they must learn in fear and trembling that the gods fought on the side of the Romans. The Latins must die in agony, suffering the punishment inflicted on them by the gods. Then having addressed all the known and unknown gods, Decius leaped onto his horse and hurled himself into the thick of the fighting. He did not live to see the end of the battle, for he was killed at its turning point. "It was as though," wrote the historian Livy, "he had been sent from heaven to expiate all the wrath of the gods and to deflect destruction from his own people onto his enemies."

The institution of the *devotio* was a peculiar one, for it involved vast and awesome claims. The consul, leading his army on the field of battle, was far more than a general. He saw himself as a religious leader in communion with the gods, possessing powers not given to ordinary mortals, capable of calling down the lightning on his adversaries; the heavens and the earth beneath were engaged in the struggle. The general became a shaman; the enemy could be cursed into defeat on condition that the general or someone chosen by him was prepared to sacrifice his life. If the man who pronounced the *devotio* died in battle, there were no further ceremonies; he was remembered gratefully in the hearts of the people he had saved. If he survived, his image was buried seven feet deep in the earth, and a guilt offering was sacrificed over the so-called tomb that contained the image of a living man. The guilt offering was made because he had not died; the gods had demanded his death, but a miracle or the word of an unknown god had saved him. In this strange war, guilt and sacrifice came together

in a rite that was at once mysterious and terrible in its consequences. Never again was the man who had devoted his life
permitted to take part in religious ceremonies either on his own
or on behalf of the state. He had become a man without an
existence, for he was neither dead nor alive, and the place
where his image lay was sacred.

The wars changed and the methods of fighting changed, for
the Romans continually learned from their adversaries. The
organization of warfare, down to its last-minute particulars,
was their constant study. Originally they had fought in the for-
mation known to Greeks as the phalanx: the heavy infantry
drawn up in an unbroken line many ranks deep, the massed
shields acting as armor, the long spears serving as their
weapons of offense. Their tactic was to crush the enemy by the
weight of those spears. After the Gallic invasion they learned
the need for greater maneuverability. While fighting the Latins
they seem to have experimented with combinations of a modi-
fied phalanx, using detached units capable of inflicting damage
and then retiring under cover of the phalanx.

By about 326 B.C. the Romans were fighting the Samnites,
sturdy mountaineers from the southern uplands of the Apennines, who fought in detachments of no more than twenty or
thirty men, armed with javelins and short stabbing swords.
About that time the Romans abandoned the phalanx and introduced the maniple, consisting of about one hundred twenty
men, as the principal unit of organization in their armies. The
small, round shield of the Roman soldier was replaced by a
larger, oblong one; the long spear, which had earlier proved
ineffective against the huge Gallic long swords, gave way to the
javelin; and the cutting sword was altered into a stabbing
weapon. The heavy javelins, nearly seven feet long, could be
hurled at the enemy from a distance of several yards before the
Romans closed for an encounter with swords. (The same princi-

ple was followed in modern wars when machine-gun fire opened the way for a bayonet charge.) Instead of the great shock of the phalanx there was now a series of shocks in rapid succession. Over the years the weapons were continually changing: new weapons were developed; old weapons were adapted, but the basic elements were retained. The Spanish sword replaced the old Roman one; the sling made of sinews became the sling staff, four feet long with leather thongs; the heavy artillery, which the Romans designated with the word *tormenta*, came into being. But it was the highly maneuverable maniples that conquered the world.

The wars against the Samnites in the Campania were long and costly, fought with a vigor and a savagery that threatened to bleed both armies white. Though many historical questions remain as to the origin and extent of this fighting, there is no doubt that over a period of many decades Rome grew vastly by subjugating these settlers allied to the Greek colonists in the south. Given the presumptive dates 343–341 B.C. for the first war, 328–304 for the second, and 298–290 for the third, the Romans remembered thirty-one processional triumphs in which they led their Samnite captives across the Forum, displaying the heaped booty to the cheering crowds; but they suffered nearly as many defeats. In 321 B.C. at the Caudine Forks, between Capua and Beneventum, the Samnites trapped a Roman army in a defile by closing it at both ends. The Romans tried to fight their way out and then realized that if they continued fighting there would be no survivors. They sought for terms, but the Samnite general was all for massacring them to the last man. Finally he was prevailed upon to save the lives of the Romans on condition that they admit defeat and not make war. The Romans were compelled to surrender their arms, their equipment, and all their clothes except their undergarments, and they were forced to bend their necks under a yoke of spears.

They solemnly signed a treaty of peace, which they later disavowed, claiming that it had been obtained under duress. War soon broke out again and continued for decades, the Romans mounting one punitive expedition after another. Then, at last, in 290 B.C. they captured the Samnite general whose magnanimity had saved them at the Caudine Forks, bound him in chains, led him in triumph through Rome, and beheaded him. The gods disapproved, for they sent a pestilence.

With the subjection of the Samnites the Romans opened the way for the conquest of all southern Italy. They had already secured their northern frontier by striking deep into the heart of Etruria. They were building military roads to the north, the south, and the west. Treasure was pouring in from the conquered territories and the ancient taste for opulence was revived. Stern republicans might offer warnings against Samnite gold, but the warnings went unheeded. The many-colored robes of the Samnite warriors, their silver scabbards, gold sword belts, and gold-embroidered saddlecloths passed into the hands of the Romans, who marveled at so much finery and learned after centuries to don it again.

Saturated with Samnite opulence, Rome began to mint silver coins, having only recently learned to mint bronze. The Forum was beginning to be crowded with the gilded statues of victorious generals. On the roof of the great temple on the Capitoline, as a visible sign of Roman dominance, there was now a statue of Jupiter riding in a four-horse chariot. Within the temple itself a new statue of Jupiter was fashioned from the breastplates, greaves, and helmets of the Samnites.

The Greek colonies in the boot of Italy held the promise of even greater loot. They were a temptation too great to resist; they were also a threat to the growth of Rome. Tarentum (Taranto) was a city of wealth, built around a great harbor, with a powerful navy composed of men proud of their Spartan descent. In 282

B.C. a Roman squadron of ten ships appeared offshore, and the Tarentines, remembering a treaty with Rome that forbade the passage of ships through their waters, decided to attack in force. All the available ships of Tarentum put to sea. Four Roman ships were sunk, one was captured, the rest fled. The Roman commander was killed in the fighting, and the captives were either executed or sold into slavery. Then, elated by the easy victory, the Tarentines turned their attention to the neighboring Greek city of Thurii, which had placed itself under the protection of the Romans, with a Roman garrison to keep the people in order. They attacked the city, forced the Roman garrison to withdraw, and returned in triumph to celebrate their victory.

These were not the acts of an excited, irresponsible mob, rather they were the result of a carefully-thought-out policy. Rome clearly intended to conquer the Greek world to the south. It could be stopped only by a superior force determined to prevent its expansion. The Tarentines, counting on the exhaustion of the Roman army after the long Samnite wars, may have decided that the time had come to assert the independence of the Greek colonists in Italy; and when a Roman envoy came to Tarentum to demand safeguards against future attacks, he was refused a hearing. We are told by Roman historians that the mob laughed at his bad Greek and pelted him with filth, and that he said, holding up his stained robe so that all could see it: "Laugh now, but this robe shall remain uncleansed until it is washed in your best blood." Rome was offering peace in exchange for domination. The Tarentines nevertheless prepared for war.

The future of the Greek colonies in southern Italy and Sicily was at stake. The Tarentines summoned help from Greece. Pyrrhus, king of Epirus, an ambitious and tempestuous prince, a kinsman of Alexander the Great, crossed into Italy with a force of 20,000 infantry, 3,000 cavalry, and 20 elephants. He, like Alexander, was tempted with visions of world empire. All

southern Italy, he thought, would fall to him, then Sicily and
Spain and Africa. He held Tarentum in an iron grip, ordered the
theatres closed, drilled the citizens, prepared to destroy any
Roman army that dared to take the field. At Heraclea in 280 B.C.
a Greek army encountered a Roman army for the first time. The
Greek phalanx was confronted by massed maniples; Pyrrhus'
force was tight and solid with its thick forest of bristling spears,
man touching man in ranks sixteen deep. The Romans stood in
open order at arm's length from one another, with their javelins
and stabbing swords. Pyrrhus kept his best weapons in reserve:
his Thessalian cavalry and armored elephants, which were
thrown into battle when the Romans were giving ground.
Pyrrhus, author of a celebrated treatise on the art of war, was a
good general, and he had calculated his precise moment of
attack to perfection. The Romans had never before seen elephants, and they fled in panic, leaving 7,000 dead on the field.
Yet Pyrrhus had lost 4,000 of his Epirote veterans. According to
Plutarch, when he returned to Tarentum to offer the spoils to
the temple of Zeus, he remarked to one who congratulated him
that another such victory would utterly undo him.

Later Pyrrhus marched on Rome, but when he was sixteen
miles from the city he decided that it would be hopeless to lay
siege to those impregnable walls and looked for another opportunity to destroy the Roman armies on the field. The opportunity came the following spring when the battle of Heraclea was
fought all over again at Asculum, in Apulia. Once more the elephants were thrown into battle and the Romans retired in
panic. But the losses on both sides were great, and Pyrrhus
returned to Tarentum. There he learned that the Romans were
allied with the Carthaginians, and the Gauls were overrunning
Greece. No more reinforcements could be expected from Epirus,
Macedonia, and Thessaly.

Carthage dominated the western Mediterranean. The power

of its empire extended from the borders of Cyrenaica, in northern Africa, to the legendary Pillars of Hercules, at the western end of the Mediterranean Sea, and beyond. The descendants of Phoenician settlers, from Syria and Lebanon, had built a fortress-city on the Gulf of Tunis and ringed it with a triple line of walls. Homer describes the Phoenicians as "greedy men, famous for their ships," by which he meant perhaps nothing more than that they were fine sailors and cautious merchants. Unlike the Romans, they were content with their possessions and had little liking for war; instead of raising a citizen army, they employed mercenaries who were led by Carthaginian officers. These mercenaries were tribesmen from the African interior, Numidian light-horsemen, Libyan archers, Balearic slingers, and there was a leavening of Gauls, Spaniards, and Greeks. Their trading centers in Spain, Sardinia, and Sicily prospered; gradually southern Spain, most of Sardinia, and all of Western Sicily fell into their grasp. But they did not want land as much as a command of the seas, and both the Romans and the Greeks knew there were sea routes forbidden to them by the Carthaginians.

When the Greek cities appealed to Pyrrhus for help, he turned his attention to the Carthaginians. He chose to fight them on land, where they were most vulnerable. He swept across Sicily, reducing their fortresses one by one. He laid siege to Lilybaeum (Marsala), the strongest and westernmost Carthaginian citadel. The city held out so long that he was compelled to raise the siege. Once again he returned to Tarentum and built up an army capable of fighting the Romans. But an indecisive battle at Beneventum in 275 B.C., in which his troops were mauled during a night attack, was the signal for the abrupt termination of his campaigns, and he sailed for home, his dream of becoming a new Alexander shattered.

On leaving Sicily after his failure at Lilybaeum, Pyrrhus is said to have remarked, "What a battlefield I have left for the

Romans and the Carthaginians!" With Pyrrhus gone, the Greek
settlements in southern Italy and Sicily were left in a power vac-
uum, and before long a confrontation was bound to take place
between the force expanding from the north and the strength
radiating from the African shore. The battlefield of this great
collision between former friends was to be not Sicily alone but
the entire western Mediterranean. The first and second struggles
of the Punic wars (264–241 B.C. and 218–201) were waged with
increasing ferocity. The contestants were evenly matched:
Carthage was larger and wealthier than Rome and could more
readily face the costs of a large navy; Rome, however, was superior to Carthage in manpower and in the enthusiasm of its citizen soldiery. No quarter was given. Savagery became a way of
life and massacre a commonplace. When the long struggle was
over, Carthage lay in ruins and the fields of Italy were a desert.

After Pyrrhus' departure, Rome and its supporting cities had
found it an easy task to put down remaining opposition in the
south of the peninsula, thereby crushing not only Greek resistance but that of the Samnites, Oscans, and Lucanians as well. In
264 B.C. the Romans stood at the Strait of Messina—but a
Carthaginian garrison stood opposite. After much debate in the
Senate, Rome responded to an appeal by the autonomous city
of Messina, on the Sicilian side, to form an alliance and protect
it against the Carthaginian attack. Once landed, Roman forces
were soon driving against a number of Punic settlements on the
island, and the war to the death had begun. In an astonishingly
short space of time the Romans built a fleet to challenge
Carthage's mastery of the sea. A Carthaginian quinquereme,
cast ashore on Bruttium (Calabria), provided the model to which
the Romans added an ingenious device they referred to as the
corvus, or "raven." This was a thirty-foot gangway, with a
heavy curved spike at one end serving as a grappling-iron,
which could be lowered from the ship's mast by pulleys. With

the aid of the corvus the Romans proposed to transform naval war into a kind of land war, the aim being not to sink the enemy ships but to board them and fight the enemy on the deck. These tactics were more successful than they had dared to hope. Early in 260 B.C. the consul Gaius Duilius encountered a Carthaginian fleet off Mylae (Milazzo), on the northern coast of Sicily, and engaged it in battle. When the two sides pulled clear, the Romans had captured thirty-one of the Carthaginian ships and sunk fourteen. The Romans had won their first naval victory with their first fleet. Gaius Duilius was awarded the honors of triumphator; the strange, savagely decorated beaks of Carthaginian ships adorned the column in the Forum where the proud admiral walked, attended by flute player and torchbearer.

Emboldened by this victory, and believing that it had acquired command of the seas in a single stroke, Rome decided to invade Carthage. Four years later an enormous fleet of about three hundred thirty ships sailed for Carthage. The Carthaginians, too, had been building a new fleet. The two fleets met off the southern coast of Sicily in the greatest naval battle yet fought, and once more the corvus settled the issue. The Carthaginians were routed; the Romans sailed on to Carthage, confident that in a few weeks they would conquer the enemy. However, when Rome demanded in harsh terms that Carthage surrender, the Carthaginians were fired to a desperate resistance. Under the command of a Spartan general they hurled themselves at the Roman lines, and the Romans fled. The first landing on Africa was a disaster; only a small remnant of the invading army was able to make its way back to Rome.

Such catastrophes occurred at intervals during the long-drawn-out war. Whole armies, whole fleets vanished. Weeks, months, years would pass while the opponents painfully reassembled their forces, and then once again they would engage in a sudden, murderous conflict, from which they

retired in disorder, bruised and broken, only to resume the
fighting when they recovered their strength. At last, in 241 B.C.,
after twenty-three years of struggle, another Roman naval victory brought about a treaty of peace. The Carthaginians were
ordered to pay an indemnity, to refrain from sailing their war-
ships in Roman waters, and to abandon all claim to Sicily. The
Romans declared they had won a crowning victory, but it was
nothing more than a truce—a truce that was to last no longer
than the war that preceded it.

The period between the first and second Punic wars was an
important one for Rome. Sardinia and Corsica became Roman
outposts, the raids of Illyrian pirates in the Adriatic were halted,
and by the conquering of Corcyra (Corfu), off western Greece,
the Romans obtained a foothold on Greek soil. These goals were
obtained with little effort. More difficult was the conquest of
northern Italy, or Cisalpine Gaul, which extended Rome's frontiers to the Alps and made it considerably more secure against
the constant threat of invasion by northern Gauls. These were the
years of the great break-through. Now Roman command posts
stood in an unbroken chain from the Alps to Sicily. Nor were the
Carthaginians resting on their laurels; they were pushing northward through Spain, bringing all the tribes under their sovereignty, securing the wealth of silver and other mines to restore
their finances and the strength of manpower for their armies.

Hamilcar Barca, a soldier who had proved himself in Sicily,
became governor of Carthaginian Spain. In eight years of brilliant activity, he built up a state, a treasury, and an army, placing
great new resources into Punic service. Some years after his
death, his son Hannibal was raised to the governorship. He was
only a youth; at the age of nine he had vowed to dedicate his life
to the destruction of Rome, and he very nearly accomplished it.

A strange impersonality attends Hannibal, for the records of
Carthaginian historians are lost and the Romans never

described his person, except to say that he was lean, hard-muscled, and possessed piercing eyes. They saw him as power incarnate, and no one else ever terrified them so much or wounded them so deeply.

Hannibal's plan was simple, effective, and deadly. He proposed to lead African and Spanish levies across the Pyrenees and across the Alps into Italy, and to strike at Rome from the north. He counted on the Cisalpine Gauls to flock to his standards, and after the Gauls, all the conquered tribes of Italy. The great expedition, supported by many war elephants, took place in 218 B.C. At first all went well. On the river Trebia and by the shores of Lake Trasimene, Hannibal tore to pieces the Roman armies sent to block his progress. At Cannae, with superb strategy, he induced the Romans to fight on his terms, surrounded them, then slaughtered possibly 50,000 of them at a cost of only 6,000 of his own men, the greater part of whom were Gauls. It was told that many of the Roman dead were found with their faces buried in the earth. They were the wounded who preferred to choke themselves to death rather than to be killed in a manner determined by their conquerors.

The army of Hannibal was intact; three huge Roman armies had been destroyed. "In five days' time," said the Carthaginian officers, "we shall dine in the Capitol." But without siege trains, and without a general uprising by the Italian tribes against Rome, Hannibal knew that he was powerless to occupy and hold the city and thus bring the Romans to their knees.

He appealed to the Italians and Greeks to join his forces, but his appeal failed; central Italy remained loyal to Rome. He learned that victory in the field is a faulty substitute for the capture of the enemy's citadel. His brother Hasdrubal crossed the Alps with Spanish reinforcements only to be defeated on the Metaurus. By 206 B.C., Roman armies had almost completely wrested Spain from the grip of Carthage. For nearly four more

years Hannibal camped in the wild and mountainous regions of
Bruttium, his veterans around him, hoping against hope that
help would come from Carthage, from Philip of Macedonia,
from the Italians; but none came.

Then once more, the Romans decided that their most promising
course would be to carry the war to the enemy's homeland. In 204
B.C. the young and popular general Publius Cornelius Scipio sailed
for Africa with an army, landed at Utica, and attempted to raise
the tribes of Africa against Carthage. He was more successful
than Hannibal in efforts at subversion; the Numidian king
Masinissa had already gone over to the Romans on the promise
of receiving an enlarged kingdom. Hannibal, undermined, abandoned Italy, sailed for Carthage with his veterans, and fought a
combined Numidian Roman army at Zama, some eighty miles
southwest of Carthage. His veterans fought superbly, but when
he threw his elephants into the battle, the Romans, no longer
frightened by those beasts, simply opened their lines and let
them pass. The half-trained Carthaginian citizen-soldiers broke;
the Numidian cavalry hammered at the wavering line; long
before nightfall it was over. Hannibal escaped from the battlefield unharmed, having lost in a day's fighting all the advantages he had gained in a lifetime of victories.

When peace was concluded in 201 B.C., Carthage was pros-
trate. Though the city was permitted to retain its African possessions, it was compelled to surrender Spain and all its
remaining foreign trading posts. The war elephants became the
property of the Romans, and the great fleet, with the exception
of ten triremes, was towed into the harbor and solemnly
burned. As the ships burned low to the waterline, the
Carthaginians standing on shore saw that their command of the
sea, and therefore their power, was gone forever. The Mediterranean was already a Roman lake.

V

A REPUBLIC DIVIDED

When a commonwealth, after warding off many great dangers, has arrived at a high pitch of prosperity and undisputed power, it is evident that, by the lengthened continuance of great wealth within it, the manner of life of its citizens will become more extravagant; and that the rivalry for office, and in other spheres of activity, will become fiercer than it ought to be.

—Polybius, *Histories*

Though the Romans had triumphed over Carthage, there must have been many who wondered whether victory had not been bought at too high a price. In sixteen years of fighting Rome had lost nearly a quarter of her population, four hundred towns had been destroyed, and half the farms of Italy had been devastated. Profound social changes had been set in motion. Slaves won by conquest flooded the labor market, and any Roman who could afford to feed them could have as many as he pleased; the number captured in the first half of the second century B.C. may have reached two hundred fifty thousand. The result was a growth of great estates worked by slaves and the displacement from the land of large numbers of independent farmers. They flocked to the towns, only to discover that they were unwelcome there, and soon became part of the restless Roman mob. A rising class of shrewd business promoters, the equites, mounted large-scale commercial ventures, taking advantage of the fact that the senators—august representatives of the old, landholding aristocracy—were prohibited by law from engaging in overseas trade. New wealth pouring in from the granaries of Sicily, the fields of North Africa, and the mines of Spain made the rich richer, but left the poor poorer.

In the past the Romans had been peasants and woodsmen, men of the countryside who brought into the towns the discipline of the seasons. They owed their strength to hard work, to the frugality of their lives, to their respect for household and public gods, and to their effort to embody such qualities as *gravitas, virtus*, and *diligentia*. But the conquest of Carthage had brought not only wealth and upheaval but subtle changes in the Roman character as well. The hard and grasping qualities that the Romans had possessed from the beginning assumed more dangerous forms. Never remarkable for their pity, they now became remarkable for their pitilessness, and victory, far from leaving them sated, only whetted their appetite for more.

Physically Rome burgeoned immensely in the period following the Punic holocaust. Despite all losses, by the middle of the second century B.C. the population of the city may have numbered half a million. In the same period national wealth is thought to have doubled or trebled. Industries, such as the manufacture of pottery, tools, cordage, and ships for the military or carrying trade, rose and thrived. According to the modern scholar H. H. Scullard, the great slag heaps discovered at Populonia, opposite the island of Elba, suggest that "an average of ten million tons of iron ore were treated each year during the last centuries of the republic." Finished goods went out across the entire Mediterranean; and in turn raw materials poured into Italy—along with some manufactured ware, and spoils and art treasures from Sicily and Greece.

To sustain a fast-growing populace and to aid the spread of Roman power, programs of public works were undertaken by official and private enterprise. Drainage canals were dug and aqueducts were built to control water supply, irrigation, and urban sanitation. Rome's paved road system, begun in the fourth century B.C. with the building of the Appian Way, grew and eventually linked all the major communities of the penin-sula in an unprecedented network. In addition to wooden bridges, the Romans built great bridges of stone—a particular feat of early Roman engineering. The Mulvian Bridge, across the Tiber, was constructed in about 109 B.C. Provisions were set up whereby the equites, who may have numbered ten thousand in the later days of the republic, could engage in competitive bidding for public contracts and set up companies in which any Roman citizen could buy a share.

In theory Rome was still a republic. In fact it was an oli-garchy ruled by the three hundred aristocratic senators, who had been elected for life and who replaced the annually appointed consuls, the tribunes, and the popular assembly as the fount of authority. The change had come about gradually as the Punic war effort demanded an increasing concentration of power. The popular assembly and the Comitia Centuriata con-tinued to meet, and the tribunes still possessed a theoretical power of veto, but all the important decisions were made by the senators, who had control of military appointments, of the treasury and the judiciary, of regulating all revenues and expenditure, and of determining foreign policy, receiving ambassadors, and ratifying treaties. Although the senators sup-posedly acted as an advisory body, they acquired supreme judi-cial authority by appointing committees empowered to act on all matters concerning the safety of the state. Though excluded from trade, they nevertheless granted public contracts, and in this way assisted the growing mercantile class. The consuls were simply the agents of the senatorial majority. The Senate was a self-perpetuating body; it was not in direct contact with the plebeian assembly, and it was jealous of the privileges enjoyed by the assembly. Edicts announced in the name of the

Senate and the Roman people—*senatus populusque Romanus*—merely represented the will of the senators.

Such a vast accumulation of power by a few privileged aristocrats could lead only to revolution, and almost inevitably it would be headed by a small and determined group within the senatorial party. The revolution, when it came, was broken because its leaders were murdered, and the remaining years of the republic only served to show that oligarchies and dictatorships were adept at employing republican forms as a means to achieving their purposes.

All the advantages were on the side of the Senate, for the plebs were without resources. Virtually unlimited power was at the disposal of the Senate; it was not burdened with a sense of responsibility to the people. It fed and entertained them with bread and circuses. To keep the people in a good temper it increased the number of public holidays and provided games, dramatic performances, and gladiatorial shows. And more games were offered by candidates for high office. The gift of bread and circuses resembled a loan secured on the good behavior of the plebs.

Entrenched in their privileges, possessing vast estates tilled by slaves, having little or no respect for the laws, the senators dominated Rome as thought it were a conquered city obedient to their whims. Of the three hundred senators, perhaps twenty formed the inner cabinet. Family ties bound them together; they rejoiced in their exclusiveness and their secrecy, so that we rarely know who was responsible for the great decisions nor do we know much about the debates that took place in the inner councils. The inner cabinet ruled, and those who defied it suffered the consequences.

Publius Cornelius Scipio, known as Scipio Africanus after his victory at Zama, both reached the peak of power in the Senate and incurred its displeasure. He was one of those rare men who combines so many virtues that the man himself seems to vanish and becomes a copy-book maxim. All the gifts were showered on him. Wealthy, wellborn, violently courageous, at times calmly meditative, scholarly, and deeply religious, believing himself close to the gods, he went through life as though he were in a dream. In his youth he had shown a girlish beauty, but no one thought he was effeminate. He wore his hair long in the Greek fashion, preferred Greek robes, and was admired for his graceful gestures, but there was a diamondlike hardness at the core. Scipio fought through the three disastrous battles of Ticino, Lake Trasimene, and Cannae and distinguished himself still further when the handful of dispirited survivors of the battle of Cannae threatened to leave Italy and take service in Greece. He held his sword over the head of the leader of the malcontents and threatened to kill him unless he went on fighting Hannibal. Scipio was then nineteen years old and already a veteran and an officer.

For generations members of his family had held high office. Within the family shrine there were said to be thirty death masks of ancestors who had held consular rank. His boundless self-confidence came perhaps from the knowledge of his aristocratic heritage, but there was a vein of mysticism in his nature which set him apart from other men and from his own family. The greatest military commander of his time, fired with visions of Rome's destiny, he was also an intellectual drawn to Greek thought and presence. Though a member of a class rooted in tradition, his personal impulses were directed toward sweeping and civilizing change.

During Scipio's lifetime Greek cultural influence was beginning to be widely felt in Rome. The conquest of southern Italy and Sicily (then filled with beautiful Greek cities) had opened the invaders' eyes to Greek art. In 212 B.C. the general Marcellus had returned from Syracuse in triumph, with statues of that

cultivated city as trophies. When Roman forces in the Second
Punic War crossed into Greece itself, closer contact with Hellenic ways resulted, along with more booty. Adaptations of
Greek plays had appeared on Roman stages in the third century
B.C., and by the middle of the second century B.C. Rome produced its first playwrights of note in the comic writers Plautus
and Terence, both of whom derived their plots from Greek New
Comedy. The poet Quintus Ennius, a profound student of Greek
literature, chronicled in dactylic hexameters the history of
Rome from its beginnings to the age of Scipio. In 167 B.C. the
consul Lucius Aemilius Paullus, another philhellene, was to
bring from conquered Macedonia the library of King Perseus
and form the first large collection of books in Rome. Greek
traders, artists, teachers, and slave-tutors converged on the city
and brought to it the testimonies of a superior culture and a
new landscape of the mind. Greek philosophy and Hellenistic
grace entered Rome; rich Roman youths went to Athens to
study and returned with a reverence for Attic thought. With the
looting of Greece's art treasures and with the importing of
Greek ideas, a more mature Rome came into being—one in
which worldliness and self-indulgence mixed with individuality
and enlightenment.

In this cultural expansion, for it was nothing less, Scipio
played a leading role. He was the innovator who threw the
gates wide open, and in time he came to be regarded as being
more Greek than Roman. Made censor and *princeps senatus* in
199 B.C., he seemed to occupy a position of unassailable authority. His family and his friends continued his Hellenizing effort.

But such men invite enemies. Scipio's most dangerous and
rancorous enemy was Marcus Porcius, who bore the nickname
Cato, which means "shrewd one." He came from a humble
background in the Sabine farm country and owed his advancement to his friendship with powerful members of the aristoc-

racy and to the courage he had displayed as a soldier in the ranks in the Second Punic War. At the age of thirty he became quaestor to Scipio in Sicily; six years later, in 198 B.C., he served as praetor in Sardinia, where he expelled usurers and made himself widely known as an apostle of strict morality and traditional Roman virtues. In another three years he achieved the consulship, and in 184 B.C. he became a censor—an office that Scipio had held. Thus he had immense influence over public morals and the disposition of offices and funds. He enlarged his functions, making himself in effect the puritanical policeman of Rome, bent on suppressing the Hellenizing and liberalizing influences of Scipio and his clan.

Farmer, soldier, lawyer, writer, political chieftain, Cato was an extraordinary presence. Robust and somewhat rustic, he had a gift for blunt speech raised to the power of genius. He had a fiery red face, steely eyes, large teeth, and a harsh, bellowing voice—vibrant and unforgettable, it commanded attention as he proclaimed his adherence to the ancient republican virtues and damned the fashionable Hellenism of Scipio and all newfangled things. As an orator Cato was among the greatest that Rome ever saw. He maintained that an orator's task was to "hold fast to the matter, the words will follow." Yet Cicero, the most polished speaker of his time, admired Cato's diatribes as showing "all the qualities of great oratory." His hatreds, which were many, belong to a recognizable type: women must be kept in their place; slaves must feel the whip; nothing good ever comes from philosophy. He liked to say that he wore homespun clothes, allowed no plaster or whitewash on the walls of his house, and drove the plow with his own hands. In his view too many people gathered in the Forum to gossip, and he wished that the Forum were paved with sharp-edged shells.

Cato was almost a caricature of the archreactionary, the uncompromising upholder of an ancient patriarchal age which

never existed except in his sturdy imagination. He was a man
without sentiment who could write in his *De agricultura* that
everything that was old and sick and worn-out on the farm
should be sold, including "old and sick slaves, and whatever
else is superfluous." Profit should be the main motive of the
good husbandman—profit, and nothing else. A farm hand
should receive a smock, a blanket, and a pair of wooden clogs
every other year, and the farmer should keep the threadbare
cloaks to make caps from.

The grave and brilliant Scipio, at home in Greek poetry and
philosophy, was confronted by the rough and spirited Cato,
who regarded Greek poetry and philosophy as luxuries that
would assuredly destroy the fabric of the Roman state. He was
even more uncompromising: he turned from reproving spiritual
luxuries to attacking extravagances in dress and jewelry. As
censor he sent his inspectors to examine the wardrobes of the
rich and taxed the contents far above their value; in this way he
earned the favor of the poor. He also saw to it that riots were
put down mercilessly—even grumbling was punished—and in
this way he earned the favor of the rich, who wanted above all
an orderly and obedient people.

By brilliantly exploiting the conflicting interests of rich and
poor, Cato became the most powerful figure in Rome. From a
soldier in the ranks and farmer he rose to become the acknowledged lawgiver and judge, giving his name to one of the buildings in the Forum containing law courts. Senators feared him
because as preserver of public morality he possessed sweeping
powers and could call for their personal records and arrest them
if he found any documents that displeased him; and everyone
else feared him too, because his inspectors were everywhere. He
was highhanded, vindictive, and always cautious, keeping to
the letter of the law.

Scipio's influence, however, remained strong. When war

broke out against Philip V of Macedonia in 200 B.C., Scipio's influence was such that the Senate gave orders to the Roman general Titus Quinctius Flamininus to proclaim to the Greeks that he had come, not as their enemy, but as their liberator from Macedonian tyranny. In 197 B.C. Flamininus defeated Philip at Cynoscephalae in a strange battle fought in the mist. The next year Flamininus attended the Isthmian games. A herald marched into the arena and spoke words meant to stir the Greeks to the depths of their souls: "The Roman Senate and the proconsular general Titus Quinctius have conquered King Philip and the Macedonians, and they now declare the Corinthians, the Phocians, Locrians, Euboeans, Achaeans, Magnesians, Thessalians, and Perrhaebians to be free, without garrison or tribute, subject to their own ancestral laws."

The Greeks had not expected the grant of freedom from the conquering Romans and became delirious with joy. Valerius Maximus says the birds in the air were stunned by the thunder of applause, and Livy says the Isthmian games came to an abrupt end because the Greeks were too happy to watch them. There was a vast outpouring of affection for the thirty-three-year-old imperator. Flamininus became the idol of the Greeks, and hymns were sung in his honor: "Hail, Paean Apollo, hail, Titus our Savior." As the months went by, it seemed as though Greeks and Romans were bound by ties of enduring friendship, and the two civilizations would fuse and there would be no more war. The philhellenes in Rome were overjoyed; the world they desired was taking shape.

Six years later, in 190 B.C., Antiochus III of Syria, known as Antiochus the Great, an eager voluptuary who had conquered the Greek cities of Asia Minor, fought a Roman army at Magnesia, near Smyrna. Scipio Africanus accompanied the army to the east, serving under the command of his brother Lucius Cornelius Scipio. Although the army of Antiochus outnumbered the Roman army two to one, the Syrian phalanx was cut to pieces by the Roman cavalry, and heavily armored troops were not even engaged in the battle. Antiochus returned to Syria and abandoned half his kingdom, saying that he was grateful to the Romans for saving him the trouble of ruling so large an empire. The triumph of Lucius Scipio was the most dazzling ever seen in Rome. In the procession that wound across the Forum there were 224 military standards, 1,231 ivory tusks, 37,420 pounds of silver, and an immense quantity of gold. Lucius Cornelius Scipio was awarded the title of Asiaticus.

The two Scipios had won the two most significant battles of their age. They were the darlings of Rome, at once conquerors and leaders of an intellectual elite. Cato, however, was biding his time. Three years passed before he decided to attack them. Although he directed the attack against Lucius by demanding an account of the spoils of victory, he was actually aiming at the far more famous brother. Such a demand had never before been made, for generals were accustomed by tradition to distribute rewards to their officers and soldiers as they saw fit, and most of the treasure automatically made its way to the state treasury. Africanus was incensed, and instead of defending himself or his brother, brought his records to the Senate and tore them into shreds in full view of all the senators. Because the official records of the spoils had disappeared, Cato could no longer press his attack.

The law, however, was on Cato's side. He knew all its intricate workings, he had his spies in the Scipionic circle, and he knew his whole future depended upon destroying the influence of his two greatest enemies, who were too proud or felt too secure to attack him. Again he waited three years, and then quite suddenly, when everyone thought the matter had been forgotten, he ordered Lucius Scipio to appear before the plebeian assembly to render his account. The great Africanus stood beside his brother. Nevertheless a heavy fine was imposed on Lucius, whose refusal to pay brought him a sentence of imprisonment. The power of the Scipios was broken; the family that had risen to such great heights was now disgraced. They were the cultivated men who had hoped to marry Rome to Greek culture; but instead of peace and friendship, the Greeks were to be offered interminable wars, which were little more than butcheries. Scipio Africanus vanished from the scene, moving to his country estate at Liternum, on the coast of the Campania, far from Rome. He never returned. Broken in health and spirit, bewildered by the ingratitude of the Romans, he died in 184 B.C. at age fifty-two. Cato outlived him by thirty-five years.

For Cato the only good foreigners were dead foreigners or slaves. His conception of the Roman empire was one of unlimited despotism, the subject nations to be ruled by an iron hand. He sowed the seeds of tyranny, scattering them in handfuls, and more than anyone he shaped a century that was to become tragic.

In 150 B.C. or shortly before, Cato, who was then in his late eighties, sailed for Carthage at the head of a commission to arbitrate a dispute between Carthage and Numidia—still being ruled by Masinissa, who was also nearing ninety. The two old men had much in common, and they shared an intense hatred and horror of the Carthaginians, who had survived defeat to become once more a great trading power. Masinissa's Numidians, loyal allies of the Romans, were in a privileged position. Since Carthage was forbidden by terms of peace with Rome to wage war on them, they could and did threaten it with impunity. They had absorbed one Punic province and were preparing to absorb another. Cato had been sent to mediate the dispute; instead he encouraged Masinissa in his designs and returned to

Rome to plead the cause of the Numidians. At the end of every speech, whatever the subject, he would add the words: "And furthermore I move that Carthage must be destroyed!"

He meant exactly what he said—the city must be wiped off the map, with no building left standing, no people permitted to live within the ruined walls. His demand was obeyed three years after his death: the Senate gave the task of destroying Carthage to Publius Cornelius Scipio, known as Scipio Aemilianus Africanus, Minor, the adopted grandson of the great Africanus, Carthage fell. For six days the Romans fought within its walls before the citadel surrendered. The thirty-nine-year-old commander watched the destruction impassively, but there came a moment when he turned to his close friend and secretary, the Greek Polybius, and said: "It is all so beautiful, and yet I have a foreboding that the same fate may fall on my own country." In the manner of a wellbred Roman he recited lines of Homer and wept a little.

For seventeen days the fires blazed over Carthage, then the buildings and walls were razed—a lengthy task, for some of the walls were nearly fifty feet high and over thirty feet broad—and then a plow was driven over the rubble and salt was sown into the furrows. Finally a solemn curse was spoken over the whole city; it forbade any crops to grow or any people to live there under pain of disastrous punishment by the gods. With the destruction of a city that had endured for about seven centuries, the long history of the Punic wars finally came to a close.

The Romans showed no interest in preserving even the vestiges of Punic culture. The libraries found during the sack of the city were scattered among the tribal princes of the interior; not a single book has survived. Little remains of their temples, their palaces, their bronzes, or their marble statues. Archaeologists must work with potsherds and a few inscriptions and with such reference to Carthaginian customs as survived in Greek histories.

Scipio Aemilianus was a cultured man of great personal distinction who could excuse his part in the destruction of Carthage by saying that he had merely obeyed the orders of the all-powerful Senate. To the end he remained a philhellene, encouraging Polybius to write his long and superbly intelligent history of republican Rome. The tragedy was that Scipio Aemilianus had had to perform the terrible acts that Cato had demanded.

It was a time of tragedies; never had the Romans shown themselves to be so bloodthirsty nor so destructive. The Greeks came out in rebellion, protesting that the promises of Flamininus were not being kept. "You pretend to be friends, but you behave like tyrants," declared the Greek philosopher Critolaus. The rebellion was put down by Lucius Mummius, who won the title of Achaicus by transforming Greece into the Roman province of Achaia. Corinth fought more furiously for her promised freedom than the rest and received the same punishment as Carthage. The walls were razed, the people were massacred or sold into slavery, and whatever was valuable was removed to Rome. For four centuries Corinth had been renowned for her arts; now all the bronze and marble statues were transported to Rome to decorate the temples, the Forum, and the private houses of the senators. To the ships' captains taking the treasure to Rome, Mummius gave the formidable instruction: "If any statue is damaged, it must be replaced by another of equal value."

But the lost statues could never be replaced, and there was little left of Roman *virtus*, by which was meant decency, sobriety, and courage. The dream of an empire founded on trust and fair dealing was going down in the blood of conquest. The march took Roman armies westward around the great bend of the Ligurian coast, past what are now Genoa and Nice, to fight off raiders threatening Rome's long-standing Greek allies

established at Massilia (Marseilles) and then in 124 B.C. to strike
up the Rhone valley and build outposts against the Gauls. Next
they set up a key stronghold at Narbo Martius (Narbonne) to
control the coastal route to Spain. To safeguard western sea
routes, revolts were put down in Sardinia and colonies were
established on Majorca, which had known the Phoenicians and
Carthaginians in turn.

In 133 B.C. most of the kingdom of Pergamum, in Asia
Minor, was annexed as a new Roman province. In the fastnesses of eastern Europe, battles were fought against the Cimbri
and Teutones in 113 B.C. near what is now Ljubljana, in
Yugoslavia. Booty and prisoners were paraded through the
streets of Rome, and the conquerors were decked out in the
robes of Jupiter. Europe and Asia bled. Those who were not
killed were treated like cattle.

The Romans too suffered from the wars. A grandson of Scipio Africanus, Tiberius Sempronius Gracchus, pointed to the
vast estates of the rich and then to the soldiers who had fought
the Roman wars, with no property they could call their own,
abandoned by the state to wander aimlessly through the countryside, unemployed, starving, and discontented. "The savage
beasts have their particular dens in Italy . . . ," he declared, "but
the men who bear arms, and expose their lives for the safety of
their country, enjoy in the meantime nothing more in it but the
air and light; and having no houses or settlements of their own,
are constrained to wander from place to place with their wives
and children." Though the Roman soldiers were called the masters of the world, he went on to say, they did not possess one
foot of ground which they could claim as their own.

Tiberius Gracchus was known for his bravery in battle and
his quiet earnestness of speech. Becoming tribune in 133 B.C.,
he proposed to revive an old law limiting the size of the great

estates, and vastly to reduce the amounts of public land that
had fallen into a few private hands and distribute it to the poor.
He made no effort to warn the Senate prior to making his
speech before the plebeian assembly. As tribune he had, or
thought he had, the right to offer bills to the lower house, conveniently forgetting that the Senate had long ago usurped this
right, employing its own docile instruments for this purpose. A
docile instrument was found. Another tribune appeared in the
assembly to veto the bill, but was thrown out. At that moment
the social war began that was to sound the knell of republican
Rome.

In defiance of the Senate, Tiberius Gracchus appointed a
board of three to supervise the breakup of the great estates. The
board consisted of Gracchus, his brother, and his father-in-law.
The selection was unwise; in the eyes of the senators the board
had been constituted illegally and represented only Tiberius
Gracchus. No funds were granted to the board, and almost no
capital was granted to the new farmers. In the following year
Tiberius Gracchus presented himself as a candidate for the tribunate for the second time. When the returns showed that he
was winning, the Senate decided to act. The young revolutionary and some three hundred of his followers were attacked by
hired bravos outside the temple on the Capitoline. All were
killed. Tiberius Gracchus was beaten to death with a chair leg.

Eleven years after the death of Tiberius, his younger brother
Gaius Sempronius Gracchus was elected tribune, and put forward further measures of land reform. He was a more vehement
orator than his brother, and was even more popular. The Senate
prepared for the inevitable moment when Gaius Gracchus
would have to step down after a year in office. Once more the
bravos were thrown at the revolutionaries. Three thousand of
Gracchus' followers made a last stand on the Aventine hill.

Gaius Gracchus either was killed or committed suicide; his followers were cut down or made prisoners, to be strangled in
their cells. The Senate acted toward the reformers as it had
acted toward Carthage; it annihilated them. A special law was
passed forbidding the wives and children of the dead to put on
mourning.

The Senate was supreme, but it was no longer respected
amid the growing division of the state. Corrupt, ingrown, and
murderous, it pursued its own purposes with no regard for the
people. The African king Jugurtha, out to win sole control of
Rome's allied state of Numidia, bribed many a senator in order
to win support for his aim. Summoned to Rome to reveal their
names, he remarked, "Rome is a city for sale, and doomed to
perish if it can find a purchaser." Finally there was open war
with Numidia; and this struggle, begun in 112 B.C., brought into
prominence the two men who were to lead Rome on a new path
to dictatorship. One was the hard and rugged Gaius Marius, the
son of a farmer from the Volscian mountains, a *novus homo*, or
"new man" who rose by his own merits without the patronage
of the Senate which he despised. The other was Lucius Cornelius Sulla, a patrician, determined to uphold the senatorial
privileges at all costs. A man of moods, dangerously impulsive,
he would order a blood bath as calmly as he would read a Greek
poem.

Marius and Sulla had been comrades, working closely
together during the Jugurthine War. Marius received the credit
for bringing it to a victorious end; but Sulla, the capable diplo-
mat, was the one who trapped Jugurtha by inviting him to a
conference, guaranteeing his safety, and then placing him
under arrest. Jugurtha, chained, graced the triumph of Marius
against whom Sulla now plotted revenge.

Both were great generals who served the republic well in
war but helped to destroy it in time of peace. Marius fought and

destroyed the hordes of barbarian Cimbri and Teutones as they descended from the north; Sulla overcame the armies of Mithridates in Greece. The two conflicting parties were bringing on a tragedy in Rome: the one intent on breaking the power of the Senate, the other on maintaining senatorial privilege. Marius, whose military reforms turned the citizens' legions of Rome into professional standing armies, was consul seven times during the last twenty-one years of his life. In 87 B.C., he and his supporters slaughtered the leaders of the Senate and thousands of members of the aristocratic class. Sulla, in turn, after winning battles against partisans of Marius after the latter's death in 86 B.C., resorted to even greater butchery, setting up lists of outlawry that gave his followers the right to kill his and their own enemies at will and take over their properties. Countless numbers perished.

Once in command, Sulla had himself elected to the ancient emergency office of dictator. He held extraordinary powers and dominated Rome in near-regal state. The people, watching him parade through the streets surrounded by his bodyguard, observed that he was preceded by twenty-four lictors—a number perhaps even greater than that which had preceded the ancient kings. His announced scheme was to write new laws that would reorganize the republic. Believing in firm government by established leaders of the upper classes, he strengthened the powers of the Senate and reduced those of the tribunes and the popular assembly; moreover, a man could now become consul only after having served in the Senate for eight years. In this way he would prevent rule by plebeian chieftains (such as Marius) or future autocrats (such as himself). But the Senate was so ineffective, and the best men of Rome in both parties were so decimated, that uncertainty lay ahead. The Senate was in fact only the instrument of the dictator's will. His chief agents, the men who carried out his laws, were ten thousand young and sturdy slaves recruited from the households of the men he had killed, owing allegiance to him and murdering at his pleasure. This brotherhood of assassins acquired the family name of the dictator: they were known as the Cornelii. The forms of republican rule continued, but under a reign of terror.

Sulla himself seemed to revel in it. He ordered the severed heads of many of his enemies to be heaped before him in the Forum and gazed on them with quiet satisfaction. One of his most brilliant lieutenants, Catiline, was sent to murder a nephew of the late Marius; the killing was performed with all the refinements of slow torture. Sulla called himself Felix, meaning that he was the happiest of men and blessed by the gods. Yet the Roman people were not equally blessed. In the wake of Marius and Sulla, other rival military chieftains—Crassus, Pompey, and Caesar—were to arise to put an end to the republic.

VI

THE COMING OF CAESAR

Therefore, my lords, strain every nerve for the preservation of the state, look in every quarter for the storms, which will burst upon you, if you do not see them in time.

—Cicero, fourth oration against Catiline, 63 B.C.

The Romans never forgot the despotic reign of Sulla when the streets ran with blood and strange portents darkened the sky. His rule, however, was mercifully brief; for after two years of it, in 79 B.C., he abruptly stepped down, abandoned Rome to its fate, and retired to his estate at Puteoli, near Naples. He offered no explanation. The historian Appian says that Sulla was "weary of war, weary of power, weary of Rome." He spent his remaining days fishing, hunting, talking with his friends, and writing his memoirs—which have perished. A cultivated voluptuary, he gave himself up to a life of pleasure. He had written comedies, and it amused him to see them performed by actors and actresses who flocked to his court. He was well guarded by the Cornelii, who had followed him into retirement. He died in the following year and received a tyrant's funeral. The Romans, having feared him during his reign, in retrospect regarded him as a man of vast audacity, worthy of their respect. His body was carried to Rome on a golden bier preceded by horsemen and trumpeters, his battle standards, and the twenty-four lictors who had attended him. When the bier reached Rome, the senators came to pay homage and carried it to the

Campus Martius, the traditional burial ground for kings. For the cremation of the body, the women of Rome provided immense quantities of spices, and there was enough left over to make a large statue of him from frankincense and cinnamon.

Sulla left no successor, only a number of ruthless and audacious followers who were determined to advance themselves. His desire to strengthen the Senate as a stabilizing force was frustrated by the rise of military chieftains and adventurers, whose rivalry led to further conquests, internecine struggles, heightened social tension, and finally to the collapse of the republic.

The era that saw the emergence of Pompey and Crassus and the ultimate triumph of Gaius Julius Caesar was not, however, one of aggrandizement and brutality only. The pursuit of wealth and power was accompanied by a rapid growth of cultivated life, literary expression, and intellectual enquiry. Although dominated by men of the sword, it was also the time of the poet-philosopher Lucretius, the lyric poet Catullus, the encyclopedist Varro, with his studies of Roman history, customs, agronomy, and the Latin language, and the versatile Cicero, who embodied the culture of the final decades of the republic at its best.

Even before Julius Caesar emerged to enlarge the Roman world, it had become far flung. By about 60 B.C. Rome ruled over northern Italy up to the Alpine passes; over southern France; over the Iberian peninsula save for its northwestern corner and part of what is now Portugal; over the Dalmatian coast, Thrace, and Greece; over a broad belt of Asia Minor fronting on the Black and Mediterranean seas and including such ancient seats of power as Ephesus, Antioch, Sidon, and Tyre; and over such North African coastal centers as Cyrene, Leptis, and the remnants of Carthage. Raw materials, together with tribute and tax money and slaves from the conquered provinces, added to Roman wealth—as did the gain of the rapacious governors whom Rome sent out.

The influx of slaves, though profitable, was not entirely a blessing. It brought in men and women alien to the old Roman stock and thereby led to its dilution. The slave population of Rome in the late republic may have numbered two hundred thousand. Of these, all were by no means farm workers or domestic servants; many of the educated slaves became tutors, secretaries, librarians, and physicians. Few passages in Roman writing are more handsome than Cicero's affectionate correspondence with his own secretary Tiro, who helped him with his writings and was given freedom, becoming after Cicero's death the guardian and editor of his literary estate. Yet the foreign slave also brought with him social unrest. In 73 B.C. Spartacus, a Thracian gladiator, fomented and led a mass revolt of slaves, including Celts, Germans, and tribesmen from his own rough country northwest of Greece. Some ninety thousand in number, these desperate men vanquished several Roman armies and threatened much of central and southern Italy before they were brought to bay by Marcus Licinius Crassus, a praetor appointed to take over the command of this newest civil war from the defeated consuls.

Despite all political and social uncertainties, life in and around the city of Rome flourished. Early in the first century B.C., the senatorial class as well as the leading equites had begun to build, on the Palatine and other heights, great mansions complete with coffered ceilings, mosaics, wall paintings, libraries, sculpture-courts, and surrounding gardens. The urban poor, their number swelled by masses of dispossessed peasants, were quartered in lodging-houses or in multistoried tenement blocks known as *insulae,* some of which lined the slopes leading down to the Forum. The Forum served as a year-round center not only of oratory but of every kind of daily commerce—buying and selling houses, produce, livestock, slaves, ships, cargoes. Since Rome was approaching a population of one million, a habit arose among the rich of erecting country retreats—villas surrounded by parks and ponds. Cicero had eight villas. Clodia, the sensual wife of consul Metellus Celer and the woman whom Catullus loved as the "Lesbia" of his lyrics, was known for holding extravagant garden and boating parties that were filled with music, gaiety, and frivolity.

Greek influence stood very high in Rome. Lucretius expounded to a Latin audience the teachings of the Greek philosopher Epicurus, with his argument that the universe consists of random atoms over which the gods themselves have no control, and that man can best overcome his fears of death and godly vengeance by equipoise and contemplation of the "majesty of things." Catullus, though trained in polished alexandrine meter, harked back to the impassioned style of Sappho of Lesbos as he pursued his beloved "Lesbia" in Rome. Cicero as orator took the Athenian Demosthenes as his model, and as moralist leaned heavily on both the conservative idealism of Plato and on the Stoics' emphasis on practical social virtues. Men like Catullus and Cicero spoke Greek as well as Latin, and their houses were filled with Greek books and works of art. The thought and style of Greece were commingling with the practical intelligence and verve of the Romans to produce an eclectic yet increasingly polished civilization.

Though the Romans were philhellenes in their acquisition of ideas and tastes, they still adhered to many of their own. Not all the influence of Athens altered, for instance, the position of Roman women—particularly the Roman matron of the upper classes, proud, dignified, often a participant in her husband's public affairs, and free from the seclusion that had shut in the Athenian wife. She was the object of high matrimonial alliances between clans; she accompanied her husband to ban-

This Roman mosaic depicts Plato (third from left) seated among his disciples at his Academy in Athens; the Acropolis is pictured at upper right. In philosophy, Rome was never to match the accomplishments of Greece and was always to look to the east for teachers. By Cicero's day, study of the Greek language and Greek thought was a prerequisite of a good Roman education.

quets and often made her voice heard in politics. Cicero's wife Terentia, a particularly gifted woman, appears to have been highly skilled at handling her husband's property and accounts.

The high role of the Roman leader's lady—one to become even more important amid the strategic marriages and divorces of Caesar and thereafter—stood in contrast to the low role of the courtesan, one very different from the part played by the gifted *hetaira* in Athenian Greece. Liaisons outside of marriage were at best furtive; and as for the prostitute, there was no talk of obliging temple hostesses such as those at Corinth. Prostitutes took out licenses at the aediles' office and thereupon donned their distinctive dress and boldly dyed their hair to denote their calling.

In this mixed and increasingly literate society, a major cultural pursuit emerged—that of oratory, which became perhaps the most characteristic vehicle of Roman self-expression. Greek manuals of oratory and Greek teachers had been known in Rome since Cato's time, and had helped to mold the style of many leading statesmen. The first Latin-speaking school of rhetoric was opened in 95 B.C.; and as political competition intensified, oratory became even more important. Studies in gesture, delivery, diction, and the effective marshaling of argument were regarded as essential training for aspiring, young men. Cicero won his consulship chiefly by dint of his marvelously sonorous and rhythmic utterances, and Julius Caesar himself was regarded as second only to Cicero in his command of speechmaking.

Barring mighty Caesar, Marcus Tullius Cicero was the most characteristic and brilliant personage of the era—and moreover the one who most staunchly defended traditional republican ideas against the swordsmen who finally destroyed him. Not of patrician birth, but rather the son of an equites who had devoted himself to literature, he began life as one of the *novi*

The ladies in the marble monochrome, above, are playing knucklebones, an uncomplicated game based on odds and evens, and are probably betting heavily. Gambling was one of the most popular amusements among the Romans, which amounted more to a passion than a pastime. They wagered on everything, and any game of chance appealed to them.

homines of the times; he was schooled by Greek tutors and dedicated himself to law. A brilliant young advocate, pleading criminal and civil cases before senatorial courts, including a brave and winning defense of a victim of the rapacity of one of Sulla's henchmen, he attracted so much attention that he was elected quaestor in 76 B.C., at the age of thirty, and thus entered the Senate; seven years later he became an aedile; then he won a praetorship, which permitted him to preside over the highest civil court of Rome; finally in 63 B.C.—a year that was to see renewed domestic tumult—he was chosen consul.

Witty, urbane, always graced with style and courage, Cicero comes down to us as the most articulate and comprehensive figure of late republican Rome. Fifty-eight of his speeches survive along with seven works on oratory, and nearly twenty on philosophy, and over eight hundred personal letters on topics ranging from high affairs of state to details of his personal life. He had no single predominant style, but wrote in many different manners, each suited to the occasion and to his audience. The gay informality of many of the letters to his friend Atticus, the vigorous clarity of his narrations in criminal proceedings, and the elegant and subtle dialogue of his books on rhetoric and philosophy stand in contrast to the orotund magnificence in which, for a denunciation or a peroration, he summons up full powers of the Latin language. His prose became a model for cultivated speech for a thousand years and more after his death.

Cicero was to defend to the death a republican system based on an alliance of his own mercantile class and the aristocracy against strong dictators above and dissatisfied masses below. But other leaders and forces attractive to the people were rising. Among Sulla's ill-assorted crowd of adventurers one stood out: Gnaeus Pompeius, who was known as Pompey. He was a brilliant and impressive cavalry officer. He had a broad head, large nose, and athletic body and was skilled in running, leaping, riding, and fencing. He was popular with his soldiers and ferociously ambitious. Born in 106 B.C., the same year as Cicero, Pompey was twenty-three when under Sulla he successfully led an army against the followers of Marius. After notable victories in Sicily and Africa, he returned to Rome and demanded from Sulla the right to enter the city in triumph, although only consuls were permitted to enjoy triumphs, and no one could become a consul until the age of forty-two. Pompey was adamant: "More people worship the rising than the setting sun." Sulla, surprised by the remark, said: "Then let him triumph!" So, he triumphed and was thereafter called Pompeius Magnus, Pompey the Great. When Sulla died, Pompey expected to be appointed the dictator's successor, but when the will was read he was not mentioned in it at all. Sulla, who had wearied of Rome, had finally wearied of Pompey.

For the next five years Pompey fought in Spain. He returned to Rome in 71 B.C. to assist Crassus in crushing the slave revolt led by Spartacus. When he arrived in the city, the Senate's two most influential men were Crassus and Cicero. Crassus, like Pompey, had been a faithful follower of Sulla and had amassed a great fortune during the time of the proscriptions by buying up cheaply the estates of the proscribed and then selling them dearly. Shrewd, affable, a skilled intriguer in the inner councils of the Senate, he was also a capable and ruthless general, tracking down the Spartacists with unexampled ferocity, crucifying the slaves who fell into his hands. He left only fugitives to be mopped up by the returning Pompey the Great.

When Pompey presented himself to the Senate he expected to hear his own praises spoken by Crassus. Instead he heard a panegyric honoring Cicero. The affront was deliberate and demonstrated that the two soldiers were now rivals for power, and that Crassus was seeking to win the great orator to his side. At the head of their armies they cowed the Senate, suspending their enmity long enough to be made joint consuls for the year 70 B.C., during which they managed to undo much of Sulla's constitution, reducing the Senate's powers and restoring those of the tribunes. Then Pompey won a sweeping command at sea and in the east, and distinguished himself by putting down pirates, by vanquishing King Mithridates of the Black Sea realm of Pontus, and by founding colonies, while jealous Crassus in

Rome worked to strengthen his own position against Pompey's return. Immensely rich, he bought the voters while Cicero swayed them with oratory; Pompey, on the other hand, by nature scrupulous and lacking a faculty for intrigue, had little to recommend him but his generalship.

Having successfully completed his tasks abroad, Pompey returned to Italy in 62 B.C., prepared to play the role of another Sulla. Completely fearless, he dramatized his return by leaving his army at Brundisium and entering Rome accompanied only by a small staff. But Rome was in no mood to receive another Sulla. Only a few months earlier one of Sulla's lieutenants, Lucius Sergius Catilina, known to history as Catiline, had made a terrifying bid for power with a plan to seize the city with the help of Gauls from the north and of a fifth column that would fire the public buildings and create panic. The conspiracy of Catiline might have succeeded if it had not been for some Gallic informers in Rome. Catiline's agents were exposed by Cicero and were arrested and sentenced to death; shortly afterward, a Roman army defeated the forces of Catiline and killed him. The horror of those days when the fate of Rome hung in the balance was vividly remembered on Pompey's return.

After Pompey's arrival in Rome the possibility of a violent clash between him and Crassus grew more imminent. It was averted, however, by the intervention and mediation of an extraordinary young leader who returned in 60 B.C. from a successful command in Spain. Gaius Julius Caesar brought together the two statesmen to form with himself the triple alliance known as the First Triumvirate. This was a fateful moment in Roman history, for it marked Caesar's first bid for power.

Before the legends accumulated around his name, Caesar was not a man who inspired any particular confidence. He was a gallant, a spendthrift, and a born conspirator, who carefully covered his traces. It was rumored and widely believed that he had been in secret correspondence with Catiline and would have been among those to seize power if that man's rebellion had been successful. He had held some minor positions in government, and in 63 B.C., at the age of thirty-seven had secured the position of *pontifex maximus*, the ceremonial head of the state clergy. Yet in that year he was still not widely known. He had not commanded any large armies—nor indeed any armies at all. Apart from a daring, youthful exploit on the island of Lesbos—he had saved the life of a fellow soldier—and a punitive expedition that he had subsequently led against pirates, he had taken no leading part in wars. At an age when young soldiers had been covering themselves with glory, he had been busily engaged in seducing the wives of politicians and practicing law. He was deeply in debt to Crassus, for with his help Caesar had been sent to Spain, where he had shown himself to be a brilliant and unorthodox general, careless of danger, restless and violently ambitious, driving his men hard and himself harder. In 60 B.C. he was back in Rome, hungry for power.

His appearance suggested much, but not all, of the inner man. The few surviving portraits in bronze and marble show an idealized Caesar, lean and suave, with high cheekbones and a mouth like a trap. Yet the coins struck in his lifetime show a thin, craggy face, a thin nose, a thin neck, set lips, knit brow, and large deepset eyes, which we know were black and very piercing. He became bald at an early age and was particularly sensitive about this condition. His skin had a curious marble-like pallor, and there is some evidence that he suffered from a mild form of epilepsy. He had an intensity that appealed to women and made some men afraid.

According to Suetonius, Caesar claimed descent from the goddess Venus and from one of the legendary kings of Rome. But in fact, his family was not a very distinguished one, though it achieved one socially important marriage when his aunt Julia wedded Marius, the sworn enemy of Sulla. During the Sullan proscriptions young Caesar had fled to save his life. Friends had pleaded for him, and Sulla was supposed to have remarked: "In that boy there are many Mariuses," suggesting that an eye might well be kept on him. Yet at another time Sulla supposedly dismissed Caesar with the remark: "He wears his girdle too loosely." Wearing a loose girdle was accounted as a sign of effeminacy.

At the age of forty, still wearing his girdle loosely, dressing with exquisite taste, brushing his few remaining hairs forward, Caesar set about to conquer Rome with the same cold intelligence and thrust that had brought about his victories in Spain. The First Triumvirate had introduced a new and hitherto untried form of dictatorship, one that could remain stable only so long as the three men's interests coincided. The triumvirs held absolute power, though the fictions of republican rule were being maintained. Consular elections were held, and Caesar became consul for the first time in 59 B.C.; his colleague the conservative Marcus Calpurnius Bibulus served as co-consul.

Also in the year 59 B.C. Pompey was given Caesar's daughter Julia in marriage. Crassus, who had offered the state a vast sum for the privilege of collecting public revenues in the eastern provinces of Asia, found the revenues disappointing and he asked the Senate for relief. The Senate refused. Caesar obligingly arranged to have a law passed requiring the Senate to offer remission to Crassus, the richest man in Rome. Pompey, in turn, was rewarded with the ratification of his eastern conquests. He had promised his veterans large areas of land, and these were now set aside for them. For himself, Caesar demanded that at the end of his consular year he obtain the governorship of Cisalpine Gaul, and when the newly appointed governor of Transalpine Gaul conveniently died Caesar asked that this province also be given to him. He raised three legions in preparation for assuming his new post and then carefully arranged to station them near Rome, ringing the city with his soldiers. The hint was not lost on anyone—certainly not on Cicero, who had declined to join the coalition of the generals. Caesar had observed that Sulla's abdication had only shown that Sulla did not know the first thing about the nature of dictatorship. A dictatorship is not something that can be put aside lightly; it must be held with all the force and all the stratagems at the leader's disposal. In stepping down from the consular office Caesar was not yielding his power. He was simply preparing for greater power—a more absolute rule over a larger empire. On a far more massive scale he was employing the ruse first attempted by Catiline: in alliance with the Gauls and with his own agents in the city he would become the undisputed master of Rome.

Caesar emerged from his year as consul with immense powers. He could select his own commanders, found colonies as he wished, push back the frontiers wherever it served his purpose, and employ the treasure of conquered peoples for his own ends. His governorship of Gaul was to last for five years, but it was renewable. The army that was entrusted to him was so powerful that it could survive any enemy. With the Gallic levies that he intended to raise, he foresaw that in a very short space of time he would accumulate more power in the form of treasure and men-at-arms than any Roman before him had been able to amass.

He spent the following nine years carving out an empire in Gaul as more and more opportunities for conquest and enrichment presented themselves to him, and thereby delayed his threatened return to Rome. He was constantly on the march, constantly putting down rebellions and extending his dominions. The poet Lucan speaks of him as a man *in arma furens* ("furious for war") and impatient to cut bloody swathes through the enemy: "He would rather burst open the city gates than have them opened for him. He preferred to ravage the land with fire and sword than to receive the farmer's permission to cross it peacefully. He detested an unguarded road, or to parade like a peaceful citizen." Caesar would have disagreed with that verdict. He would have said that he waged war in a spirit of analytic enquiry, without rage, his sole object being to bring greater glory to Rome by force of arms. In *De bello Gallico*, his commentaries on the Gallic war, he presents himself as a man of single-minded purpose, who regards war as an exercise of the mind, with Roman brain power pitted against that of the barbarians. Above all else, Caesar was interested in the mechanics of conquest—the unrelenting march of the war machine once its precise purpose had been established and its goal had been calculated.

Caesar's commentaries do not reveal the whole man. His hesitations, doubts, and complexities are glossed over. The report is written in a style so plain that it seems to be without art; no rhetorical devices are employed. Sallust, on the other hand, in describing the Jugurthine war, gives the hot breath of the campaign, the rush and roar of the cavalry, the sense of human beings engaged in dubious conspiracies and hand-to-hand combat. Caesar describes his stratagems or battle plans in stark and precise terms. His crowning achievement was the defeat, in 52 B.C., of the Gallic army led by the chieftain Vercingetorix. Caesar appears on the scene wearing his blood red cloak:

His coming was known to the enemy by the color of his cloak—that cloak which he was accustomed to wear as his distinguishing mark in battle—and then they saw the cavalry squadrons and the cohorts, which he had ordered to follow behind him, these being plainly visible from the heights: so they joined the battle. From both sides came battle cries, which were taken up by the men on the rampart and along the whole length of the entrenchment. Our men threw down their spears and got to work with their swords. Suddenly the enemy saw the cavalry in their rear; fresh cohorts were coming up. They turned and fled, and the cavalry cut off their flight. There was great slaughter. . . . Seventy-four standards were presented to Caesar; only a few of that great army succeeded in reaching their camp safely. When they saw from the town the slaughter and flight of their countrymen, they surrendered to despair and recalled their troops from the entrenchments. As soon as they heard what had happened, the Gauls fled from their camp. . . . Our cavalry pursued them and caught up with them about midnight; a large number were taken and killed; the survivors made for their towns.

The next day Vercingetorix addressed his war council. "I have not undertaken this war for my own ends," he said, "but for our common freedom. Since I must accept my fate, I freely offer myself to you. If you want to kill me in order to make amends to the Romans, do so, or surrender me alive." A deputation was sent to Caesar to decide what should be done. He ordered them to lay down their arms and surrender their chiefs. He sat down at the fortifications in front of the camp, while the chiefs were brought to him. Vercingetorix surrendered, and the arms were laid down.

In this terse, compact way, never raising his voice, Caesar describes the fall of the fortress town of Alesia, which brought to an end his long battle with Vercingetorix. The most remarkable qualities of the description are a certain suavity and ease. He was not writing for schoolboys, but for the men of his own class—the aristocracy of generals who were the real rulers of Rome. His deliberate understatements, the sense of order that he quietly imposes on chaos, and the calm superiority that he displays throughout the passage arise from a peculiar attitude of mind that is proud, austere, and intensely ambitious.

Caesar's ruthlessness is barely masked by the restrained tone of his memoirs. He sometimes reports not only the slaughter of enemy warriors but the systematic butchering of their families to the last man, woman, and child. On one occasion he had his legionaries cut off the right hands of several thousand rebellious Gauls. Vercingetorix, whose nobility in defeat Caesar makes no effort to disguise, was kept imprisoned for six years to serve as a living exhibit at Caesar's triumph, and after being paraded through the streets of Rome, was put to death.

Cicero, who was always uncomfortable in Caesar's presence, called him "an instrument of wrath, terrifying in his vigilance, swiftness, and energy." What was most terrifying was Caesar's insatiable appetite. Not content with conquering Gaul, he went on to attack large areas of what is now Flanders; he crossed the Rhine and went into Germany; and twice he invaded Britain, though these brief campaigns were scarcely more than reconnaissances in depth. The final conquest by Rome was still to come.

The triumvirate had long since collapsed. In 53 B.C. Crassus had led an army against the Parthians of the east only to suffer the loss of seven legions in the greatest Roman defeat since the battle of Cannae, and to meet death himself; his severed head and right hand were presented to the Parthian king. With Crassus gone, Caesar prepared to confront Pompey. The ties that had bound them had been broken in 54 B.C. after the death of Caesar's daughter Julia, wife of Pompey. The two men had no love for one another, though they protested their friendship. "When the clash comes," wrote Cicero, "every man on earth will be involved." Pompey was serenely unconscious of danger: "I have only to stamp my feet, and armed men will start from the soil of Italy," he is said to have declared. In January, 49 B.C., contrary to the wishes of the Senate, Caesar and his troops crossed the flooded Rubicon—the frontier between Cisalpine Gaul and Italy—and all of Pompey's and Caesar's protestations of friendship were seen to have been merely the preparations for a duel to the death.

Pompey with his troops slipped across the Adriatic to Illyria while Caesar stormed into Rome and seized the state treasury. Pompey's generals were in command in North Africa and Spain, and in addition Pompey had command of the seas. Caesar decided to strike first at Spain, where he quickly defeated an army loyal to Pompey. Then he turned to the east, and in August, 48 B.C., at the battle of Pharsalus, in Thessaly, a heterogeneous force supporting Pompey was decisively defeated; over a hundred standards were captured and Pompey fled. Appian gives a hair-raising account of how the opposing armies, after invoking the gods and sounding their trumpets, marched toward each other "in stupor and deepest silence." Lucan tells the story that on the following morning Caesar ordered a luxurious breakfast to be prepared for him on the battlefield, and as the sun was rising he calmly contemplated the faces of the dead around him.

The triumph of Caesar was not complete, for Pompey had escaped. Caesar was determined to rid the world of him, and three days later, having learned that Pompey was making his way toward Egypt, he set out in pursuit. Pompey could have gone to North Africa, where there were armies loyal to him, but he seems to have chosen Egypt quite deliberately in the hope of raising an Egyptian army to protect himself against Caesar. In the past he had shown many favors to the Egyptian royal house; he knew the country well; and its capital, Alexandria, was regarded as impregnable. He made a mistake by sending heralds to announce his arrival, for the Egyptians were in no mood to receive a defeated Roman general. He had scarcely set foot on the sandy shore when he was stabbed in the back. His head was cut off and removed to a safe place; his body was stripped and left lying on the sand until someone thought of providing a funeral pyre by setting fire to an abandoned fishing boat.

When Caesar reached Alexandria he was civilly received. Shown the head of Pompey, he wept; it was one of his rare moments of sentiment. But Egypt only awakened his appetite for conquest, and soon there was war between his small army of some three thousand and a much larger Egyptian force. He first seized the city's famed lighthouse on the strategic island of Pharos, opposite the harbor, thus giving his ships access to the port; but Alexandria remained in Egyptian hands, confining him. For six months he was in deadly peril. The conqueror of Gaul, the master of the Roman empire, found himself in command of some fifty houses along the seacoast, and nothing more.

At some time during this period Caesar encountered the princess Cleopatra, who was a member of the house of the Ptolemies and a descendant of the half brother of Alexander the Great. As Plutarch recounts the story, the beautiful princess sailed secretly to Pharos during the night and was carried into Caesar's presence wrapped in a carpet. She stepped out from the carpet and announced that she had come both as a friend and an ally. He was immediately captivated by her. "By this ruse," says the historian Plutarch, "Cleopatra caught Caesar in her toils."

It is possible that he had been captivated by her long before;

they appear, at least, to have been in correspondence. Caesar was fifty-four, Cleopatra was nineteen. They were well matched in cunning, and both possessed an imperial manner, sharing a common belief in their divine ancestry—Cleopatra believed herself to be the incarnation of the goddess Isis, as Caesar held himself to be descended from Venus. The alliance they formed was to have an incalculable effect on the destiny of Rome.

For all her youth Cleopatra had the instincts of a veteran. Her beauty was one of the weapons she employed with consummate skill. To charm Caesar she gave magnificent banquets at which she appeared splendidly caparisoned, and even after Roman reinforcements came and Alexandria finally fell, he stayed at her side in Egypt. She appears to have induced him into taking a long journey with her up the Nile as far as the borders of Ethiopia. Altogether he spent nine months in Egypt. A few weeks after he left her, she gave birth to his son Caesarion.

More fighting was still to be done. In 47 B.C. he marched northward through Syria to Pontus on the Black Sea. Near Zela he destroyed the army of King Pharnaces, the son of Mithridates the Great, four hours after sighting it. After this battle Caesar sent to Rome the words that were later displayed on the banners at his triumphs in Rome: *Veni, vidi, vici* ("I came, I saw, I conquered").

In Roman Africa there remained an army of Pompey's followers, allied with the forces of the kings of neighboring Numidia and in open resistance to Caesar. After a brief stay in Rome, early in 46 B.C. Caesar sailed for the Carthaginian coast to put down their rebellion. A story was told that when he came ashore he slipped and fell, and a cry of horror went up from the soldiers, who thought the fall of their commander could only presage defeat; but he had the presence of mind to say: "So I possess thee, Africa!" There were continual skirmishes, but few pitched battles. Though superior to his own veterans in number, the enemy mass of Gallic, Spanish, and African cavalry was elusive. Provisions threatened to run out. Caesar himself was ill, suffering, according to Plutarch, an epileptic attack. Yet the outcome, given his brilliance and aura, was never in doubt, and Numidia, too, now fell into his hands. He returned to Rome in 45 B.C. to receive a greater triumphal celebration than any Roman general had ever known. He had conquered Gaul, Egypt, the Pontic realm, and much of North Africa, and there was a triumph for each victory. Four days of celebrations followed: carts were overflowing with booty, and huge paintings were carried aloft depicting the scenes of his battles and the conquered towns in flames. Wearing a gold helmet and the robes of Jupiter, carrying the eagle-topped ivory scepter, his face glowing with red paint, he presented himself as triumphator to the multitude.

Almost every power that Caesar could desire was now bestowed on him by an obedient Senate. In 46 B.C. he was made dictator for a ten-year term—with command of all armies, sole control of all public monies, and authority to determine the lists of senators, equites, and the citizenry as a whole. Immune from veto of the tribunes, he could issue decrees without consulting the public assembly. He could afford to ignore that assembly; his vast personal power rested on the solid base of his mass of legionaries, each of whom, on his return from his quadruple triumph, was awarded a grant of 20,000 sesterces (with benefits reaching as high as 200,000 sesterces for individual officers). By this time the revenues of the Roman state and Caesar's own immeasurable spoils from his conquests—including as a major item the sale of innumerable captives—had become so intermixed that the great mass of Romans saw him as their personal benefactor.

Thus armed, he devoted the second half of 46 B.C. to a phe-

nomenal exercise of civil leadership. He settled a great number
of veterans on lands in Italy and outside. He revived Corinth
and Carthage as commercial centers and sent experts to Corinth
to plan a canal across the isthmus. With the dictator's affection
for vast building schemes, he redesigned the Forum and drew
plans for new suburbs, new temples, new libraries; and because
there were areas where the Tiber overflowed its banks, he
decreed that the river's course be altered. In his priestly role as
pontifex maximus, which gave him authority over the calendar
and festivals, he decreed a massive reform of the calendar
Romans had lived by for centuries, but which had fallen far out
of step with the solar year. The new Julian calendar, introduced
in January, 45 B.C., was based on the studies made by Egyptian
astronomers and has survived, with only slight modifications,
to our own day.

In December of 46 B.C., however, when Caesar's triumph was
complete and when civil strife had ended at last, news came of
a revolt in Spain. Many survivors of the defeats in Africa had
found refuge there, and Pompey's sons had marshaled still
another force seeking to overthrow Caesar. Hurrying to Spain,
the dictator defeated the rebels at Munda, near Cordova, in a
battle which he very nearly lost. For a moment his troops pan-
icked, and Caesar, who only a few months before had the world
at his feet, gave way to terror at the thought of dying on some
remote Spanish battlefield. Men remembered that he had "the
look of death on his face" as he plunged into battle; his sudden
appearance stemmed the rout. "On other occasions I fought for
victory," he said, "but today I fought for my life." The Roman
historian Velleius Paterculus writes that the battle was the
bloodiest and most perilous Caesar had ever fought. It was also
to be his last.

Either before or after the battle, Caesar was joined by his
eighteen-year-old grandnephew Octavian. The youth had risen

from sickbed, and Caesar appears to have been deeply moved
by his courage. They traveled together by carriage through
Spain. Mark Antony claimed they were lovers; Caesar certainly
felt a greater affection for his sister's grandson than for anyone
else. Soon after this when he was writing his will, Caesar named
Octavian as the principal heir to his fortune, his honors, his
title, and his power.

Caesar was back in Rome at the beginning of October, 45
B.C., celebrating his fifth triumph. In theory it was a triumph
over Spain; in fact it was a triumph over the followers of Pompey, who were Romans. Among the crowds watching the procession were many who had lost fathers and sons in Spain.

Once more the senators vied with one another in heaping
new honors upon the conqueror. He was given the right to wear
the purple toga of the Roman kings, to appear everywhere in a
laurel crown, and to sit in a gold chair. His image was to be
borne in procession among the images of the gods and set up in
a prominent place in the temple of Jupiter. He was hailed as the
Father of the Country, and a statue of gold was erected to him
on the speaker's platform in the Forum. An order was given
that in every temple in Rome and in all the towns of the empire
there should be statues of him. The anniversaries of his birth
and his major victories were to become holidays. His likeness
appeared on coins in 45 B.C. and 44 B.C.; also in 44 he was made
dictator for life, and his person was declared sacrosanct and inviolate. Senators swore to defend him at the cost of their own lives.
Caesar accepted the new honors as his right, but seems to have
been unconvinced that his person was sacrosanct, for in December when he went to visit Cicero in his villa at Puteoli, near
Naples, he was surrounded by a guard of two thousand men.

As the days passed Caesar became increasingly remote, arbitrary, and authoritarian. Once, holding court in the portico of
the temple of Venus Genetrix—erected to honor his adopted

ancestor—before the gilded statue of the goddess modeled on the body of Cleopatra, he failed to rise when the senators presented themselves. Toward the end of January, 44 B.C., a crowd meeting him on the Appian Way cried, "*Rex!*" He replied that he was not a king but Caesar, but when the ringleaders among the crowd were arrested, he was incensed and ordered the arresting officers removed from their posts. In February, at the ceremony of the Lupercalia, the consul Mark Antony laid a crown of laurels interlaced with the white ribbons of the royal diadem at his feet. The laurel crown was lifted to his head. Few applauded then, but there was deafening applause when Caesar removed the crown. He asked that the crown be taken to the temple of Jupiter and that there should be inscribed in the public records the following words: "At the bidding of the people, Antony, the consul, offered to Caesar, the perpetual dictator, the kingship, which Caesar refused."

Yet during the following days a statue of Caesar was crowned by his supporters, and it became known that he had consulted the sacred books. Caesar had been planning the conquest of Parthia, and the sacred books said the Roman army could conquer Parthia only if commanded by a king. By this time there were few who had any doubt that Caesar intended to become king and to found a dynasty. Cleopatra, whom he had brought to Rome with their son Caesarion, was living in a villa on the bank of the Tiber. The Romans despised Cleopatra and were irked by the presence of the statue modeled after her in the temple of Venus Genetrix. They may have wondered whether Caesarion might not inherit the throne. Caesar knew he was in danger, but perhaps he was too ill, or too tired, or too proud, to care.

The plot to murder Caesar was devised by men he favored and to whom he had granted high positions. Gaius Longinus Cassius was a veteran who had been named praetor in 44 B.C.; Gaius Trebonius had been approved as consul the previous year; Decimus Junius Brutus was about to take command of Cisalpine Gaul; Lucius Tillius Cimber had been promised the government of Bithynia; Marcus Junius Brutus had fought for Pompey, but had been pardoned by Caesar. Most of the conspirators belonged to patrician families—the Old Guard of the perishing republic. Their motives were mixed. They feared his plays for popularity among the masses and the soldiery, handing out enormous sums as doles and veterans' benefits; they were repelled by the venality of some of his favorites, fatting on his spoils; they longed for the liberty and class order of past days; above all, most of them being senators, they were affronted by his claim to absolute and arbitrary power, reducing the Senate to an ignominious servant of his will.

Altogether some sixty men were involved in the plot, and inevitably rumors reached Caesar's ears, but he dismissed them haughtily. On the evening of March 14, he dined with Marcus Aemilius Lepidus, the commander of the armed forces, and possibly they discussed the rumors, for when the conversation turned to the best way in which to die, Caesar is said to have answered: "Suddenly."

During that night he was restless, and once all the doors and windows burst open in a gust of wind. His wife Calpurnia begged him not to leave the house next morning for the meeting of the Senate. He laughed at her fears, but to please her he called in the diviners, who performed their solemn rites. The omens were unfavorable. Yet he was looking forward to the Senate meeting to be held in the portico of Pompey's theatre on the Campus Martius—a meeting that was to ratify his use of *rex* as his title when he was outside of Italy. In three days he intended to leave for Apollonia, on the Illyrian coast, where a vast camp had been prepared for the veterans who would take part in the Parthian campaign. There, too, he would be able to see Octavian, whom he now regarded as his adopted son.

It was just after eleven o'clock in the morning when he stepped into the portico to receive the salutes of the senators, who rose to greet him. A moment later Lucius Tillius Cimber approached him to plead that his brother be recalled from exile. Caesar refused to listen to him; Cimber insisted, and as he did so the other conspirators gathered round, pressing themselves against Caesar, completely surrounding him. Twenty-three dagger thrusts felled him at the foot of Pompey's statue.

Borne to his house by slaves, the body of Caesar remained there for several days, while the conspirators debated what should be done and made speeches in self-justification, calling upon the gods to witness that tyranny was dead and the republic would be restored. They had planned to throw the body into the Tiber, but Mark Antony had taken possession of it, along with Caesar's treasure and private papers, including the will, and thereby made his own claim for power. In the famous speech he delivered over Caesar's body when it was placed in the Forum, he brought the crowds to such a pitch of excitement that they took possession of the body and insisted that it be burned in the Forum before their eyes. Women tossed their jewelry into the pyre, musicians and actors who had taken part in his triumphs removed the embroidered costumes they wore for the occasion, tore them to ribbons, threw their shields and swords into the fire, which burned all night. It was such a funeral as might be given a barbarian chieftain.

A day or two before the funeral, the mother of Octavian sent a letter to her son in Appollonia. "The time has come when you must play the man, decide, and act," she is said to have written him, "for no one can foretell the things that may come about." No one, least of all the conspirators, could have foretold that power would soon pass into the hands of Octavian—the emperor Augustus.

VII

THE TRIUMPH OF AUGUSTUS

At the age of nineteen I raised an army on my private initiative, and at my private expense, by means of which I liberated the state from the oppression of a tyrannical faction.

—Augustus, *Res gestae*

Octavian is an excellent boy, of whom I personally have high hopes for the future.

—Cicero, letter to Gaius Trebonius, 43 B.C.

The day of Octavian began when he received his mother's letter informing him of his great-uncle, Caesar's, death; he was eighteen and studying in Apollonia, in Illyria. It ended fifty-eight years later when, revered as Father of his Country, he died after a reign of four and a half decades that far surpassed in political accomplishment, in the accumulation of national wealth, and in the flowering of the arts any period the Romans had known before. At the time Octavian received his mother's message, Rome was in a state of civil disarray. Caesar had failed to unite his people and to bring them lasting order. But when Octavian, under the title of Augustus, reached the end of his years, a great national revival had come about, imbued under his leadership with the spirit of patriotism and of return to the virtues of republican ancestors. In the outcome, the republic itself finally vanished, giving way to the personal rule of a long line of emperors, of whom he was the first and

This idealized portrait of the emperor Augustus, above, captures the god-like qualities attributed to him by his subjects. Control of the military, a vast fortune, and brilliant statesmanship enabled him to bring a long-lasting peace to Rome, which in turn fostered prosperity and the expansion of the empire.

one of the most enlightened. Under him, institutions were both altered and stabilized; imperial boundaries were extended and secured. Above all, as a sovereign artist of politics, he laid the basis of a structure of power and relative concord that was to make possible a century and more of pax Romana.

Sculptors portrayed young Octavian as having grave nobility and calm. With his broad, unfurrowed brow, high cheekbones, finely chiseled lips, and determined chin, he resembled those young princes among the successors of Alexander the Great who carved out kingdoms for themselves in the east and minted coins showing their almost too-perfect profiles.

To the end of his life there was a strange remoteness about him, as though he held himself deliberately apart and never quite fitted into the Roman scene. Possibly there was Greek blood in him, for some of his ancestors supposedly lived in the Greek colony of Thurii, in southern Italy. His tutors were Greeks, and throughout his life he was devoted to Apollo, the god of light and lucidity. Saturated in Greek culture, Octavian wrote plays in Greek. His weapons, too, were the Greek weapons of guile and the sudden, oblique thrust—though in his mastery of organization and in his ruthlessness he was thoroughly Roman.

When Octavian set out from Apollonia for Rome in 44 B.C. he knew what had to be done: he would avenge Caesar, and he would go about it cautiously, stubbornly, with the sobriety of a man possessing a single purpose. He crossed the Adriatic Sea in a small boat and landed in an obscure port not far from Brundisium. There he learned that Caesar had named him his adopted son and the inheritor of three-fourths of a vast estate and of a name that was a title to power. Calling himself Gaius Julius Caesar Octavianus, he presented himself to the garrison at Brundisium, where he was received with acclamation. Then with a small armed guard he continued on his way to Rome.

Near Naples Octavian met his mother and stepfather, who were all for abandoning his enterprise of claiming his patrimony, for they were fearful of Mark Antony's power in the capital. There, too, he met Cicero, who found him friendly and deferential, though Cicero complained that the companions of Octavian kept addressing the young man as Caesar and were breathing slaughter against the conspirators, who were Cicero's friends. Octavian was a remarkable visitor, well mannered, but absolutely determined. Cicero, who was soon to be publicly complimenting the youth, appears, at this first meeting, to have reacted to him with suspicion. His fears, though premature, were to prove justified.

The distinguished band of conspirators had failed to make concerted plans for succession to the rule after the assassination; there was still a party and an army that had been loyal to Caesar—and Mark Antony, the surviving consul and self-proclaimed guardian of Caesar's legacy, had strong appeal to it, as did Octavian. Soon after Octavian's arrival in Rome, the conspirators were either in hiding or in full flight, leaving the city to the mercy of the two men about to become deadly rivals. A third contender for power was Marcus Aemilius Lepidus, whose positions as Caesar's master of the horse and as *pontifex maximus* gave him an official rank next to Antony's, and who as governor of Narbonese Gaul and Hither Spain controlled a body of troops in the provinces.

Antony and Octavian were utterly contrasting figures. Antony, at the age of thirty-nine, was a man in the prime of life. He had powerful shoulders and a bull-like neck, and his strong jaw, fine forehead, and aquiline nose made him look like a matinee idol, and there was much of the actor in him. He had high coloring and drank heavily; drink seems to have been the stimulus that aroused him to action. He was brave and immensely ambitious, and he claimed to be descended from

Hercules. He amused himself by walking about the streets of Rome naked to the waist, a broadsword at his side, talking to all he met. His soldiers adored him, for he was always generous to them and seemed to enjoy their company. He liked making grand gestures. Once he ordered his steward to pay twenty-five "myriads" of money to a friend. The steward thought that if he piled the coins in a great heap Antony would be ashamed of his liberality. Instead, Antony took one look at the mountain of coins and said: "It is such a little pile! Give him twice as much!" But his bluster and posturing were the mask of a man beset by uncertainty.

Octavian, on the other hand, was a pale and sickly youth. When he presented himself to Antony to claim his inheritance, he was so reserved he could barely bring himself to speak in public. At first Antony would have nothing to do with Caesar's callow grandnephew, who had only a small following. Although Octavian claimed a proud lineage, Antony spread the rumor that he was descended on his mother's side from a great-grandfather of African birth, who had kept a perfumery and then a bakery at Aricia, and that his paternal great-grandfather had been only a humble ropemaker. It may have been true, but to despise Octavian was folly in view of Caesar's will. A few days after the meeting, Antony complained that some of the followers of Octavian had attempted to murder him. This, too, may have been true. Octavian, quiet but steely-eyed, may have been readying his sword.

The duel between Antony and Octavian would last for thirteen years. It would be fought across the length of Europe with no quarter given. But there were long periods of truce when the adversaries were too exhausted or too comfortable to fight.

Octavian had begun raising a private army by paying many of Caesar's veterans the amounts promised them in the dictator's will. Then he placed himself and his forces at the disposal of the Senate against his rival and made overtures to Cicero, who was convinced that Antony was more dangerous to Rome than Octavian. In a remarkable speech known as the *Second Philippic* Cicero attacked Antony with astonishing force, describing him as a forger, an embezzler, a lecher, and a drunkard who consorted with criminals and actresses and spent his days and nights in orgies. According to Cicero, Antony was responsible for all Rome's troubles because he had offered the crown to Caesar, and his death would be a suitable offering to the shades of Caesar. Cicero called the senators to witness that not even Catiline had been so menacing to the Roman state. For a few more weeks the civil war was fought in words, and passions mounted. Octavian, by his mere presence in Rome, demonstrated his confidence in ultimate victory.

In the winter of 44 B.C., at the end of his consulship, Antony slipped out of Rome, raised an army of his own, and marched northward in the hope of raising an even larger army in Cisalpine Gaul, to which he had laid claim. A series of confused struggles followed between Antony and Octavian and their partisans. The Senate, which under republican influence had declared Antony a public enemy, became alarmed by the energy of the young man whom it had pitted against him. Cicero declared that Octavian should be "flattered, used, and pushed aside." But in 43 B.C. Octavian shrewdly countered: he marched on Rome with his army of eight legions to support his demand for the consulship for the following year (42 B.C.)—an office that was promptly awarded him. It was to be the first of his thirteen consulships, which formed the basis of his power, and it gave him a strong position from which to continue his struggle for power with Antony.

In the midst of the rivalry, however, there was Lepidus, who was able to swing his force of some seven legions to either contender. The Senate had hoped to use him against Antony as it had used Octavian, but Lepidus decided to join Antony's side, for which he in turn was proscribed. Then, rather than fight intramural contests among themselves, with republican enemies ready to take advantage of them, Antony, Octavian, and Lepidus decided they had better suspend their differences as Pompey, Crassus, and Caesar had done before them, and accordingly they formed a triumvirate, claiming supreme power over public affairs. A cowed Senate confirmed their status in late 43 B.C. for a period of just over five years, thereby abdicating what little power it still possessed. On a small island near present-day Bologna, under conditions of extraordinary secrecy, Antony, Octavian, and Lepidus met and entered upon a compact to divide the Roman world among them. They were alone except for their legions, which lined the banks of the river; they could surrender to whatever impulses they pleased, and for three days and three nights they indulged themselves by drawing up harsh laws and engaging in sophisticated intrigues. Finally they were able to announce that Transalpine and Cisalpine Gaul would go to Antony; Spain, to Lepidus; Africa, Sardinia, and Sicily, to Octavian. Since the state treasury was empty and they needed bounties for their troops, they drew up lists of proscriptions: the rich were to be killed and their estates confiscated; old debts were to be paid off, and the slates wiped clean.

Among those whose names were on the death lists was Cicero, who had exulted over the death of Caesar, attacked Antony, and sought to undermine Octavian. He could expect no mercy. He was in his litter, not far from one of his villas near the seashore, when the assassins caught up with him. For a few moments he gazed at them keenly, leaning his chin on his left hand, and then calmly bared his throat to their swords. His head and hands were hacked off and presented to Antony, who ordered them nailed to the speaker's platform in the Forum as a warning to others. Plutarch says the Romans shuddered: "And they believed they saw there, not the face of Cicero, but the image of Antony's own soul."

Octavian was to regret his connivance in this crime against one of the greatest of Romans. One day, many years later, he found one of his grandsons reading a book by Cicero. On seeing Octavian the boy did his best to hide the book, but it was taken from him. For a long time Octavian pored over the pages, and at last he handed the book back, saying gravely: "My son, he was a learned man, and he loved his country."

Here and there resistance flared up against the triumvirs. The conspirators Cassius and Brutus were raising armies in the East, marching through Asia Minor, and ordering every city they entered to surrender its treasure so that they could pay bounties to their troops. But in 42 B.C., a year after the meeting on the island, the forces of Antony and Octavian met the forces of Brutus and Cassius at Philippi, in northern Greece, and under Antony's leadership defeated them; both Brutus and Cassius committed suicide. The republican cause finally perished.

Once again there was a division of the spoils. Italy was to be ruled in common; Transalpine Gaul and all the lands east of the Ionian Sea were to go to Antony; and Octavian was to receive Dalmatia, Sicily, Sardinia, Africa, and Spain. (Lepidus was ignored until Octavian ceded Africa to him in the year 40 B.C.) The twenty-one-year-old heir was sometimes reminded that he owed his vast realm to the generalship of Antony.

The next years saw efforts to stabilize a system of joint leadership and division of rule, but also the gradual heightening of the tension between Octavian and Antony that was to lead to their climactic clash at Actium. A new, disturbing element appeared in the person of Sextus Pompeius, a son of Pompey the Great, who had been outlawed by the triumvirs after raising his own army in Spain and briefly holding fleet command under the divided Senate's orders, only to re-emerge as chief of a piratical force that raided the commerce of the Italian coast. His success at this was such (he had moreover seized Sicily and Sardinia) as to force the triumvirs to come to terms with him and treat him almost as an equal, awarding him the islands he had occupied, and Corsica as well. Amid this accommodation Lepidus virtually vanished. Then in 38 B.C., a year that saw Rome in straits of confusion, Octavian took up arms against Sextus, whom he accused of violating agreements, and asked Antony for support in putting down the intruder.

Antony and Octavian failed to meet in time, and the latter was alone when he was defeated by Sextus—a humiliation that cast a pall of doubt over the year 37 B.C., in which Antony's and Octavian's joint supreme powers were renewed for another five years. In 36 B.C., the pall was seemingly lifted when Sextus was beaten at sea by Octavian's lieutenant Agrippa and forced to flee to the east, where he was put to death by one of Antony's commanders. Upon Sextus' defeat, Octavian proclaimed a new era of peace and prosperity, and the day of the victory was made an annual religious holiday. The person of Octavian him-self—*divi filius*, or "son of a god," ever since Caesar had been deified in 42 B.C.—was declared sacrosanct and inviolable. But despite Octavian's claim that he had brought peace and order to the empire, the final act in the drama of rivalry was still to come, shaped in large part by the matrimonial alliances and sexual interests of its chieftains.

To pacify Antony, Octavian in 40 B.C. had promoted a marriage between his sister Octavia and his rival. At about the same time, he himself wedded a twice-married woman related to Sextus—Scribonia, who gave him little joy. On the day of their daughter Julia's birth, he divorced her—"because," as he wrote, "I could not bear the way she nagged at me." Octavian then fell in love with Livia Drusilla, the nineteen-year-old wife of

Tiberius Claudius Nero, a republican leader and veteran soldier who had fled to Greece after attempting to raise an army of former slaves against Octavian. Livia was pregnant by her middle-aged husband. Nero, however, complacently divorced her, and she married Octavian and remained faithful to him all the years of their marriage, dying in extremely old age in the reign of her son Tiberius Claudius Nero Caesar.

What had attracted Octavian to Livia was her serene, aristocratic beauty and perhaps a certain loftiness of manner. She had, if one can trust the statues, a commanding presence, features of perfect regularity, enormous eyes, and thick, wavy hair. She practiced the old republican virtues of chastity, obedience, and silence, though she could sometimes unbend: when Octavian heard that she had seen some men parading naked in the street, he flew into a rage, only to soften when she answered that to a woman like herself naked men were no different from statues. No one else had so great an influence on Octavian, who carefully made notes on the subjects he wanted to discuss with her—a remarkable tribute to her critical intelligence. She gave him no children, but he never divorced her for a more fertile bride. After Octavian's death she was pronounced *mater patriae*, the Mother of her Country, and when temples were erected to honor her husband she was invariably honored by being included in the dedication. Her greatest service to the Romans lay in her devotion to Octavian and in the civilizing influence she brought to bear on him.

Meanwhile Antony, too, had come under the influence of an extraordinary woman—Cleopatra. She had escaped from Rome in 44 B.C., after the murder of Caesar, and returned to Egypt. In 41, before his marriage to Octavia, Antony had summoned Cleopatra to Tarsus to answer a charge of aiding the republicans: the penalty for such a crime was death. When she presented herself to him, she was attended by all the seductive panoply of an actress in full command of the stage. "She came sailing up the river Cydnus," wrote Plutarch, "in a ship with a golden stern and outspread sails, while silver oars beat time to the music of flutes and fifes and harps. She lay under a canopy of gold cloth, dressed as Venus in a picture, while beautiful boys like painted cupids stood on each side and fanned her. Her maids were dressed like sea nymphs and graces, and some were steering the rudder while others worked the ropes. All manner of sweet perfumes were wafted ashore." Such is the description that Shakespeare was to adapt into the most splendid passage of his *Antony and Cleopatra.*

Whether Antony fell under her spell at that meeting or at subsequent ones remains a matter of conjecture. The impulses of Cleopatra, having been Caesar's mistress and having perhaps entertained a hope of becoming his wife, appear to have been to make a matrimonial and dynastic alliance with this new powerful man of Rome and thereby preserve her kingdom. She succeeded. The Romans learned in 37 B.C. that Antony, who had been living openly with Cleopatra, had married her, divorcing Octavia to do so. Moreover, he had given her as a wedding present much of the eastern half of the empire that was under his dominion and legitimized the children she had borne him. It was an affront to Rome and to Octavian in particular because Octavia was his sister.

After campaigning victoriously against the Parthians, Antony returned from Armenia in 34 B.C. for a curious triumphal procession through the streets of Alexandria. In triumphs held at Rome, it was customary for the conqueror to lay his laurels on the lap of the great statue of Jupiter on the Capitoline hill. Antony, however, placed his on the lap of Cleopatra as she sat on a golden throne, wearing the robes of the Egyptian goddess Isis. On that same evening there occurred a solemn celebration of the self-proclaimed divine rulers, Cleopatra-Isis and Antony-Osiris. This, an outrage to Roman ideas, served to emphasize the new division of the empire that Antony announced to the Egyptians. Cleopatra was declared queen of kings and of the sons of kings, and the fourteen-year-old Caesarion, her son by Caesar, was awarded the title of king of kings.

In 32 B.C. Antony committed a fatal error. He sent Octavia formal letters of divorce, and a messenger was dispatched to Rome with instructions to deposit his will in the temple of the vestal virgins. Once deposited, such wills were sacrosanct, and only at the writer's death could the seals be removed. Yet Octavian seized the will and read it to the Senate. The senators noted its provision that if Antony died in Rome, he desired his body to be taken to Alexandria and given to Cleopatra. The implications were clear. He had turned his back on Rome, which had brought him to power, and had become so infatuated with Cleopatra that he no longer had a mind of his own. Octavian was determined on war, and Antony's perverse affection for an oriental princess provided a suitable excuse. At a ceremony in the temple of Bellona war was formally declared.

Romans would have preferred to fight on Italian soil, and they even suggested that Antony ferry his troops from the East to Italy. The coast would be cleared, and he would be given time to regroup his forces. Antony, suspecting that such a chivalrous offer concealed treachery, refused, but agreed to fight in Greece and set up his headquarters near Actium. Octavian ferried an army across the Ionian Sea and landed it close to Antony's. Antony may have had over five hundred ships, including one of Cleopatra's squadrons. At noon, on September 3, 31 B.C., the two fleets met and there was some desultory skirmishing, with the lighter Roman ships buzzing around the slow-moving, heavily armored ships of Antony, while the two armies took up their positions along the shore. Several of

Antony's squadrons surrendered, and Cleopatra precipitously sailed away, abandoning Antony to his own resources. When Antony saw the purple sails of her flagship vanishing into the distance, he did what no other commander had ever done before—he fled from his army and fleet to run after a woman.

Before he made his decision to follow Cleopatra, Antony had the destiny of the world in his hands. He commanded nineteen legions on the shore twelve thousand horse, a mighty navy, provinces with inexhaustible supplies of treasure and manpower, and a capital in Egypt that rivaled Rome in wealth and splendor. By the time he climbed on her flagship he had lost them all. We are told that he made his way to the prow and sat there for three days, his hands covering his face—possibly he was drunk.

The collapse at Actium was followed by the suicides of Antony and Cleopatra when the victor eventually reached Alexandria. Italy and the western provinces had already sworn allegiance to Octavian in 32 B.C.; now the entire eastern empire fell into his hands as well, rich Egypt becoming a domain that he ruled as the successor of the Ptolemies. He was virtually the master of the Mediterranean world, and all that was left for him to do was to put down surviving resistance among Antony's followers and to consolidate a new order in divided Rome. The first task was readily accomplished; the second he had set for himself was more difficult, however, and his solution revealed all his artistry of power.

When he returned to the capital in the summer of 29 B.C. to celebrate a three-day triumph, parading the spoils of Egypt through the streets, he was greeted as peacebringer by a war-weary people whose economy and very city had become badly run down. He immediately suggested measures of encouragement and reform. Rome's huge army of some sixty legions was slashed in half, and Octavian's income from Egypt was applied

to settle veterans on plots of land. Unpaid back taxes were for-
given and records were burned. A general amnesty for Antony's
followers was declared. The Senate, swollen by Julius Caesar's
liege men, was judiciously cleansed and cut back in size. All
this—along with the start of a vast program of urban renewal
and rebuilding that was to change the face of Rome—was
accomplished on the basis of Octavian's commanding prestige
and presence, though he held no regular office other than that
of annual consul, with the additional title of princeps, or first
citizen. In effect, he controlled the state through his money and
his well-rewarded soldiery. Yet ostentation and the trappings of
power had no interest for a man so absorbed with the substance
of power. In a time of self-indulgence he set an example of a
return to republican austerity, living in a small house on the
Palatine, his bedroom hardly larger than a cell, and wearing
simple robes woven by his wife. Deliberately he presented himself as a man utterly without vanity, even without ambition,
who remained at his post only because he regarded it as his
duty to impose order on the empire.

In theory his power reposed in the fiction that he had
restored the republic. Coins were struck honoring him as LIB-
ERTATIS P[*opuli*] R[*omani*] VINDEX, ("vindicator of the liberty
of the Roman people"). Although he also proclaimed himself to
be that, he had not the least intention of restoring the republic,
and he was to destroy the vestiges of its liberties by reducing its
governmental forms to mere extensions of his authoritarian
rule. In one of the craftiest moves ever made by a statesman, he
appeared before the Senate in 27 B.C. to announce that he
wished to relinquish his power, having led his people to peace
and well-being: "I shall lead you no longer, and no one will be
able to say that it was to win absolute power that I did whatever has hitherto been done. . . . Receive back also your liberty
and the republic; take over the army and the subject provinces,

and govern yourselves as has been your wont." He was careful to remark, however, that "nothing in the world would deter me from aiding you when you were in danger . . . I gave myself to you unstintingly . . ."

The Senate was filled with Octavian's adherents and they became his willing accomplices. His seeming self-denial was actually a bid for the confirmation of even further power, backed by his prestige or what he was to refer to in his memoir, the *Res gestae*, as his auctoritas. Almost everything a chief of state could desire was granted him by the listening Senate. He was to hold a ten-year proconsular imperium over Gaul, Spain, Syria, and Egypt; this involved control of the bulk of Rome's army. To consul and princeps, a third title was added—*augustus*, or "worshipful"—suggesting an exalted, priestlike presence and indicating prophetical knowledge and divine favor; its connotations dated back to Romulus, who had established Rome *augusto augurio* ("under the most favorable augury"), so the chronicler Ennius said. The Senate also voted to place laurels and a wreath of oak leaves on the door of his house, and to hang in the Senate a gold shield inscribed with a tribute to his valor, clemency, justice, and piety.

Though Augustus—this being the name under which he was from then on to be known—refused such titles of majesty as king and emperor and shrewdly preferred the simple one of princeps, he found in 23 B.C. that to run the vast affairs of Rome efficiently he needed even more power than he had already obtained. Refusing what would have been his twelfth consulship, he was given overriding proconsular power throughout the empire and was named tribune for life, a position that gave him power of veto. This was the highest peak of unchallenged authority yet reached in Rome.

Though chilly and reserved, Augustus did not exercise his principate in lofty isolation. He had close and gifted advisers—

none more influential than Marcus Vipsanius Agrippa, who was his faithful deputy, and Gaius Cilnius Maecenas, who never held public office, but who was a trusted counselor, diplomatic agent, and friend of many years, besides being, with his wealth and culture, a patron of the arts, which Augustus was anxious to further as a reflection of his regime.

Born of an obscure family, Agrippa had been Augustus' boyhood friend; he was in Apollonia when news came of Julius Caesar's murder and was one of the first to advise the young man to make a bid for power. Then he had distinguished himself against Sextus Pompey and at Actium and had put down uprisings in Augustus' behalf in Gaul and Spain. Surviving portraits show his rugged, strong-jawed, granitic features. "In him," says the historian Velleius Paterculus, "there was no difference between thought and action." We are told that he was utterly impervious to danger and absolutely loyal to Augustus. An outstanding general and a man of considerable learning, he was also a brilliant administrator, organizing cities such as Heliopolis in the East, constructing a vast new water-supply system for Rome, and supervising the building of a road network in southern Gaul. When in 18 B.C. the Senate renewed Augustus' extraordinary powers for five years, Agrippa was named his co-regent, sharing his tribunicial authority. There was no question, to be sure, as to who the actual ruler was; but Agrippa was both the second man in Rome and probably first in line for a dynastic succession, since Augustus himself had produced no male heirs and had given his daughter Julia to him in marriage. When Agrippa (born in the same year as Augustus) died at the age of fifty-one, he left a great gap in the life and surroundings of the emperor, who was to survive him by a quarter of a century.

Maecenas differed sharply from Agrippa in background and personality. Descended from a noble Etruscan clan, he was a patrician of great charm and style, calm and gentle, and particularly bent on exerting a restraining influence on Augustus, in whom he had detected a streak of unnecessary cruelty. Tolerant, urbane, brave, he was a liberal in an authoritarian age. If Agrippa was all for action, Maecenas was for caution and moderation, and so they admirably complemented one another. Gathering poets around him at his country estate, Maecenas encouraged Vergil and Horace to place their talents at the service of Augustus. Vergil, the elegiac writer raised in the Mantuan countryside, became through Maecenas' sponsorship a confidant of Augustus, who asked him on occasion to accompany the imperial household on trips abroad and at one point appears to have suggested that he might write an epic on the late wars. Instead, Vergil wrote the Aeneid—the epic purporting to describe the finding and conquest of Italy by Augustus' ancestor Aeneas, but also intended to celebrate Rome's illustrious destiny and the moral foundations of the peace and order Augustus had achieved. The triumph of Aeneas was the triumph of Augustus, who appears in the poem in a prophetic vision of his great ancestor. In this vision Augustus is seen enthroned within the temple of Apollo as he inspects the tribute offered him by all the peoples of the world, and these gifts are hung on the gleaming white temple gates. Again and again Vergil insists that it was not for plunder or lust of battle that the Romans came to dominate the world; they were to dominate it because the gods had decreed that rule should be given to the righteous, the just, and the blessed.

Once in a mood of despair Vergil wrote to Augustus to complain of the difficulties of composing the *Aeneid*. "It is so shapeless a thing," he wrote, "that I think myself mad to have embarked on it." It is true that it lacks the clear contours of the *Iliad* and was evidently written with immense difficulty by a poet burdened by the magnitude of his theme and its demands of style. He was continually rewriting, "licking it into shape," Suetonius remarked, "as the she-bear does her cubs." Even with the epic completed, except for the finishing touches, he was so dissatisfied that he begged his friends to burn the manuscript when he died. However, Augustus ordered that Vergil's wish be disregarded, and the epic was published as it was left, with half-lines uncompleted and awkward passages unchanged. Vergil had claimed that he needed three more years to perfect it, and it is possible that if he had been given those years he would have ruined it.

What survives is the proudest literary monument ever offered to an emperor. Although Vergil celebrates the noble achievements of Aeneas, he has a quite un-Roman pity for Aeneas' fallen enemies. Indeed, pity and terror are major themes in the epic. It is almost as though Vergil had been granted prophetic powers, seeing Rome as both conqueror and victim, tyrant and slave. Augustus looked outward at the world at peace. Vergil looked inward and saw that the peace was delusory and impermanent and at the mercy of dark forces.

Horace, both a witty amorist and a traditional moralist, exquisitely deft in the use of his words, was invited to compose a hymn for the secular games announced for 17 B.C. to celebrate the first ten years of Augustus' principate. This he did in the form of the celebrated poem *Carmen saeculare*, which opens with an invocation to Apollo and his sister goddess Diana to keep Rome under their protection. Addressing them, the poet proclaims: "*Roma vestrum est opus* (Rome is your handiwork)." He was undoubtedly writing in praise of Augustus, who had taken Apollo for his special patron.

For three days and three nights the games were held, with vast processions moving through the city; at night, under the full moon, there were torchlight marches; finally, a choir of youths and maidens sang Horace's hymn outside Apollo's tem-

ple on the Palatine. All classes gave homage to the durable victor and leader who had brought peace, prosperity, and a wiser
distribution of the spoils or rewards of growth to Rome.

Augustus, both in his early and later years, was aware of the
far boundaries of his empire, advancing some, consolidating
others. In 19 B.C. he organized campaigns to subdue what
remained of resistance in Spain; he spent some three years in
Gaul, organizing it and making Lugdunum (Lyons) its capital;
he advanced Roman power across the Alps into the Bavarian
plain and along the Danube to Vindobona (Vienna) and the
Hungarian grassland; he sought for a stable northeastern border along the rivers Weser and Elbe, but was finally stopped in
A.D. 6 by Teuton tribes. In the east, meanwhile, he had reached
a settlement with Parthia whereby the Euphrates was recognized as the border between two empires.

In 18 and 17 B.C. Augustus instituted reform legislation at
home that was designed to improve morals and restore republican virtues, though he had no intention of restoring republican
institutions. Laws against adultery, coupled with restrictions on
luxury and ostentation, emanated from him. In order to stabilize marriage and promote offspring, benefits were bestowed
upon the parents of large families, and a candidate for public
office could win precedence because of the sheer number of his
children. Ancient rites and domestic rituals that had fallen into
decay in a time of Roman absorption with cults of the east were
restored. Augustus is described as having been particularly
engaged in reviving respect for the lares and penates and for
the vestal virgins. Though he had shown favor to Ovid, the
liveliest and naughtiest poet at his court, this puritan emperor
eventually banished him. Augustus' vast public works program—restoring old temples and providing a new forum—was in
large part an effort to provide work for the unemployed.

During the rest of his reign Augustus ruled in austere

majesty, his powers being periodically renewed by a compliant Senate. He was the fount of honor, the chief magistrate, the commander of all armies (which had taken an oath of personal allegiance to him), the holder of the treasury, and after 12 B.C. when he became *pontifex maximus* after the death of Lepidus (previous holder of the office), the head of the state religion as well. He could issue edicts and judicial decisions without review. He had been given the right to make treaties and thus conduct foreign affairs as he saw fit. His personal income was immeasurable, drawn in great part from revenues from various parts of the empire that he governed through his deputies as provinces of his own. As in the case of Caesar before him, his own treasury and that of the state were intermixed. His power of patronage, of appointment, and of reward was oriental in its extent.

Yet with this vast concentration of might in his person, he was wise enough to see that he would do well to share it or delegate a considerable part of it to others. A great empire could not be well managed by a supreme potentate alone. It needed the skillful and devoted hand of men who would share the responsibility for it. It needed, in short, a high administrative class. One aspect of the genius of Augustus lay in recognizing in the humbled Senate, now no longer the lofty and contumacious arbiter of Roman fortunes, the basis of collaboration with himself. He paid courtly deference to the senators, rising in their presence and repeatedly referring matters to them for further consideration. Anxious to secure both their loyalty and their talents, he extended their functions, encouraging them to take over legislative and judicial roles from the popular assemblies, the tribunes, and the judges, and to share with him the burdens of imperial management—all subject, to be sure, to his final veto. Some laws were left to the Senate to promulgate; many provinces were left to it to administer; and the basis of membership in the Senate was broadened to attract promising young men of the class of equites whom he wished to recruit for careers in public office. Augustus was in need of trained men to serve as quaestors, aediles, praetors; all positions from which they could rise to become legion commanders, governors, and prefects. Using the Senate as his base, he offered longterm, salaried appointments to such men, as against the volunteer and amateur system of the republic. In effect, the Senate and the senatorial order became his administrative right arm. He himself, both magisterial and deft, combined the ways of a dictator, a constitutional monarch and an American President calling upon the "advice and consent" of the Senate, while building a formidable bureaucracy.

Almost uninterrupted peace under Augustus led to even greater prosperity. Rome, which had previously resembled a large sprawling village, became amid his rebuilding of temples and monuments a splendid city, and the wealth of the empire flowed into it. Not long before his death Augustus remarked: "I found Rome built of sun-dried bricks; I leave it clothed in marble."

In 9 B.C., midway in his reign, the Ara Pacis, an altar to the Augustan peace, was dedicated on the Campus Martius. Augustus, who had built numerous large temples to the gods, could no doubt have raised one in his own honor; instead he allowed the Senate to erect a rather modest shrine less than forty feet long to commemorate his greatest achievement. Although richly decorated with symbolic friezes and carved portraiture (one can recognize Augustus and Agrippa, Livia and Augustus' daughter Julia) the altar reflects a certain restraint—a quality lacking in many of Rome's later emperors.

When he died at seventy-six in A.D. 14, having also outlived Maecenas, Vergil, Horace, and his only two grandsons—his daughter Julia's children by Agrippa—no further memorial in

The Ara Pacis, above, the altar of Augustan peace, was erected on the Campus Martius by the Roman Senate to commemorate Augustus' return from Gaul, where he had been living for three years. The reliefs that adorn the altar are among the greatest works of art produced in the early empire.

marble was needed. The empire itself, unchallenged, masterful, and bearing the imprint of Augustus' firm and lucid mind stood there for all to see. For centuries the Romans were to look back on the Augustan age as a period when their world was divinely blessed, when peace was as familiar as daily bread, and hope was the commonplace of daily lives.

VIII

ARCHITECTS OF EMPIRE

*Fare thee well, Tiberius, most charming of men, and success go
with you, as you war for me and the Muses. Fare thee well, most
charming and valiant of men and most conscientious of generals,
or may I never know happiness.*

—Emperor Augustus, in a letter to his adopted heir,
as reported by Suetonius

T he coming of the emperors brought profound and cumu-
lative changes in the institutions, the mores, and the very
physical appearance of Rome. Many old public organs,
along with many old buildings, survived. But new structures of
power were overtaking the former, while vast new undertakings
in stone overshadowed the latter. The Senate survived in its
ancient dignity, but its authority was much altered and dimin-
ished. Tiberius, Augustus' successor, sought in his reign (A.D.
14–37) to continue his stepfather's policy of encouraging the
Senate to collaborate with the ruler in the management of the
empire; but with the disappearance of political parties, and
thereby of public debate, the Senate's old role as the vital center of Roman statecraft was gone. Great new speakers' rostra
were erected, but under the new order there was no Cicero to
exhort the citizens from them.

The consuls were still annually elected, but they were hardly
more than ceremonial relics of the past, their powers long
superseded by those gathered into the hands of a single head of
state, who ruled by virtue of a grant of tribunicial authority

(*tribunicia potestas*) and through his control of the army and of political patronage. The civil service, which Augustus had founded on the basis of the senatorial class and the equites, was to be developed by Tiberius and to be organized into a great imperial bureaucracy by the brilliant though sickly Claudius, who as emperor (A.D. 41–54) established three or more executive bureaus and went so far as to invite freedmen rather than aristocrats to head them. In 27 B.C. Augustus had created, from among the bodyguards that had surrounded individual generals during the republic, a corps of soldiers that was to enjoy special status as protectors of the emperor, his clan, and the imperial order of rule. These picked professionals, the Praetorian Guard, rapidly became a formidable new power in the state—one that on occasion could be decisive. Claudius owed his accession as emperor to them, at a time when the Senate was debating whether or not the republic should be restored. As Edward Gibbon remarked succinctly, "While the Senate deliberated, the Praetorian Guards had resolved." In years to come, the protectors of emperors sometimes became their captors.

Such shifts in power affected the whole character of the age. Political interest, once so broad and intense, now tended to become narrow, if not passive, and to concentrate on the ways of emperors and on the rise and fall of their favorites. Cornelius Tacitus, the historian of the new era, was in large part a chronicler of court intrigues and imperial eccentricities, of which there were many. It was a time of decline of popular participation in government (elections were taken out of the hands of the assemblies and placed in those of the compliant Senate, possibly at about the time of Augustus' death) and of the rise of great imperial monuments and gifts to the people that were very often provided from the emperor's own treasury.

Of the major rulers who followed Augustus in the first century A.D.—Tiberius, Claudius, Nero, Vespasian, Titus, Domitian—

each set his individual seal upon the development of the state and upon the face of Rome itself. The physical transformation of the capital, begun by Caesar, was only a part—though the most spectacular part—of that astonishing flowering of architecture and engineering that studded the empire near and far with aqueducts, bridges, paved highways, ceremonial arches, stadiums, open-air theatres, and large public halls, or basilicas. If Romans no longer expressed themselves individually in politics, they did so collectively and magnificently in stone.

By Caesar's time the Roman Forum, wedged in among the hills, had become so crowded that he had ordered the building of a new one to the northwest of the old. He had also chosen the area known as the Campus Martius, beyond the Capitoline hill and beside the river's bend, as the site for future public buildings; and on this land were to rise the Pantheon, the baths of Agrippa, the mausoleum of Augustus, the baths of Nero, and the stadium of Domitian. Caesar had also enlarged the Circus Maximus, between the slopes of the Aventine and Palatine hills, into an immense stadium some two thousand feet long and able to accommodate two hundred fifty thousand people, who came to watch chariot and horse races and gladiatorial shows. But the spaciousness and splendor begun by Caesar still left most quarters of Rome a nest of old and narrow streets jammed with traffic and so short of living space as to result in the construction of tenements for the poor—rabbit warrens consisting of six and seven stories of cubicles that were usually rented out by the room at exorbitant rates. Augustus wisely limited the height of these *insulae*, as they were called, to seventy-five feet, since they were firetraps and collapsed frequently.

It was not until after the great fire of A.D. 64, which leveled many parts of the city, that what we might term a program of general urban renewal was begun. Tacitus, recounting the disaster, speaks of "those narrow winding passages and irregular streets, which characterized old Rome"; but he adds that some citizens did not like the cutting of new and broader ways through the rubble nor did they like the creation of open spaces, and thought the old order "had been more conducive to health, inasmuch as the narrow streets with the elevation of the roofs were not equally penetrated by the sun's heat, while now the open space, unsheltered by any shade, was scorched by a fiercer glow."

Though Augustus himself has been estimated to have either built or rebuilt over one hundred public buildings, his interests did not lie in the direction of devising a new city plan. He did, however, reorganize the city's management in a manner that again revealed his administrative mastery. He divided the sprawling metropolis into fourteen *regiones*, or wards, and over two hundred fifty precincts. To maintain public order he set up a police force of three cohorts of a thousand men each, reporting to the city prefect. To guard against fires, Rome's greatest daily hazard, he established a corps of seven cohorts of professional firemen, or *vigiles*, who also had the power to make arrests. To maintain its public buildings, to safeguard its water supply, and to oversee the maintenance of the roads, he appointed separate boards of commissioners known as *curatores*.

In its new and refurbished buildings, the Rome of the Augustan age reflected the character of Augustus, who was determined that his city should tower over all others in the world. All authority came from there; it was to be the visible center of all men's loyalties, the lodestar by which they lived, the place of ultimate judgment and reward. At the same time, because Augustus considered himself to be a man of studied moderation, wearing homespun and living in his small villalike mansion on the Palatine, there had to be a limit to ostentation.

Stateliness rather than opulence was his theme, and he liked to stress the utilitarian nature of his improvements. This the architect Vitruvius did also, and he dedicated to Augustus the ten books of his *De architectura*. After acknowledging the superhuman intelligence of Augustus, Vitruvius goes on to remark that the emperor had embarked on a program of general welfare, the establishment of public order, and the provision of public buildings intended for practical use.

To accomplish his aim, Augustus enlarged Rome's central meeting area by adding a third forum next to the one built by Caesar. He turned his attention to an important element in "useful" building—the basilica, or the assembly hall, of which a number had been rising in Rome as well as in other cities of importance. These halls were usually roofed and offered far greater protection against weather than did the open colonnades that surrounded public squares in Greece, though the design of the basilicas may have been of Greek origin. Usually they were rectilinear, with lines of columns within their walled enclosure, and with a raised platform at one end on which the presiding official sat, often against the background of a tall, curved apse. They were both governmental and social meeting places, protected against summer's heat and winter's storms; in time the Christians would adapt the design of the basilica, transforming the hall into a church and placing an altar where the dais had been. Augustus, for his part, rebuilt for the second time the Basilica Aemilia, after Caesar's reconstruction of the even earlier building had been damaged by fire. On a far larger scale Augustus rebuilt Caesar's Basilica Julia, on the south side of the Forum, giving it a long central space that has been calculated at about two hundred seventy by fifty feet, with lines of interior columns on all four sides. All but the foundations of Augustus' basilicas have disappeared; one can only speculate as to what Pliny meant when he wrote that the reconstructed Basilica Aemilia was one of the three finest buildings in the empire.

In the eyes of Augustus, temples were useful too: their building or rebuilding was an act of piety to the gods who had granted him victory, but it was also an affirmation of national faith in the divine protectors. He was not deeply religious in the spiritual sense; but it was practical to favor the gods who had favored him. Since he believed that he was protected by Apollo and that the god had presided over his victory at Actium, he built on the Palatine a temple of Carrara marble, dedicated to his tutelary god, with pillared portico and inlaid ivory doors, with a statue of Apollo, and equipped with two libraries—one of Greek books, the other of books in Latin, as if to symbolize a marriage between the two cultures.

In support of the oath he had sworn at Philippi in 42 B.C. that he would build a great temple to Mars the Avenger if he won the battle, he raised a shrine to the god of war in his forum, and with wings that contained not books, but military relics. Among the noblest relics was the sword of Julius Caesar. Augustus no doubt planned that the temple of Mars should assume many of the functions previously fulfilled by the great temple of Jupiter on the Capitoline, across the way. In this new temple the conquering general would deposit his laurel wreath after his long triumphal procession; here was to be the center where the record of Roman valor and glory under arms would forever be preserved. Only three columns and a fragment of architrave survive.

Other temples were to come forth in profusion, such as those of Concord and of Castor, rebuilt from a decayed state by Tiberius after he became Augustus' heir. At the base of the Capitoline, in an area which Augustus is thought to have given over to the arts, a great theatre was completed, with two tiers of

arcades and a seating capacity of some twenty thousand. Dedicated to Augustus' young son-in-law Marcellus, this open-air
auditorium was a vast improvement over early Roman theatres,
which were built of wood. Spectators had been offered little in
the way of comfort in those earlier structures; they were forced
to stand before a wooden stage to watch a play. The theatre of
Marcellus was revolutionary in other ways, too, for it greatly
exceeded in size what was probably the first masonry theatre in
Rome, built only forty-two years earlier by Pompey.

Augustus and Agrippa, his adopted son and right-hand
man, together had presided over the centennial games that
marked the city's dedication to Apollo in 17 B.C., and together
they had planned the city's rebuilding. Livy spoke of Augustus
as "the founder or restorer of all the temples of Rome"; yet a
great deal of the practical work lay in the hands of Agrippa, a
brilliant organizer who was also a great engineer. He built
aqueducts, erected one of Rome's major public baths, and provided the city with one of its most extraordinary temples—the
stately Pantheon. After two ruinous fires, the Pantheon was to
be rebuilt by the emperor Hadrian as a lofty, domed, circular
shrine; it has survived as one of antiquity's most noble buildings, and to this day no one can be certain how much or little
of Agrippa's own work was preserved in its stones. Hadrian, in
any event, must have felt deep respect for what his predecessor
had wrought when he set his own architects to work on it, for
he caused an inscription to be carved in huge letters running
almost the entire length of the pediment: M · AGRIPPA · L · F ·
COS · TERTIUM · FECIT—meaning that Agrippa had made this
edifice in his third consulship. Such tribute to an earlier
designer was indeed unique. Hadrian, possibly one of the most
thoughtful and accomplished of Romans, evidently realized
that he was in the presence of a master builder.

Agrippa was, in fact, one of the major practical geniuses of

Rome. The city's needs for a sure water supply for its fast-growing citizenry were immense, and they had been ably met before his time by four aqueducts that brought in a constant flow from watersheds in the Alban hills. Under Augustus, Agrippa added two more and united and administered the whole system, which has been estimated to have provided some three hundred million gallons for the city every day, or about one hundred fifty gallons for each man, woman, and child. These aqueducts were the life-bringers to a metropolis unable to rely on the muddy Tiber for cleansing and recreational baths, and Romans regarded them as their supreme engineering achievement. Above all, they were practical—not simply ornamental. As Sextius Julius Frontinus, the governor of Britain who became a prominent engineer, remarked: "Will anybody compare the idle pyramids, or those other useless though renowned works of the Greeks with these aqueducts, these many indispensable structures?"

Under Augustus and his successors, the engineers came into their own, developing three major architectural elements that were to become distinctive of Roman architecture—the arch, the vault, and the dome. These forms were not original to Rome; Egyptians and Mesopotamians had raised arches and vaults, and small clay domes may have been built in the Near East from early times. But the Greeks, for their part, relied almost entirely on the post-and-lintel system of construction, and it remained for the Romans to exploit arched forms as the means of spanning large spaces. That they were able to accomplish this was due largely to their innovation in the making of concrete: they used lime mortar, a far stronger binding material than the traditional clay. This was a revolutionary departure in building techniques. Using temporary wooden supports, curved brickwork mixed with liquid mortar could be laid aloft, to become as secure as any masonry when the mixture set, and much lighter. Though huge stone blocks were still generally used in erecting a wall, it was also found that a wall could be just as strong and much less bulky and costly in carrying the thrust from above if composed of courses of broken stones and brick fragments bound with the new mortar. All that remained was to mantle the walls for appearance's sake with ornamental glass, stucco, or face-brick, and coffer the interiors of arches and ceilings with ingenious designs.

Yet the great buildings, erected with extraordinary skill and attention to balance and detail, were the product of a somewhat limited background. There is no evidence that the architects and engineers were trained in mathematics; they worked, as Vitruvius says, *ex fabrica et ratiocinatione*, which may be translated as "on the job and with hard thinking." They used models extensively, drew levels with plumb lines, and employed simple surveying instruments, together with huge wooden cranes worked by treadmills and pulleys. But their equipment was not notably superior to that used centuries earlier by Assyrian kings, who also built roads, aqueducts, and buildings that created awe in the minds of their subjects. The Roman contribution to architecture was expressed mainly in a dramatic magnification of scale, made possible by the most imaginative use of forms and materials. Near the end of the first century A.D., a palace was built on the Palatine for the emperor Domitian; it contained a lofty hall with a lengthy barrel vault more than one hundred feet in span—the precursor of the colossal vaulted enclosures of the baths of the later emperors Caracalla and Diocletian. Agrippa's Pantheon, moreover, when it was rebuilt and possibly enlarged by Hadrian early in the second century A.D., was roofed by a dome almost one hundred fifty feet in diameter—an engineering feat that pointed the way to the ever greater experiments that were to culminate in the vast dome of the church of Hagia Sophia, in Constantinople.

The new order of building spread rapidly across the empire as an embodiment of Roman strength and leadership. Soon every major provincial capital had its basilicas, its roofed baths, its monumental arches, its paved roads, and often its aqueducts too. The Romans also inspired their allies to emulate them. When Herod the Great of Judaea determined to found a new seaport on the barren coast of Palestine, to which he had fallen heir as head of the Hyrcanian dynasty, he decided to show his friend Augustus that he, too, could build a city on the Roman scale. Enormous blocks of limestone, fifty feet long, were lowered into twenty fathoms of water, to provide a sea wall. The new city's public buildings included a theatre, an amphitheatre, and a hippodrome; aqueducts brought water from a distant river; there was a large and complex drainage system operated by tidal power. Here is the Jewish chronicler Josephus' description of Herod's seaport, which was to become the administrative capital of Judaea under Roman rule and to maintain that role during the three centuries and more that saw the Romans in power there.

At the harbor mouth there rose three colossal statues supported on pillars on both sides, and the pillars on the left of the ships entering the harbor were supported by a massive tower, and those on the right by two upright blocks of stone clamped together, even higher than the tower on the other side. Adjoining the harbor were houses, also of limestone, and the streets of the city, which were laid out at equal distances apart, led to the harbor. On rising ground, facing the harbor mouth, stood Caesar's temple, which was of exceptional size and beauty, containing a colossal statue of the emperor, not inferior to Olympian Zeus, and there was another statue dedicated to Roma, comparable with the Hera of Argos.

Herod dedicated the city to the province, the harbor to those who sailed the sea, and to Caesar went the glory of the new creation; therefore he called it Caesarea.

A chief uniting element of the empire was, of course, the complex road system radiating from Rome and begun centuries earlier with the building of the Appian Way, which crossed the Pontine marshes on an embankment as it headed in a straight line to Capua, in Campania. By Augustus' time the network had been extended as far as the Rhine and Danube frontiers; mileposts marked the distance from Rome, or within the provinces, the distance from the nearest provincial city. A road had been pushed on from southern France across the Pyrenees to the river Ebro; the greater and lesser St. Bernard passes, in the Alps, had been opened for traffic to Switzerland and the Rhine, and to the highlands of Provence. Whether Romans carved out entirely new routes or adapted earlier tracks, surfacing and ballasting them, remains a matter of some debate. In any case Roman roads were built very straight and often they measured three feet in depth, consisting of a foundation of rubble supporting tiers of stone and concrete and topped by a pavement to support heavy-wheeled traffic.

The accession of Tiberius, in A.D. 14, upon Augustus' death at the age of seventy-six, brought to the principate another man of brilliant military background, who under the tutelage of his imperial stepfather had become a builder of provinces as well as of great architectural structures. Yet Tiberius, fifty-five when he came to the throne, was a soured person, having lived perhaps too long in the shadow of Augustus, who had shown him little affection. Son of the republican officer Tiberius Claudius Nero and of Livia (who divorced Nero to marry the rising emperor), Tiberius accompanied Augustus on campaigns in the east. In 11 B.C. he had subdued the Pannonian tribes along the Danube; he had also distinguished himself in the fighting in Germany. But Augustus, after the death of his son-in-law Agrippa and of his own grandsons, chose Tiberius as his successor only with reluctance. To cement the family bond, he had required that Tiberius divorce his wife and marry Agrippa's widow Julia. A hesitant man, forced into an unhappy marriage, now came to power.

Tiberius immediately disclaimed any desire to receive the same sweeping authority that Augustus had enjoyed, by telling the senators that he was unequal to the whole burden of the state. Furthermore, he told them: "A well-disposed and helpful princeps should be the servant of the Senate. I have looked upon you as just, kind, and indulgent masters, and so regard you." Tacitus thought Tiberius was hypocritical in making these obeisances to the senators, who at the same time were making obeisances to him in their search for a leader. He may have been sincere in his protestations, however, sensing only too well that he could not carry the full responsibilities of Augustus. But the reluctant new princeps, who finally accepted all the titles and honors of office, including a lifelong proconsular imperium, was not to view the senators in such a self-effacing way for long.

In his first years he gave Rome a civil rule of high quality, appointing men of merit to key posts, awarding the Senate increased administrative functions in line with Augustus' scheme, and ensuring freedom for the little public debate that remained. In his later years, however, his troubles accumulated, exacerbated by his lack of public appeal, his failures in tact when dealing with the Senate, his growing indifference to public affairs, and his involvement with dynastic rivalries and household favorites. Augustus was so popular that he could walk about Rome unprotected; Tiberius feared for his life. Augustus chose to live in an unassuming private house;

Tiberius, for all his professions of humility, built himself a sumptuous palace on the Palatine, along with a huge barrack to house his Praetorian Guard.

There are few Roman emperors stranger than Tiberius, for he was endowed with high qualities, and might but for some flaws of character and wounds of experience have continued the tradition of his stepfather. Outwardly his reign was a period of prosperity and generally prevailing peace. The empire continued along the course mapped out by Augustus, with the momentum the great princeps had given it. Trade flourished, especially with the east. More and more roads were built across North Africa, a vast program of city planning was begun in Antioch, and wealth flowed from the silver mines in Spain into the hands of their owner, the emperor. Tiberius' nephew Germanicus, campaigning beyond the Rhine frontier, restored among the German tribes the prestige that had been lost by the defeat of Varus' legions in the Teutoburgian Forest. Minor rebellions in Africa and Gaul caused barely a ripple on the surface of the imperial order.

Yet in the emperor's own household and in his own person there was increasing disarray. Young Germanicus, whom he had made his son by adoption, caused him trouble through unruliness and ambitious seeking of popularity; Germanicus' death under mysterious circumstances while he was in the East raised unanswerable questions. Tiberius' only son, Julius Caesar Drusus, died suddenly in A.D. 23, leaving him no recourse but to hunt for heirs in the family of the late Germanicus. A miserable family feud broke out in which Agrippina, the headstrong widow of Germanicus and mother of three sons, became the center of intrigues against the emperor. By this time Tiberius had fallen under the sinister influence of Lucius Aelius Sejanus, the prefect commanding the Praetorian Guard, who promoted the quarrel, and with his men concentrated in the permanent barrack near Rome's gates, plotted to win the succession for himself. It was Sejanus who, evidently aware of Tiberius' increasing melancholy and instability, persuaded the emperor to withdraw his seat of residence to the island of Capri, while he himself would oversee affairs in Rome—a division of actual and seeming power that led to the tragic dissolution of Tiberius' once-promising reign.

By nature studious, tolerant, and lethargic save for the pursuit of military affairs, Tiberius did not have in him the qualities of a tyrant. Yet he became a tyrant in spite of himself, turning with brutal force against Agrippina and her sons and finally against his favorite Sejanus too, and invoking the law of high treason against his enemies or suspected enemies until there were few people in the empire who trusted him or whom he could trust. Much of this he accomplished from his southern island retreat, a haven into which he disappeared only to emerge from it on occasion with corrosive and unpredictable force. In his Villa Jovis, perched high on the cliffs of Capri, he secluded himself from the world as he presided from a distance over his dominions. Suetonius observed that no magnificent architectural works marked Tiberius' reign. He left unfinished his effort on two major monuments that might have commended him to posterity, the great temple to Augustus the Divine in Rome and the restoration of Pompey's theatre. Yet his eyrie on Capri was one of the most spectacular constructions of the age—a sprawling, fortresslike mass built about a central courtyard with four rain-catching cisterns, with reception rooms and galleries arranged in a semicircle fronting on the sea, with baths and libraries in the wings. In the most remote section of the villa were the emperor's private chambers, reached through labyrinthine corridors beyond the quarters of members of his court. Kitchens were relegated to still a different wing to avoid the intrusion of cooking odors, and in a remote terrace annex there was still another set of living quarters—perhaps the most private of imperial chambers.

The emperor possessed other villas as well on the island of Capri, which became his private domain, with no one permitted to land on it without his express permission. In summer he would retreat to a cool grotto on the mainland overlooking the Gulf of Amyclae—in itself a small palace with its marble basins, fountains, pools, and collection of statuary. As Suetonius recalls, "But after the loss of his two sons, of whom Germanicus died in Syria and Drusus at Rome, he [Tiberius] withdrew into Campania; at which time opinion and conversation were widespread that he would never return and would soon die. And both turned out to be nearly true. For, indeed, he never returned to Rome, and a few days after leaving it, when he was at a villa of his called 'The Cave' near Terracina, during supper a number of stones fell from above killing many of the guests and attendants, but he almost miraculously escaped." Several more years were given to him, but the empire had all but lost sight of him when he died in A.D. 37.

Augustus, for all his wise statecraft, had produced no clear-cut program for the succession, with the result that an emperor could choose an heir according to whim, trusting in the Praetorian Guard to assist the changeover when the moment came. From the offspring of Germanicus, Tiberius had picked Gaius, who was to become a disaster for Rome. Gaius, who was known as Caligula—Little Boots—from the child's version of soldier's boots he had sported as a youngster, was a handsome man of twenty-five, popular with the soldiery, and the hope of a people weary of Tiberius' ways when he was acclaimed princeps in A.D. 37 with Guard support. For a short while he ruled ably; then for three years he ruled like a madman until he was stabbed to death by a Praetorian officer, the prefects of the Guard being party to the murder plot.

In his early months he seemed the bringer of a new, liberal dispensation. He recalled political exiles, suspended treason trials, banished informers from his court, made public the accounting of the empire's finances (a practice instituted by Augustus but abandoned by Tiberius), held games, and launched a large building program. Then, from a model prince, he quite abruptly changed into an autocrat of exceptional cruelty and irresponsibility, moreover desiring that he receive the honors accorded to a god. A severe illness, which he is known to have suffered, may have deranged him; or it may have been his high office that caused him to fall victim to delusions of grandeur. No previous princeps had permitted a cult of emperor worship; Caesar and Augustus had been deified only after their deaths. Caligula, however, erected a temple to himself with a life-sized statue of himself in gold, and every day the statue was dressed in the clothes identical with those he was wearing on that day. He formed his own priesthood, which offered prayers and performed the appropriate sacrifices—for which he had a nice taste, urging those who wished to worship him to offer up flamingos, peacocks, woodcocks, and pheasants on certain days. According to Suetonius, he communed with his fellow gods: "When the moon shone full and bright he always invited the Moon-goddess to his bed; and during the day would indulge in whispered conversations with Capitoline Jupiter, pressing his ear to the god's mouth and sometimes raising his voice in anger. Once he was overheard threatening the god: 'If you do not raise me up to Heaven I will cast you down to Hell.' "

Meanwhile he resorted to indiscriminate murder. On a whim he caused his father-in-law to slit his own throat. He was suspected of incest with his sister Drusilla. He squandered state funds: Tiberius had left the state a fortune of twenty-seven million gold pieces, but Caligula spent it all and left the treasury bankrupt. Abroad, his perversities and follies were also notori-ous—mismanagement and oppression brought Mauretania and Judaea to the brink of revolt. He lined up a great array of his troops on the Channel coast to invade Britain, but changed his mind and marched them away again. The news of his death, in a capital seething with humiliation and indignation, was greeted with relief.

What Caligula had undermined was more than restored by his successor, Claudius, during the thirteen years of his rule. The new emperor was physically handicapped. Early in life he may have suffered many illnesses; he walked with a tottering gait, trembled continually, slobbered, and spoke in a manner that was difficult to understand. A nephew of Tiberius (Caligula himself had left no heir), he had long been overlooked for the succession because of his infirmities, and his elevation was largely a matter of chance. Following Caligula's assassination, members of the Praetorian Guard had found him in hiding in the Palatine palace, and its chiefs had decided that this all but forgotten man could serve them well as an emperor beholden to them. Thus Claudius, with his weak chin, weak knees, and shak-ing head, became at fifty-one the successor of the line of the handsome Augustus. But though his body was weak his mind was not, and his intellect overcame his limitations. Suetonius remarked that for all his infirmities, he "possessed majesty and dignity of appearance." Claudius was an intellectual and indeed a scholar. He had written voluminously on Etruscan history, and he composed forty-one "books" or chapters on the reign of Augustus. No other Roman emperor ever knew so much about the Roman past, and Claudius' love and respect for it made him, in turn, a follower of Augustus' aim of judicious distribution of functions in an imperial state, as against Caligula's oriental despotism.

Pursuing a policy of measured growth, he was able to add

five provinces to the empire: Mauretania (once a satellite kingdom, later split into two); Thrace, Lycia, and Britain. Almost a century had passed since Julius Caesar's first assault upon England. But Rome's foothold in the distant island had remained tenuous since that time, while on the other hand the emerging Britons had considerably advanced themselves, setting up small tribal kingdoms, trading with Gaul, attracting Gallic settlers, and absorbing Gallic influences as well. In A.D. 43, responding to an appeal from the Kentish chieftain Verica, who had long lived in Rome and professed to be friendly to the empire, Claudius dispatched four legions numbering some forty thousand men to put down the local rulers and organize their territories into a major province. A legion commander named Vespasian distinguished himself against the British tribesmen, and Claudius arrived in time to lead the final assault and accept their submission, permitting some of their petty kingdoms to survive within the imperial boundary he had set up between the river lines of the Severn and the Humber.

In his governing Claudius tried to follow Augustus' method of accommodation and balance, seeking to befriend the Senate. Intent on public improvements, he instituted a building program that was not as decorative as Augustus', but considerably more utilitarian. A new harbor was built at Ostia, north of the Tiber's silted mouth. Two aqueducts were completed for Rome. In many parts of the empire major roads were added to the existing system, some running to the Channel coast, and one of them extending for three hundred fifty miles from the Adriatic across the Brenner Pass to the Danube in Germany. Most ambitious of all among his engineering projects was that of reclaiming valuable farm land south of the capital: thirty thousand men were employed for eleven years in draining the Fucine Lake and in driving a tunnel three miles long to carry off the surplus water.

Yet, for all his merits, Claudius had shortcomings in leadership. Of necessity, because of the increasing complexity of the empire's business, he developed the bureaucracy begun by Augustus to the extent of setting up a group of private secretaries, who conducted themselves virtually as ministers of state and vastly enriched themselves in the process. He failed to impose a restraining hand on them and let himself be unduly guided by them; the fact, moreover, that these palace favorites were non-Roman freedmen was not reassuring to the Senate. And, most tragically for himself, he lived under the influence of two ill-chosen wives. The first was the promiscuous Messalina; the second was the imperious Agrippina, daughter of Germanicus and the elder Agrippina, who persuaded him to adopt Nero, her young son of an earlier marriage. In A.D. 54 Claudius was murdered by his ambitious second wife, who thus cleared the way for Nero and for herself as matriarch.

No novelist could have invented Nero; as an emperor he all but exceeds the bounds of credibility. Yet in his virtues and vices he was typical of his age, brilliant and decadent, elegant and gross. In his youth he was conspicuously handsome, with his finely chiseled nose, square chin, thick curls powdered with gold, and a physique well made except for his thin short legs. In time he would become a travesty of himself, grown fat, pot-bellied, thick-lipped with self-indulgence. The beginnings of his reign were promising. After the years of the physically grotesque Claudius, the young Nero, coming to the throne at seventeen, appeared to be one of those youthful rulers who ushers in a new age. He was burning with the desire to please and delighted in his popularity. Schooled by his tutor Seneca, the philosopher, he was well read and intelligent; moreover he was a gifted lyre player, a poet, and a singer. (The word *Nero* is derived from a Sabine word meaning "valiant" or "manly.") In the first years of his reign he was prodigal of his good behavior

Nero, immortalized in this bust, above, became infamous for his personal indulgences, his indirect involvement in the burning of Rome, and consequently the persecutions of Christians.

and showed a proper respect for the opinion of others, being especially attentive to the Senate. There was nothing to suggest that he would soon demonstrate massive incompetence, a passion for self-worship, and unbridled cruelty, becoming the murderer both of his mother and of his wife, along with countless others.

Some of the evil in this unstable man can probably be traced back to his domineering mother, a lecherous woman so spoiled by wealth and high position that she regarded her slightest impulse as a command to be obeyed, even if it meant that the entire resources of the state must be placed at her disposal. Agrippina amused herself by liquidating personal enemies and corrupting her son, and she succeeded so well that Nero lost respect for everyone, most of all for his mother. She is shown beside him on one of the first coins struck during his reign, and she made efforts to sit beside him in state on public occasions. Nero, however, grew resentful of her domination at court and had her banished from it, and in A.D. 59 had her put to the sword, declaring that she had planned his assassination. He received the congratulations of the Senate and the Roman people.

For a certain period the people had reasons for applauding him: he fed them well from his own grain ships, he entertained them with his own songs and by taking part in chariot races, and he refused to engage in unnecessary wars. Some virtuous Romans objected to the fact that the emperor made a public display of himself, performing in the theatre, dressing as a racing-chariot driver, and surrounding himself with singularly unpleasant companions—but there were not many virtuous Romans left. For a time he rode the tide of popularity.

Soon, however, there were wars in Britain and Armenia, and Nero began to debase the currency in order to pay for them. Wealthy nobles were put to death on suspicion of opposition,

while the emperor relaxed among Greek and oriental favorites
of low birth. By A.D. 64, virtually all elements in Rome were
united in enmity for him—so much so that when a ruinous fire
broke out that year, he was accused of setting it. All the buildings on the Palatine were destroyed; of the fourteen wards or
districts of Rome, three were burned to the ground and seven
were largely destroyed. Suetonius reports that "pretending to be
disgusted by the drab old buildings and narrow, winding
streets, he [Nero] brazenly set fire to the city." But he appears,
in fact, to have been absent from Rome at the time, and hurrying back when the disaster struck, to have directed the fire-
fighting. The story of his fiddling or singing while Rome burned
is most dubious. What remains, however, is the fact that in
order to divert suspicion of arson from himself he caused it to
be cast upon a sect of Jewish heretics who had been holding
secret services in the city and who were already the object of
enmity. As Tacitus puts it, "Nero fastened the guilt and inflicted
the most exquisite tortures on a class hated for their abomina-
tions, called Christians by the populace. Christus, from whom
the name had its origin, suffered the extreme penalty during the
reign of Tiberius at the hands of one of our procurators, Pontius
Pilatus. . . ." The "exquisite tortures" included being thrown to
wild beasts in the amphitheatre or smeared with pitch and used
as living torches to illuminate Nero's nocturnal festivals.

The emperor at one time or another took to identifying himself with various gods—Apollo, Hercules, and Helios, deity of
the sun—and coins were struck depicting him with a radiating
crown. He did, to be sure, order the rebuilding of the ruined
areas on new and open lines, with greater protection against
fire hazard, and paid for much of this out of his own imperial
purse. But he also squandered incalculable sums on the creation
of a sumptuous palace and pleasure ground for himself between
the Esquiline and Caelian hills. Known as the Domus Aurea

Nero was genuinely interested in the arts, but when his interest mani-fested itself, an egotistical rather than a creative act always seemed to take place. Above is the Octoganal Hall in the Domus Aurea, built to be Nero's palace. Situated in a mile-square park in central Rome, the build-ing itself covered over twenty acres; descriptions of its sumptuous and often very vulgar decorations defy belief.

because of its rich decorations, it was an immense complex centering about a vestibule lofty enough to house a gilded bronze statue of Nero himself, one hundred twenty feet high, and surrounded by parks, artificial lakes, and colonnades, one of which was reportedly a full mile in length. One of its ban-queting halls was circular and equipped with a revolving ceil-ing; its rooms were richly painted and set with jewels and mother-of-pearl; the ceilings of ivory were pierced with pipes that sprayed perfume upon the banqueters. Tacitus described Nero as a man who desired the impossible—*incredibilium cupi-tor*—and it was clearly Nero's aim to stagger men's imagina-tions by the sheer immensity of his performance. But the spell was already broken. Incompetent in the face of a revolt in Judaea, despised by the army, abandoned by his provincial administrators, hated by all classes, he stood virtually alone. A Gallic governor named Julius Vindex got in touch with other commanders and raised revolt against Nero, denouncing him among other things as a bad lyre player. The Senate roused itself to declare him a public enemy. Beset by fears, he killed himself in A.D. 68.

Nero's successors, some of whom shared his grandiose tastes, lacked his mania for self-indulgence. The Domus Aurea became the victim of the wreckers, who set about leveling it. Where the private palace had been, there arose public bath-houses and a circus; where Nero had built an artificial lake, there stood the Colosseum. Nothing made by Nero was permitted to remain; and the ancient rite of *damnatio memoriae* was invoked to remove any lingering respect for his memory: his images were destroyed or mutilated, his name was erased from inscriptions, and his public acts were rescinded. Nevertheless for nearly two thousand years his memory has remained fresh as the epitome of the tyrant ready to waste the wealth of an empire for his own pleasure.

His suicide left the succession in doubt. Through maternal lineage he was the great-great-grandson of Augustus; but he had left no heir. The line of emperors known as Julio-Claudian, rulers of a century of glory mixed with perfidy and disaster, had reached its end; the field was now wide open for new candidates for the principate to stake their claims—by force. After a brief period of anarchy, power fell into the hands of Vespasian, the legion commander who had distinguished himself in Britain and who was proclaimed emperor after his troops in the east had hailed him as such. Vespasian was not a man of Julio-Claudian refinement or learning; born of an obscure plebeian family, he had risen in the army through sheer ability and native intelligence, and he disliked the aristocrats. A friendly, down-to-earth man of simple tastes, bullnecked, thickset, he was adored by his soldiers because he spoke their language, and the plebs of Rome liked him for the same reason. Rising to his responsibilities he became, as princeps, one of the major builders of Rome and its empire.

His armies fought successfully both to expand and to consolidate the empire's frontiers. The revolt that had broken out in Gaul upon Nero's death was put down. Roman power was advanced to Scotland and Wales. The rebellion in Judaea, also provoked by Nero's mismanagement, was broken by a 139-day siege of Jerusalem that resulted in the city's surrender to Vespasian's able son Titus. In A.D. 70 Vespasian could claim that peace had been restored along the far-flung borders of the empire. The gates of the temple of Janus were closed to celebrate this, and a new temple to peace was erected, recalling in purpose Augustus' altar of peace, the Ara Pacis.

Only three columns of Vespasian's temple survive. In its time it was apparently the largest of all Roman temples and the most skillfully designed. And this was only one of the magnificent new buildings provided for Rome by an emperor who was frugal in his own tastes, scrupulous, honest, and anxious to restore both Rome's fortunes and its morality. The temple of Jupiter on the Capitoline had burned down; Vespasian rebuilt it along more sumptuous lines than it had possessed before. He also built most of that barbarous masterwork, the Colosseum, though he himself had no particular liking for gladiatorial displays. The structure had been planned originally by Augustus, and Vespasian simply carried out the intentions of an earlier age.

Though Rome had its Circus Maximus—essentially a long race track—it lacked, until Vespasian's time, an amphitheatre large enough to give many tens of thousands of spectators a good view of the spectacle in the arena. The form of the Colosseum was not new to Rome—there had been other circular or oval structures in Italy—but its dimensions and its engineering were unprecedented. Three steeply rising tiers of seats, capable of holding perhaps forty-five thousand people, were raised by an intricate system of piers, arches, vaults, and cross vaults, with surrounding corridors. A top-story colonnade, added under Titus and Domitian, brought the oval to an outside height of nearly one hundred sixty feet. As we see it today, a ruin that seems to be sinking deeper into the ground, its travertine facing in most part removed long ago, its archways bare, its pilasters crumbling, the floor of the arena broken up to reveal the network of subterranean passages and pens for wild animals, the Colosseum still suggests some of the savage grandeur it once possessed. Its high walls, once topped by masts, shut out the world. Vast and brilliantly colored awnings, scarlet, blue, and yellow, stretched across the auditorium and held off the glare of the sun. Gilded bronze statues stood in the archways. The colored light, passing through awnings, cast a theatrical gleam upon the spectacle; the shouts of the audience echoed off the stone galleries.

Though not an intellectual, Vespasian furthered the arts and education, establishing, for instance, chairs of Greek and Latin rhetoric in Rome. His urge to found his own family dynasty, with his sons Titus and Domitian next in line, brought him into collision with a group of agitators who identified themselves with the Stoic and Cynic philosophers and who accused him of autocratic intentions. This led to some cruel meting out of punishment on the part of a man who had otherwise shown himself tolerant.

There was to be a dynasty known as the Flavian from Vespasian's family name, but it was short-lived. Titus, the handsome, popular conqueror of Jerusalem, had been made virtual co-regent by his father in preparation for the succession; but when he came to power in A.D. 79, he was to have only two years of rule. As openhanded as his father was parsimonious, his liberality and pleasant ways delighted all classes. When he died at the age of forty-two, he left a triumphal arch of modest but exquisite proportions, a new public bath, a record of great aid to the sufferers of a new fire and plague in Rome, and a memory that caused him to be deified alongside Caesar, Augustus, and his father. Suetonius spoke of him as the "darling of the human race." No one was to say the same of his brother Domitian, who came to the throne to be the last of the Flavian line.

The second great fire in Rome, however, was preceded by the eruption of Vesuvius, which buried the prosperous city of Pompeii under some thirty feet of lava and volcanic ash in the first year of Titus' reign. Suddenly overwhelmed, the city was preserved as though in amber for the spades of archaeologists. As a result we know more about the day-to-day details of the lives of Roman citizens in the years of Vespasian and Titus than in any other period of the empire. When Vesuvius erupted, the shops were open, and children in school were scribbling their letters on wax tablets. We can visit the slaves' dormitories, the stockyards, the prostitutes' quarters, the shops of butchers, bakers, jewelers, and dyers, and if we want to know how cloth was dyed, we have only to look at the wall paintings showing dyers at work.

Pompeii, first settled by descendants of neolithic people of Campania, had come under the influence of the nearby Greek colonies along the coast; this no doubt accounts for the early refinement of its arts. Etruscans and Samnites had in turn occupied it, each contributing their strains of culture and growth. Finally came the Romans, under whom it became an important port, trading center, and resort, combining a certain Greek delicacy in its villas with Roman weight in its baths and other civic buildings.

There were paintings everywhere—on store fronts, inside factories, and in private houses, where they sometimes decorated the rooms from floor to ceiling. Ubiquitous, lively, and devoted to even the frankest personal detail, these tell of a population in love with color, amusements, and self-representation. Many of the Pompeiian paintings have been regarded as provincial in execution and as many were also coarse in theme; but great Rome itself left no comparable array neither in quality nor quantity.

In individual buildings, too, there was evidently much originality and vigor in this mixed community. The small Pompeiian temple of Apollo, an adaptation of Hellenistic design, was one of the most exquisite of Italian constructions. The Stabian baths, dating back to perhaps 120 B.C., included what may have been the first dome erected on Italian soil, roofing its *frigidarium*. The dome did not converge on a point at its apex, but left a large circular opening at the top to admit light and air—thus prefiguring the much vaster dome, with a similar opening, that the emperor Hadrian was to mount on Rome's Pantheon.

Domitian, who came to power in A.D. 81, was as taken up with great building as his late father and brother had been, laying out a new stadium in the Campus Martius, commencing a new forum that was to become known by the name of his successor, Nerva, and raising on the Palatine a vast palace of his own with walls ten feet thick, topped, it may have been, with a colossal barrel vault. Yet Domitian, unlike the other Flavians, was a singularly forbidding figure. In foreign matters he conducted himself ably, intent on strengthening, and where possible, advancing frontiers. In Britain he pushed them ahead, chiefly through a five-year campaign led by Gnaeus Julius Agricola, father-in-law of the historian Tacitus. In central Europe he improved the Danube boundary by establishing advanced outposts along its tributary river Main. In eastern

Europe, along the lower reaches of the Danube, in what is now Rumania, he faced and withstood the threat of Dacian tribes, though not without paying them a bounty for peace. In his choice and control of provincial officials, he appears to have been astute; in his administration of revenues and taxes, demanding but fair. In his everyday confrontations with leaders and the public at home his performance became disastrous.

Embittered perhaps by jealousy of Titus and his own wait for power, he turned to tyrannical arrogance and display. He demanded of his subjects the subservience due to an oriental monarch: they were to revere him as a god and on one occasion he held out his hands for a kiss. He degraded the Senate in particular by assuming the role of *censor perpetuus*, thereby making himself master of its composition, and requiring it to endorse all his actions. As these became increasingly capricious and cruel, conspiracies formed against him, and his own wife took part in a palace plot that in A.D. 96 did away with him. He left no children.

So passed the second dynasty to rule over imperial Rome. Both had brought forth highly gifted men as well as unstable ones; both had seen the brilliant use of power as well as the abuse of it. Cruelty and at times venality had played their familiar parts. Yet, amid many occasions of disorder, all the major emperors save Nero had contributed in one way or another to the enlarging and strengthening of the imperial structure. All saw themselves as builders In both the governmental and the physical sense; even Nero, public disaster that he was, was too alert to public building and rebuilding to be entirely despised. The satirists Juvenal and Martial mocked the ways of Domitian, and pockets of republican opposition to the trend toward absolute monarchy persisted. But the centers of agitation were now confined to a small group of intellectuals who claimed for themselves the mantle of the Stoic tradition of thought, and both Vespasian and Domitian had virtually silenced them by banishment. By and large, the people seemed to feel that their emperors, for all their faults and favorites, had served to restore confidence in Rome as a permanent institution, not just the plaything of contending generals, and that one would do best to trust in their foresight, or *providentia*. The true Stoic, meanwhile, could draw strength from the memorable lines that Horace had written:

> *Not the rage of the million commanding things evil,*
> *Not the doom frowning near in the brows of the tyrant,*
> *Shakes the upright and resolute man*
> *In his solid completeness of soul.*

The Pantheon, above, is thought by many to represent near perfection in interior design. The temple was not built to be imposing from the outside. The Greek-style porch, strangely appended to it, is perhaps from Agrippa's temple, the structure that Hadrian's Pantheon replaced.

With the Flavians extinct, a new line of leadership was to arise, and it was to be Rome's good fortune that a new century brought with it two such wise and spacious statesmen as the emperors Trajan and Hadrian. The foundations for their rule, for all the cracks in the wall, had been generally well laid. Trajan was to increase the size of the empire by his victories over the Dacians and Parthians and others; Hadrian was to consolidate it further by his administrative mastery.

The success of their reigns was to be made immediately visible to all citizens of the city, for it was demonstrated by structures that were in themselves the culmination of the greatest art of the Romans, their architecture. Trajan, in addition to completing a new forum and erecting new baths, was to supervise the design of the spectacular column that celebrates his campaigns by means of a winding, carved scroll some six hundred twenty-five feet long. Hadrian, in addition to building his famous villa at Tivoli—a complex employing domes and vaults around a central mansion beside a miniature lake—was to order a marvelous new temple to be erected on or beside the foundations of Agrippa's burnt-out Pantheon. Perfectly round, of unprecedented proportions for such a shape, its internal diameter is precisely equalled by its height. Its interior is fitted with marble panels, niches, and alcoves; its coffered vault is pierced at the top by a great circular "eye." It was perhaps the most brilliant building erected since the Parthenon in Athens had brought the building program of Pericles to its peak. One of few Roman structures to be preserved without any appreciable loss or fault, the Pantheon was to remain an embodiment of Rome's highest imagination and triumph.

IX

THE ROMAN PEACE

If a man were called to fix the period in the history of the world during which the condition of the human race was most happy and prosperous, he would, without hesitation, name that which elapsed from the death of Domitian to the accession of Commodus. The vast extent of the Roman empire was governed by absolute power, under the guidance of virtue and wisdom. The armies were restrained by the firm but gentle hand of four successive emperors whose characters and authority commanded involuntary respect.

—Edward Gibbon, *The Decline and Fall of the Roman Empire*

For some two hundred years following the accession of Augustus, the Mediterranean world was virtually at peace. War, when it was waged at all, was confined almost entirely to frontier areas. Never in human history had there been so long a span of general tranquility, and never again was peace to be maintained so steadily among so many people. One mighty state seemed almost to embrace the world, with only the savage tribes of northern Europe and of central Africa and the mysterious nations of the Orient living beyond the pale. The *pax Romana*, the Roman peace, extended from Scotland to the vast Sahara Desert, and from Portugal to the borders of Persia. Throughout much of the empire, men lived out their lives in quiet contentment, safe from marauding armies, going about their affairs in the knowledge that they were sheltered by Rome, a stern but generous master that demanded unyielding obedience to its laws, at the same time granting to each community the right to adapt those laws to local circumstances. Under Roman protection trade flourished, cultivation was extended, and prosperity was brought to regions that had never before progressed beyond mere subsistence.

There were times when Romans appeared to be awed by the scope of their success. Pliny the Elder speaks of the immense majesty of the Roman peace (*immensa Romanae pacis maiestas*) as though he could scarcely bring himself to believe that so great a thing had been accomplished. He was, after all, contemplating a world in which Britons and Africans were speaking the language of Cicero and Vergil, a world in which Spaniards and Syrians were building Roman roads, using Roman weights and measures, and swearing allegiance to a Roman emperor. On a continent lacerated for centuries by local and general wars, there was suddenly peace.

The legions that had imposed Roman rule were not, of course, gone or forgotten. Few Roman subjects dared to break the peace for fear of punishment almost too severe to contemplate. Those who did revolt—such as the hapless nationalists of Judaea—served as a terrifying example for any others who might be so inclined. Rebels could hope for no outside help, for as yet there existed no military power that could seriously challenge that of Rome. Although the empire was anything but an armed camp, the element of compulsion was never entirely absent.

And the peace was by no means a perfect one. Occasionally some mad emperor—a Nero or a Domitian—would grope his way to the throne, create sudden confusion at the heart of the imperial complex, and send a succession of shudders through the Roman world. But the administrative machinery was well oiled; the civil services continued to function, and the very immensity of the empire ensured that it could not all come apart at once. To the mass of Romans the occasional murders in the imperial palace, the sporadic uprisings in Britain, Gaul, or

Africa, the revolts of the Jews were little more than ripples on the surface of a peaceful lake. With the advantage of hindsight, historians have been fond of comparing this era—and particularly the quiet years of the mid-second century A.D.—to a sunny afternoon in late summer during which storm clouds are gathering ominously on the horizon. To many Romans, however, it must have seemed that Vergil's dream of a world of plenty, in which men went about unarmed, was about to become a reality.

The Mediterranean had become a Roman sea, its shores white with Roman temples and crowded with Roman *municipia*. Roman ships patrolled the Atlantic and roamed the Black Sea. Since all roads ended in Rome, the Romans were able to buy silk from China, spices from the East Indies, perfume from Arabia, glassware from Tyre and Sidon, marble from Greece, porphyry from Egypt, tin from Britain and Spain, and furs from the far north. Epicures had their choice of figs and dates from Syria, tunny from the Black Sea, oysters from Britain, and sausages from Gaul.

For two centuries the lands bordering the Mediterranean were intensely cultivated. The Sea of Galilee, today surrounded by a half-moon of scalded rocks and another half-moon of patchy fields, was then green with the reflections of innumerable trees. The forests of cedars in Lebanon ranged for mile upon mile and were carefully guarded since they provided timber for the Roman fleet. The Fens of England were cornfields; so, too, were the plains of La Camargue, in southern France. Spain, which Pliny the Elder described as overflowing with silver and gold mines, exported not only precious metals but lead, iron, and copper in addition to textiles, wine, olive oil, and the celebrated fish sauce known as garum. From the many cities of Asia Minor and Syria came a constant supply of luxury clothing and linens, leather products, drugs, perfumes, spices, and dyes.

The painting, above, probably represents Stabiae, one of the three ports that served Rome; at upper right four boats are anchored in the beautifully decorated and well-equipped harbor.

By enriching the empire, trade provided a cement that bound the provinces together. Generally the expense of transporting goods over long distances did not prevent a growing exchange of products. But when it did discourage trade, it also fostered local self-sufficiency and prosperity by stimulating the development of manufactures in areas where such industries might not otherwise have developed. Thus, glassmaking centers arose in Europe to compete with Sidon (where the art of glass blowing was invented during the early Roman empire), and Gaul became the foremost producer of the pottery known as *terra sigillata*, once a specialty of the Etruscan city of Arretium. Ironically, prosperous Italy was among the least self-sufficient regions, for it depended on huge imports of grain from Egypt, Africa, Sicily, and other provinces to feed its growing population.

The exchange of goods between neighboring provinces and localities was immensely facilitated by the proliferation of paved roads. The Roman highway system grew steadily during the first and second centuries A.D., its tentacles extending to the borders, and sometimes beyond the borders, of the empire. The Romans were so addicted to roadmaking that they even built a highway along the Nile River from Alexandria to what is now the Aswan area, in southern Egypt, although the Nile itself constituted a more practical artery of transportation. The roads were extremely well constructed originally and were kept in constant repair by the cities and provinces that they served. Not until the fall of the empire were they left to decay. Some, crumbling and overgrown, were rediscovered centuries after they were built, by peoples who attributed them to giants or the devil or gnomes. Other roads were attended to through the ages, and a few of them are still in use today. The breadth and solidity of these roads, and the frequency with which they were repaired in some parts of the empire, hint at the volume of the traffic that they must have accommodated during the time of the Roman empire.

Although the Romans did not have a seafaring temperament, and their ships and sailing methods did not match their other accomplishments, there was nevertheless a development of sea traffic, for transport by sea continued to be the most practical means of moving bulky quantities of goods over great distances. Some of the vessels plied regular routes through the Mediterranean—particularly those that carried grain from Alexandria to Ostia. Trade was not confined within the imperial borders. Hoards of Roman coins found in Scandinavia, India, and Ceylon testify to the initiative of the merchants of that era. Trade with the Orient became a significant source of wealth for such Syrian cities as Palmyra and Bostra, to which caravans brought silks, spices, and other goods from ports on the Persian Gulf and the Red Sea. Roman gold and art objects are known to have moved eastward into India and the lands beyond. In the late second century A.D., Greco-Roman merchants presented themselves at the court of the Chinese emperor, claiming to be envoys from the Roman emperor.

Provincial life during the first and second centuries A.D. was generally calm and orderly. Civic affairs were conducted with a degree of independence that no one could have hoped for at the time of the conquests. At the head of the administration in each province was a governor, issuing orders in the name of the emperor, protected by a personal guard, and assisted by a staff of civil servants that, from the time of Vespasian, was often recruited from among the most gifted provincials rather than exclusively from Rome's aristocracy. Most of the provincial governors seem to have been well chosen. Though occasionally rapacious, they were seldom tyrannical, and as a rule, respected both the rights of the people they governed and the customs of the ancient cities where they had their headquarters.

When the governor sat in judgment, local assessors would often sit beside him to explain the customs of the land and to advise him on native law, for the provincial laws were still operative where they did not conflict with Roman ones. In the western provinces, general assemblies met once a year in the provincial capital to offer sacrifices to Rome and the emperor; those formal ceremonies were followed by debates and discussions on the state of the province, after which complaints and suggestions might be handed to the governor. This was not democracy, for only the leading members of the provincial communities attended the one day parliament, but the process may at least have served to persuade Rome's subjects that the empire was not merely a tyranny devoted to the glorification of Roman power.

Because the Romans urgently wanted peace, they were prepared to offer to the subject peoples the gift of Roman citizenship as the supreme reward for good behavior. Provincials who served in the army would receive the citizenship upon discharge, and whole cities might receive citizenship from the hands of a grateful governor or from a general who wanted to reward a city that had placed its resources at his disposal. The gift of citizenship was not lightly regarded. When Saint Paul claimed Roman citizenship he was claiming the full protection of Roman law over the local law of the province of Judaea; and his cry "I appeal to Caesar" was the cry of a provincial who knew himself to be especially favored and protected by the emperor. He claimed the right to be tried by the emperor or by a judge responsible to the emperor, and his person was inviolate until the trial had taken place.

Cities had always served, in fact, as the basic political building blocks upon which the Roman administrative pyramid rested, and for many years, the granting of citizenship to non-Roman municipalities was one of the major tools by which the Romans established consent among the governed. Under the republic, the franchise was extended to colonies that had been established by Roman citizens on foreign soil. After the creation of the empire, it became the practice to "colonize" by granting citizenship to foreign communities in return for services rendered or for conspicuous progress toward Romanization. This approach was especially effective during the first hundred years of the empire, and it was an important part of the emperor's political arsenal during the second. As time passed, however, the Romans became less discriminating in

their application of this policy, with the result that the number
of citizens increased enormously. In A.D. 212, remarkably soon
after the collapse of the Roman peace, the emperor Caracalla
granted citizenship to all of the inhabitants of the empire but
the slaves. By that time, the burdens of citizenship—and particularly, heavy taxes—had begun to outweigh its advantages.

The penetrating power of Roman civilization in any given
province—the degree to which the Romans succeeded in stamping their own political and social brand upon a subject people—
was largely determined by the characteristics of the society that
they conquered. The essential differences between the western
and eastern provinces were so marked that it seems that there
were two empires long before any formal division into eastern
and western branches took place. In Britain and Gaul and in
parts of Spain and North Africa, civic life itself might have been
described as a Roman invention. Many of the major cities had
started their histories as Roman colonies, and the Romans could
claim, with some justice, that they had brought the blessings of
civilization to the land. Latin was the lingua franca in all European lands that were situated to the west of the Illyrian shore of
the Adriatic and in that part of Africa that extended westward
from Cyrenaica.

East of this line Latin never replaced Greek. There lay the
Hellenistic world, an incredible complex of ancient lands and
peoples, a world united briefly under Alexander of Macedonia,
imbued with Greek learning, and tinctured by Greek institutions. To these lands—to Greece, to Egypt, to Asia Minor, to
Syria, and to Judaea—the Romans came not as civilizers but as
soldiers and representatives of a rude young culture. This was a
world of cities, many of them prosperous, some of them several
centuries older than Rome. Administration of the eastern
provinces, with their various ethnic groups and their strange
but sophisticated religions and their ancient customs, took all

of the political acumen that Rome could muster. At times, as in Judaea in both the first and second centuries A.D., the task proved too much even for Roman administrative genius. Roman hegemony was to survive in these regions long after it had been expunged in the West; yet the several centuries of Rome's eastern rule were to produce, in the Byzantine empire, a world that was not truly Roman, but an amalgam of Rome, Greece, and all that had gone before.

There were also great differences in the treatment of specific provinces, and there seems to have been a strong tendency to allow early precedents to guide subsequent policy. For example, the inhabitants of Narbonensis, the most Romanized of the Gallic provinces, enjoyed the special favor of Augustus and consequently found themselves in possession of certain extraordinary rights. These rights were seldom abridged by later rulers. In the middle of the first century A.D., the emperor Claudius, praising the people of Vienna (Vienne), spoke of a long-established right of the citizens of "this most ornate and worthy colony" to appoint their own senators to Rome—a privilege that raised provincial Vienna to the status of a Roman city.

Other provinces seem to have borne for decades and even centuries the marks of imperial disfavor. Egypt was exploited unmercifully, being regarded merely as a granary that must produce sufficient corn to feed the Romans. Later imperial policy followed that of Augustus, who treated the province as his own preserve to be mulcted of all its wealth and treasure as he pleased. Only Alexandria, the second city of the empire and the only major city in Egypt, escaped the crushing weight of Roman exploitation largely by virtue of its importance in trade. The province itself experienced an inevitable economic and social decline. An Egyptian in the third century A.D. wrote an anguished protest against the slow destruction of his country, crying out that the gods had deserted it and that soon "this most holy land, the very seat of shrines and temples, will be full of the graves of men."

Many provinces, of course, were governed without any particular evidence of favor or disfavor, and there were also some that suffered briefly under a hostile emperor or enjoyed temporary advantages under a friendly one. Hadrian's special love for Greece, for instance, resulted in great benefits to this highly regarded but somewhat impoverished realm.

Of the histories of the provinces during these relatively placid centuries, Judaea's must stand out. Because the religious nationalism of the Jews presented a peculiarly difficult problem, the country was permitted to retain a high degree of independence under the leadership of an aristocratic priestly caste; its Roman governors, however, were not loath to assume full military powers and rule by martial law at the first sign of intransigence. Judaea was to serve as an example of both Roman liberality and Roman severity. Although the Judaean rebellions are often attributed to the peculiarly virulent nature of the Jewish nationalism of that time, there may have been other, equally important reasons. Josephus remarks in his introduction to *The Jewish War* that the Romans feared the Jews would make common cause with the Parthians, Rome's hereditary enemies in the east, and that Rome was prepared to go to any lengths to safeguard its foothold in Palestine. Whatever the causes, Judaea was racked by great revolts, which were followed by exceptionally ruthless repressions. Jerusalem was captured, looted, and razed in A.D. 70 by legions under the future emperor Titus. An even more brutal clash occurred between A.D. 131 and 135. A widespread rebellion provoked the Romans to wage a war of annihilation in which the land was devastated and a large part of the Jewish population was put to the sword. This slaughter was carried out at the order of the emperor Hadrian, who, but for this, is remembered as one of the most generous and enlightened of Roman rulers.

The Roman army went about its work of destroying Judaea like a pitiless machine, and there is no doubt that it wielded terrible powers. Yet it was rarely used as a suppressor of rebellion within the empire during that era. It was not, in fact, the least admirable of Roman institutions. Largely recruited from the provinces, it was pervaded with democratic feeling. As a rule, men rose by merit, not by special influence, and the accidents of birth had little to do with advancement. Because the legions were often rotated a soldier at the end of his career might find that he had served in most of the provinces of the empire. We hear of Spaniards serving in Lower Moesia (northern Bulgaria), of Carthaginians serving in Britain, of Germans serving in Palestine, and of Gauls serving in Italy. Provincial differences tended to disappear within the overwhelming uniformity of army life, and the contact of the legions with the people of the many provinces helped knit the empire together, although in later times each legion was almost entirely comprised of men from the provinces in which it was stationed.

The camps and fortresses followed an unchanging pattern: vast, drab, walled-in squares with watchtowers. One large building was reserved for the camp commander, and nearby there would be the heavily guarded treasury and shrine of the standards. There were long lines of wooden barracks, but the grim uniformity of the camp was broken by the presence of granaries, kitchens, ovens, horse-lines, latrines, punishment cells, the surgery and the hospital block, the armorer's and the leather-worker's shops, and perhaps a building for the veterinary. There was a parade ground, and somewhere outside the camp there were baths, an amphitheatre, and merchants' booths. Often there was an underground Mithraic temple where devotees were initiated in a small cramped pit as they were "cleansed" in the dripping blood of a bull that had been butchered on an iron grating above their heads.

These permanent camps, however, represented only one aspect of Roman military might. There were also veterans' organizations, which could be called upon to serve when danger threatened. In the provinces these auxiliaries formed a reserve of trained men that could be thrown into battle at the bidding of the prefects, who served as chief officers in the district camps. In the city of Rome there was the Praetorian Guard, several thousand strong. In theory it was the bodyguard of the emperor, but in reality it constituted a force that discouraged raids upon the city from without and revolutionary uprisings from within. The Praetorian Guard was an elite corps, well paid and granted special privileges. On occasion it had the power to bring to office the emperors it was designed to serve; the rest of the time it remained a decorative but effective discouragement to troublemakers.

The legions were stationed along the frontiers at the extreme limits of Roman power. Through the first and second centuries A.D., except during a few brief intervals of anarchy, these units were entirely responsive to the will of the reigning emperor. Twenty-five legions existed at the death of Augustus. As the empire became larger, their number increased, but the rate of increase was not precipitous. Because these units were rarely at full strength (a full complement consisting of about 5,000 men), the standing army of Augustus amounted to little more than 115,000 men and that of Trajan to perhaps no more than 150,000. The task of defending so vast an empire would have been impossible without the use of provincial auxiliaries, local militias, and the armies of the vassal states. Yet even when all these are included, it would appear that Rome never had more than 350,000 armed men at its disposal. The cost of maintaining such an army was not generally a prohibitive burden on the treasury of the early empire; the *pax Romana* released the latent wealth of the world, and in order to maintain itself in a position of overwhelming power, Rome needed to appropriate only a fraction of the emerging riches. With this modest portion, it was not only to support an army but was also to become wealthier than any city that had ever existed.

The new riches, however, proved to be inducements to luxury; indeed luxury had become a way of life. It was not unusual for a rich man to possess four or five country retreats and a town house in Rome. But there was nothing new in luxurious living. Under the republic Cicero had collected country houses as other men collected Greek sculptures, and he showed no notable signs of decadence. Pliny the Younger, the inheritor of three fortunes, possessed a country villa as large as a palace, but lived a life of exemplary dedication. Luxury, such as it was, was often the inevitable corollary of peace. Satirists made much of the vulgar and ostentatious feasts given by a certain kind of intemperate Roman, and there are some accounts of women wearing fabulously costly gowns and of entertainments so expensive that they would have beggared anyone less wealthy than a millionaire, but history has also recorded great benefactions to worthwhile projects by men aware of the obligations of wealth.

Wealth under the empire was not limited to the senatorial class and the equites, nor even to Romans and Italians. It could be found in all the parts of the Mediterranean. (The names of Greeks, particularly, appear with monotonous regularity in imperial inscriptions relating to wholesale dealers in various seaside cities.) And, to some degree, luxury had seeped down even to the lowest of the urban classes, who were entertained by free games supplied by the state and fed on the free wheat granted to them by the emperor from the government granaries.

At the beginning of the empire Agrippa had built the first

free baths. Soon there were hundreds of public baths scattered across the empire. The gift of a bathhouse, with money for its upkeep, came to be expected from the citizen who had amassed wealth and wished to be remembered by his fellows. These buildings were monuments to leisure. They were to be found in remote towns on the borders of the empire, and even in villages. In Rome itself they came to be as large as palaces and as sumptuously adorned. The baths of Diocletian covered about thirty-two acres, those of the emperor Caracalla were spread over thirty-three acres.

The baths were more than buildings; they were whole cities dedicated to the principle that many forms of leisure could be housed in a single setting. The bathhouses became a center of Roman social life. The Roman who visited one of these establishments went first to the *apodyterium*, where he undressed; his body was rubbed with oil in the *unctorium*; a warm bath called the *caldarium* was followed by a stay in the *laconicum*, or steam room; the visitor then cooled off in the *tepidarium* and had his plunge in the *frigidarium*. Such was the ritual of the citizen intent only on the bath, but other forms of amusement were offered, too. There were gardens, courtyards, colonnades, shops, restaurants, reading rooms, libraries, art galleries, debating halls, rest rooms, gymnasiums, massage rooms, and promenades. There were wrestling rooms and swimming pools. Sometimes there were gambling rooms and clusters of rooms set apart for prostitutes. Very often—and this was true particularly in the provinces—the baths served also as lodginghouses, and a man who wished to could spend most of his life under that welcome roof.

Although the public bath was dedicated to leisure and cleanliness, it could, and often did, become a noisy, squalid, and debilitating place abounding with cutthroats and catamites. Seneca, who once lodged above a bathhouse, was appalled by the continual noise, and in his puritanical fashion wondered why people wanted to bathe in hot water. "Do they want to parboil themselves?" he asked. Yet, like the Greek gymnasium, a bathhouse could also serve as a place of spiritual refreshment, and a man with a scholarly turn of mind could enjoy the museums, the art galleries, libraries, and lecture halls without once encountering a bather. The great palaces of entertainment served all tastes and admitted almost anyone.

The Roman taste for grandeur found its perfect embodiment in the immense and splendidly decorated baths, with broad colonnades, pleasant gardens, and a welter of statues and paintings. Here the extremes of luxury were cultivated with fastidious taste. Marble-encrusted columns reached dazzling heights, and gilding was extensively employed.

The public bath was a benefit of Roman affluence that was not denied to the poor. An ill-paid workman living in a hovel on the top floor of an overcrowded *insula* might spend the afternoon splashing in the water beside the aristocrats. Senators frequented the public bathhouses, and sometimes in a show of democratic feeling the emperor might bathe with the citizens, over whom he had the power of life and death. A kind of democracy existed among the citizens of all classes; emperor and workman saw themselves as belonging to the same *communitas*. But that sense of equality extended only to citizens and freedmen. Outside of this society, and in a somewhat ambiguous relationship to it, were the masses of slaves.

At the end of the first century A.D., there must have been nearly four hundred thousand slaves in Rome, constituting about a third of the city's population, but their number was declining. The great wars were over, and slaves no longer marched into Rome in vast processions to be sold, one by one, to the highest bidders. Slave-capturing expeditions patrolled the Barbary Coast, and slaves could still be bought in adequate numbers in the slave markets at Alexandria and on the Aegean island of Delos, but generally the price of purchase was high.

The character of slavery was changing with the times. Slaves were often brutalized, but far more often they were treated with respect and consideration, and sometimes almost seemed to be members of the families who owned them. Under Hadrian a law was passed forbidding the master to kill, torture, or mutilate a slave. As late as the time of Nero, the Senate had seen fit to sentence to death all the slaves of an official murdered by only one of them—a form of punishment with ancient precedents—but for the most part, those days had passed. The slave was coming to be regarded as a human being whose dignity was to be respected. This change was due, in part, to the Stoic doctrine that all men were equal before God; by the second century that doctrine had become an article of faith among the educated.

But even before this liberal trend in private and official attitudes had made itself felt, the increasing influence of the slaves had introduced a disturbing element into the larger society of free Roman citizens. Pliny the Elder uttered a great cry that reverberated through the long years of the Roman peace: "*Vincendo victi sumus; paremus externis* (By conquering we are conquered; we are servants to foreigners)." That dependence, that sense of gradual loss of power to a foreign element, was felt strongly during the first century when there were more slaves than in later times. Although many slaves labored in mines and factories or on the great estates, a few achieved exalted status as imperial secretaries or advisers. Juvenal complains bitterly against slaves who were the great officials' doorkeepers and who had to be bribed to permit a supplicant to enter. Such slaves did not remain slaves for long; after a year of doorkeeping they were usually wealthy enough to buy their freedom.

In fact enough slaves bought their freedom to cause Tacitus to remark ruefully that if freedmen were regarded as a separate class, they would outnumber the freeborn. So many freedmen rose to positions of wealth and power that they actually did form a special group. They were the new blood pouring into the veins of the citizenry, causing its gradual and subtle transformation.

Freedmen were everywhere, in all the trades, in all the professions, in all the armies on all the frontiers. By A.D. 200 many who were Roman citizens were the descendants of former slaves. The bloodlines of Europe, Africa, and Asia fed the mainstream. The process had been at work for centuries, and the poet who spoke of "the Orontes flowing into the Tiber" was hardly overstating the case. Rome was indeed a great melting pot.

By the time of Domitian's assassination, in A.D. 96, Rome had become quite a different place from what it was when Augustus had established the principate. Not only had the city itself changed almost beyond recognition, but the temper and character of the Romans had changed too. They demanded more luxuries, and were avidly searching for new experiences. The threat of war and the tumult of political upheaval were largely absent; Romans could now expect to die in their beds. To them the empire seemed secure. There were in fact many pressing problems; among the most important were the growing restlessness of the people and the absence of a common faith, a common purpose. Oriental religions were proliferating on Roman soil. New and startling divinities were being worshiped. For many Romans, apparently, the joy had gone out of life, and the long peace had become unendurable without the consolation of religion. The empire had certainly not reached the point of becoming politically unmanageable, but there was no Augustus to give it grace and distinction, and no philosopher-king had arisen to give it meaning.

The post-Augustan emperors of the first century A.D. were rarely imaginative rulers. It is doubtful that they speculated about the possible connections between the triumph of imperial absolutism and the paralysis of the popular will. They tended to believe that bread and circuses answered the people's needs, and indeed there was ample bread, and the circuses grew more splendid every year. In fact these emperors needed little sophistication. They reigned during a magical era in the empire's history, an era when prosperity was increasing, when taxes were relatively light, and the civil service was small, efficient, and staffed by able men who needed little guidance. What was perhaps most important was that they reigned at a time when no great enemies or powerful hordes of barbarians were pressing against the frontiers. It was not surprising then that the terror of a Domitian had little effect outside the capital and that it failed to shake the imperial foundations. And because the emperor who followed Domitian initiated a process of adopting a successor without regard to blood relationship, there was no recurrence of such terrors for the better part of a century; Rome entered a prolonged period of good government such as a few other states have enjoyed.

The beginning of this era was signaled by the Senate's election of one of its own—the sixty-six-year-old Marcus Cocceius Nerva—to the vacant imperial throne in A.D. 96. The aging senator reigned less than two years, but instituted some much-needed reforms including the new "law" of succession that resulted in the elevation to the throne of the four able rulers who were to guide Rome's fortunes through the succeeding eighty-three years—years that saw the empire reach its height. These four men—Trajan, Hadrian, Antoninus Pius, and Marcus Aurelius—were of markedly varying temperaments, but all of them possessed *gravitas* and *aequanimitas*, the qualities of dignity and authority and of calm impartiality that were traditionally associated with enlightened leadership. They cared deeply about the welfare of the people they ruled and were serenely aware of their responsibilities. The general tone of their administrations was anticipated by Nerva during his brief reign.

With his withered skin, enormous beaked nose, and firm, pointed chin, Nerva did not look like a Roman emperor; he looked like an eminent jurist, which is what he was. As a youth he acquired a reputation as a poet. But it was not his poetry that commended him to the Romans when they decided to grant him supreme power. They wanted another Numa, a stern and kindly judge, a man who would represent sanity in a world that had been ruled disastrously by the morbidly insane Domitian. They chose Nerva because he seemed incorruptible and yet very human and because he was a distinguished lawyer and the scion of a family steeped in the traditions of imperial service.

Nerva accomplished all that the Romans could have expected of him. He confirmed the senators in their powers, forbade statues of himself, restored the estates confiscated by Domitian, and allotted lands to poor peasants. Detesting the gladiatorial shows, he issued an edict restricting the amount of money that could be spent on them, and revived the theatre. Because Domitian had raided the treasury and the empire was nearly bankrupt, Nerva embarked on a campaign of retrenchment, selling many of the imperial estates to the highest bidders. Similarly he ordered the auctioning of the hoards of jewels, vestments, and furniture that his predecessors had collected.

The most notable of the emperor's innovations was a scheme for the support of poor children at public expense. This grant, known as the *alimenta*, was financed by the interest from government loans to landowners and municipalities. The *alimenta* amounted to sixteen sesterces a month for boys, twelve for girls. Nerva hoped by means of the program to relieve poverty, to encourage the peasants to remain on the land, to increase the birthrate, and to eliminate the wild bands of waifs that roamed the countryside. He succeeded to a considerable degree.

In October, A.D. 97, in a formal ceremony at the temple of Jupiter, Nerva adopted Marcus Ulpius Trajanus, the military commander on the Rhine, as his son and successor. The emperor died three months later. Shortly before his death he said: "I have done nothing in my life which prevents me from retiring and living in safety the life of a private citizen." Tacitus, who admired the man warmly, said: "He combined two things once irreconcilable—the authority of the prince and the freedom of the people."

Trajan, a Spaniard, was the first provincial to occupy the Roman throne. He was in Colonia Agrippinensis (Cologne) when he learned of his succession, and months passed before he journeyed south. When he reached Rome he entered the city on foot, with only a small escort. He had no use for the grand gestures. He took command of the empire unobtrusively, like an experienced engineer who slips quietly into the cab of a giant locomotive.

Trajan was a progressive ruler. He was a professional soldier and the son of a professional soldier, a broad shouldered man, powerfully built, with finely shaped features, a look of keen intelligence, an easy smile, and furrowed brows. The Middle Ages were to regard him as the perfect emperor. His portraits are rarely idealized. We see him—in the sculptures on Trajan's column and on the triumphal arch at Beneventum—moving quietly among the soldiers, with no flamboyance, no hint of any great enjoyment of his exalted status. Like many emperors he enjoyed building, and the ruins of the gigantic forum of Trajan, with its libraries, its basilica, its famous column, its shops, and its colonnaded square, testify to his determination to build on as large a scale as possible. These vast architectural schemes, however, did not take the form of private indulgence; he built no Domus Aurea nor Hadrian's villa for himself. He liked the ordinary things of life.

Trajan's military campaigns were the last by which the Romans appreciably extended the geographic limits of their empire. Twice the emperor led his armies against the Dacians, a powerful tribe of cattle breeders who lived in the inaccessible highlands of Transylvania and were in the habit of demanding tribute to keep the peace. The Dacians, defeated in A.D. 102, were granted liberal terms, which they soon broke. A second campaign, four years later, ended with the destruction of the Dacian army and the incorporation of Dacia into the empire as a province. Trajan was granted a sumptuous triumph, and for a brief time, the silver and gold found in the Dacian capital flooded Rome, and Dacian prisoners of war flooded the slave markets and the gladiatorial games. Toward the end of his life Trajan led successful expeditions against Parthia and Arabia and looked at last upon the Persian Gulf, as Alexander the Great had done centuries before. The *pax Romana* hand reached its furthermost bounds.

These eastern conquests, however, had brought the Romans into a new and unfamiliar world, a world in which even Hellenic influences were negligible and in which the Roman presence was regarded as utterly alien. No firm or lasting Roman administration was ever to be established in such lands as Mesopotamia and Armenia. Even as the conquest of Parthia was being completed, revolts occurred among the recently subjected peoples to the rear of Trajan's advancing legions. About the same time, there were uprisings of the Jewish communities in Syria and Egypt. These disturbances forced Trajan, who may have been contemplating an invasion of India along the route once followed by Alexander, to retrace his steps and recapture several cities that he had taken only a few months earlier. During this campaign he fell ill. He was apparently on his way back to Rome when he died in Asia Minor.

Though remembered for his military exploits (he was the first outstanding Roman general to occupy the throne), Trajan was no less impressive as a political administrator. He probably gave more attention to the details of government operations than had any emperor before his time. Within a context of humanitarian aims, he concerned himself above all with the efficiency of administrative processes and bequeathed to Hadrian, his brilliant successor, a tradition of excellence both in the conduct of government and in the staffing of the most important positions in the imperial civil service, whether in Italy or in the provinces.

As a personality Trajan disarms us by his simplicity and honesty. These qualities are in evidence in a famous letter to Pliny the Younger, who, as the governor of Bithynia, had sought the emperor's advice about measures to be employed against Christians. Trajan wrote, in part: "If a Christian offers prayers to our gods, he must be pardoned, however suspect his past conduct may have been. Anonymous pamphlets must not be used as a basis for accusation, for they create the worst kind of precedent and are entirely out of keeping with the spirit of the age."

Trajan died in A.D. 117 at the age of sixty-four, after having ruled for nearly twenty years. Hadrian, whom he had adopted on his deathbed, was another Spaniard and another soldier, a relative, and trusted lieutenant who had assisted the emperor in both military and political capacities. Hadrian was fair-skinned, with bluish-grey eyes, thick curly hair, and a well-trimmed beard—he was the first emperor to wear a beard. He was, like Trajan, scrupulous, adventurous, and curiously modern, but it cannot be said that simplicity was one of his virtues.

Hadrian possessed all of the talents and was one of the few

supremely cultivated men who had ever occupied a throne. He had an expert's knowledge of painting and sculpture, spoke Greek and Latin with equal proficiency, and to the end of his life remained boundlessly curious about everything. Tertullian, a Latin ecclesiastical writer, called him *omnium curiositatum explorator*. He was a scholar, philosopher, poet, aesthete, and architect, and yet he appeared to enjoy sharing his meals with common soldiers and could walk with them twenty miles a day in full armor. Above all, he was an exceptionally gifted administrator, blessed with an extraordinary memory, boundless energy, a subtle imagination, excellent judgment, and great decisiveness.

Hadrian's first important act was to abandon Trajan's conquests east of the Euphrates on the sound theory that the administration of such realms as Parthia, Armenia, and Mesopotamia would over-tax imperial resources. He spent the better part of his twenty-one-year reign traveling restlessly through his newly consolidated empire, applying his genius for government to the drafting of countless reforms in the provinces. No less expert in military matters, he improved the discipline of the army, invented new tactics, and studied the economics of camp life, reducing unnecessary expenses. In about A.D. 122 he crossed to Britain and personally surveyed the line from the Tyne to the Solway Firth, establishing the seventy-three-mile Wall of Hadrian as a defense against the wild tribes of the north. He revised the system of tax collection, and his reign saw the completion of a great codification of the Roman law. He was responsible for few wars, the fierce uprising and destruction in Judaea representing one of his rare failures to control the flow of events by peaceful methods.

The glory of Hadrian's building program was the Pantheon, a miracle of symmetry, composed entirely as an interior and designed to capture, through the circular aperture in the dome, the golden rays of the sun and the pale glow of the moon. If the Pantheon expresses the subtlety of Hadrian's imagination, the villa at Tibur (Tivoli) hints at his refinement and complexity, and his gigantic mausoleum, completed during the reign of his successor, reveals that he could be grandiose. He clearly intended that this huge tomb on the right bank of the Tiber should be even larger and more imposing than that of Augustus. It was in fact so massive that it served as a fortress in the Middle Ages. The huge, cylindrical structure is known today as the Castel Sant' Angelo.

The last few years of Hadrian's reign were not his happiest. Pederasty was not an unusual vice among the Romans, but Hadrian's love of a particularly charming and handsome Bithynian youth named Antinoüs appears to have been obsessive. When the boy drowned in the Nile, probably by suicide, the emperor seemed shaken to the point of madness, ordering that a great city (Antinoopolis) be built at the site of the drowning and commissioning innumerable art works in memory of his favorite. There are indications also that the emperor's late years were marred by disease, that he grew increasingly severe and intolerant, and that he tried to take his life. The great Judaean war belongs to these years. Hadrian died at last in A.D. 138, but not before he had composed a peculiarly delicate little poem of farewell. Its lines, which commit his "gentle, wandering little soul" to the underworld, are like the plaintive song of a lonely shepherd.

Some months before he died, Hadrian chose as his successor a tall, thin, courteous man who was to reign for twenty-three years—Antoninus Pius. On coins, his ravaged face is oddly disturbing, for he looks like a Christian saint. He was gentler than Hadrian, more of the scholar, less of the adventurer. He quoted the words of Scipio that it was preferable to save a single citizen than to slay a thousand foes. He would have thought a triumph a mockery of everything he stood for. The historian Julius Capitolinus said: "He looked after all things and all men as if they were his own." He was passionately addicted to good works, with the result that "the provinces all prospered under him, informers were abolished, and only one man was condemned to death for aspiring to seize the throne." However, he seems to have taken few measures to stave off future troubles other than building a new defensive wall in Britain. Historians are inclined to regard him with a kind of lurking disfavor, for it seemed as though history stood still during the years when he occupied the throne. There were minor uprisings in Britain and North Africa, the Tiber flooded, and parts of Antioch and Rome burned down, but this seems to have been the limit to the excitement that can be discovered in his reign.

Before he died at seventy-five, Antoninus heeded Hadrian's decree that he adopt both Marcus Aurelius (a young favorite of Hadrian's) and Lucius Verus (Antoninus' nephew), but Antoninus did not make Lucius a co-emperor. Marcus alone succeeded to rule. Marcus possessed Antoninus' equanimity in a more robust body. He was a skilled athlete and hunter and was credited with considerable gifts as a painter. He had the Stoic temperament, and they said of him that neither in grief nor in joy did he change countenance. Such austerity in an emperor would be almost beyond belief if we did not have the testimony of his *Meditations*, a work that celebrates the Stoic virtues and documents his heroic search for self-knowledge. In it we find the man who ruled the greatest empire on earth recording such thoughts as these: "Think of the universal substance, of which thou hast a very small portion; and of universal time, of which a short and indivisible interval has been assigned to thee; and of that which is fixed by destiny, and how small a part of it thou art."

Marcus needed all of his austerity. Soon after his accession,

Of the enlightened rulers who guided Rome during most of the second century A.D., *Marcus Aurelius, cast in the statue, above, was the last. An emperor skilled in the management of both civil and military affairs, he was also a philosopher, leaving in his* Meditations, *a record of the Stoic principles by which he lived.*

in A.D. 161, the Parthians attacked the eastern frontier. Although this threat was repelled, a more terrible enemy, the plague, accompanied the soldiers on their return to Italy and subsequently raged through the empire for many years. Before the Parthians had been completely pacified, and while wagons carrying the bodies of plague victims clattered through the streets of Rome, hordes of German and Sarmatian tribesmen—pressed from the north and east by Goths and other migrants—broke through Rome's undermanned defenses along the Danube, swept into Italy, and besieged Aquileia, at the head of the Adriatic Sea. The wars against these invaders, notably the Marcomanni and the Quadi, were to continue to take place during most of the emperor's reign. The enemy was driven back, but the victory was a hollow one. Those great movements of northern European and Asiatic peoples that were soon to threaten to engulf the empire were beginning. Marcus died in Vindobona (Vienna) in A.D. 180, at the age of fifty-nine, before he could achieve his dream of securing a more practical line of defense by advancing the imperial frontier northward to the Elbe River and the Carpathians.

Self-knowledge did not make Marcus the best judge of others. As one of his earliest acts, he made his worthless adoptive brother Lucius Verus co-emperor, generously honoring a claim that was of dubious validity. Lucius was a profligate and an incompetent general who might have done much damage to the empire if he had not died in A.D. 169. Far more serious was Marcus' decision to be the good father and to elevate Lucius Aelius Aurelius Commodus, his son, to a share of the government, for he thus turned his back on the adoptive principle that had given Rome its greatest rulers. With Commodus, who became emperor at nineteen, insanity returned to the Roman throne, and the greatest period of *pax Romana* came to an end.

Nerva, Trajan, Hadrian, Antoninus Pius, and Marcus Aurelius had followed one another against all probability. So much intelligence and grace among emperors would have seemed almost too much to hope for at the end of the first century. In about A.D. 150, when it seemed that the peace might continue forever, the Greek rhetorician Aristides declared that the Romans were the only rulers known to history who reigned over free men. "The luster of your rule is unsullied by any breath of ungenerous hostility; and the reason is that you yourselves set the example of generosity by sharing all your power and privileges with your subjects, so that in your day a combination has been achieved which previously appeared impossible— the combination of consummate power and consummate benevolence. Rome is a citadel that has all the people of the earth for its villagers." Marcus Aurelius wrote: "For me as emperor, my city and fatherland is Rome, but as a man, the world." At the death of Marcus, the great dream faded. Commodus stands at the beginning of the empire's long decline.

X

AN ERA OF EXCESS

Nevertheless, this emperor, the most cruel of men, and, to include all in a single phrase, a fratricide and committer of incest, the foe of his father, mother, and brother, was raised to the rank of the gods by Macrinus, his slayer, through fear of the soldiers, especially the Praetorians.

—*Historia Augusta*, description of the death of Caracalla

Seldom in history has so speedy and tragic a reversal taken place as that which followed the era of the "good emperors" of second-century A.D. Rome. Despite tensions and wars along its frontiers, the empire of Marcus Aurelius stood at the zenith of stability and liberal order when his death, in A.D. 180, left it in the hands of the gross and dull-witted Commodus. In the next generations it was to decline into a condition approaching disruption. Military adventurers and usurpers followed each other to the throne; civil wars broke out; a police state was established, and political agents and soldiery swarmed like locusts over the land while foot-loose robber bands scoured the countryside. The treasury was looted periodically, trade stagnated, and Goths, Franks, and Persians overran the uncertain frontiers. After the sun of Rome's late summer, storms arose on every side; the signs of decay, corruption, barbarity, and fear lay across the entire Roman world.

At rare intervals an emperor with sufficient strength and intelligence would arise to halt the steady corrosion for a few months or years. New ideas would be brought forth to reconsti-

Commodus, son and successor of the revered Marcus Aurelius, considered himself the incarnation of Hercules and had himself portrayed, above, with the attributes of that god: a club and a lion's skin. He cared more for the games of the arena than for statecraft; his incompetence and extravagance led to anarchy and ushered in a century of military rule.

tute the weakened state. But the process of decomposition was never wholly arrested. At the center of its causes lay the very nature of absolute monarchy, with no remaining civil body able effectively to restrain it: all could be well under a strong and magnanimous emperor; all could go wrong under a venal and predatory one who had been hoisted into power by his soldiery. This was the era that saw a vast increase in the power of the military as a whole, over and beyond that of the emperor's Praetorian Guard. Increasingly massive provincial armies had come into being, permanently stationed in far parts of the empire and composed more and more of non-Roman levies. Each of these armies—the greatest being those in Britain, in the Danube-Balkan area, and in Syria—saw in its successful leader a potential emperor, and on occasion, rival armies would proclaim rival emperors. The result was to be the first steps toward division of the empire on one hand and total militarization on the other.

Commodus, last member of the dynasty founded by Antoninus Pius, made way for this military era by instituting his own regime of terror—one so unconscionable and savage that many leading citizens looked to the armies for relief. Not since Nero had so odious and degenerate a person appeared at the top. Priding himself on his physical prowess, yet without a shred of courage, Commodus found his best friends among gladiators; it amused him to appear in the arena in gladiatorial costume and slay unarmed opponents. He regarded himself as the embodiment of the great Hercules and appeared in the streets with the lion's skin and club—attributes of the god—borne before him. He slaughtered senators at will and permitted his pampered favorites in the Praetorian Guard to run daily affairs of state as they pleased. He established a large harem for himself, paraded in women's garments, publicly kissed his male favorites, and delighted in inventing degrading punishments for his officials.

He even thought of changing the name of Rome to Colonia Commodiana. A palace cabal finally got rid of him by causing Commodus' wrestling partner to strangle him. The Senate, which had lived in mortal fear of him, uttered a unanimous and prolonged curse on his memory:

> *He who killed all men, let him be dragged by the hook!*
> *He who killed young and old, let him be dragged by the hook!*
> *He who killed men and women, let him be dragged by the hook!*
> *He who set aside wills, let him be dragged by the hook!*
> *He who plundered the living, let him be dragged by the hook!*
> *We were the slaves of slaves!*

Commodus was evidently unbalanced and had let matters go too far. He was not exceptional in that age in his wanton love of cruelty. The least attractive trait of the Romans was a traditional blood lust that delighted in witnessing death in the arena and that led, perhaps inescapably, to the murderous excesses of a Nero or a Commodus. The Greeks, though relishing the sight of human combat, had expressly forbidden games involving weapons, and they long refrained from building any amphitheatres in which spectacles of man against beast were to be presented. But the Romans, deriving their interest in bloody exhibitions from Etruscan funeral games, enjoyed the fight to the death. Gladiatorial shows (duels of armed men against men) as well as wild animal shows (hungry beasts pitted against each other or faced by men with spears and dogs) had been familiar in republican times. Even the most civilized emperors had not only continued them but had also enlarged them in scope as entertainment for the public.

Thus Augustus recorded that during his reign he had given the people twenty-seven gladiatorial shows in which 10,000 fighters appeared. He also gave them twenty-six spectacles of

African animals in which about 3,500 beasts were killed. Whereas 320 pairs of public duelists had fought to the death during the aedileship of Julius Caesar, no less than 5,000 pairs were put in the ring during a festival celebrating a triumph of the emperor Trajan. Even so calm and civilized a Roman as Pliny the Younger spoke gravely about the necessity of offering gladiatorial displays to the public.

The fighters were in large part prisoners of war, condemned criminals, or slaves bought for the purpose of exhibition. Yet free men sometimes became gladiators for the same reasons that have prompted adventures in modern times to find refuge in the French Foreign Legion: they join because they are ruined or desperate or because they want to live the lives of complete dedication and obedience, remote from normal responsibilities. The would-be gladiators were placed into schools run by professional trainers, who were either employed by the state or working on their own as suppliers of arena manpower. When a man entered such a school he lost all claim to life by taking an oath that said he was prepared to be whipped, burned, or killed by his trainers. If he displayed cowardice during his training he was put to death. For minor infractions of the rules he was put in chains. The gladiators' barracks at Pompeii held about a hundred men. Sixty-three were in chains at the time of the eruption of Mount Vesuvius.

Gladiatorial games had their own carefully contrived ritual and routine. There were prescribed methods of killing and being killed. Some men fought with two swords, some with one, some with a trident and a net; some were helmeted, some were not. To a gladiator who had fought bravely there would come the welcome cry from the Colosseum crowd, "*Mitte* (Let him go)!"; those who had fought less bravely heard the roar, "*Jugula* (Throat)!" According to the accepted routine, the losing gladiator was killed by being stabbed in the throat; even the way in

Carnage in a Roman arena is depicted in a fourth-century A.D. mosaic (above). Two gladiators have already been killed, and another is about to receive a fatal thrust from his adversary.

which he would stretch out his neck was taught him in the schools. Later, one of the attendants would come running with a hot poker, prodding him to make sure that he was dead.

Under the emperor Domitian, the last ruler of the Flavian dynasty, the cult of the gladiator had reached a new height of excess. Even women appeared as combatants and dwarfs were made to fight dwarfs. In a travesty of taste, Domitian's gladiatorial school was provided with rich mosaics and marble columns. The time of the mass persecutions of Christians, when believers were sent into the arena to fight each other or face professional killers and hungry beasts, still lay ahead; but this ultimate savagery was simply the result of a brutalizing process that had begun long before.

During early decades of the second century A.D., many distinguished jurists flourished, expounding and developing principles and fine points of Roman civil law and procedure. But laws themselves were being flouted at every turn by the use or the threatened use of the sword. After the liquidation of Commodus, in A.D. 192, near chaos ensued: within three months a successor named Pertinax, who had been installed by the Praetorians, was in turn killed by them (he had shown himself too friendly to the Senate); in another two months, yet another successor died, leaving the way open for the strongest man with the biggest army.

Members of the Praetorian Guard, the elite of the army, drew three times the pay of the legionary and in addition received large handouts, or *donativa*. This led to increasing tension between the Praetorians and the polyglot forces in the provinces, and finally to the overthrow of the Guard when Septimius Severus, the general commanding twelve legions in southeastern Europe, marched on Rome after being acclaimed emperor by his troops at Carnuntum, on the Danube. Reaching the city's gates with host reinforced along the way, he surrounded and overpowered the Guard. Thereafter, it was no longer recruited from Italy and the thoroughly Romanized provinces, but was diluted with foreign elements; often its men came from the least civilized parts of the empire. The center of power was moved from an elite army to a mass army.

Intelligent, versed in both Greek and Roman literature, the African-born Severus was nevertheless a soldier through and through, incapable of thinking in any but military terms. He had commanded armies in Gaul, Sicily, Pannonia, and Germany, and there was hardly another man in the empire who had so wide a knowledge of military affairs. The government he imposed on Rome was nothing less than a military dictatorship based entirely on the power of his troops. It followed that in order to keep them in hand, very large amounts of money would have to spent on them and special favors bestowed on them. This led to what was in effect a scheme of mass bribery, with resultant burdens on the state. Severus increased the pay of legionaries by almost a third; great masses were quartered on the land, drawing requisitions of foodstuffs, transport, and housing. Finding the treasury nearly empty, he resorted to confiscations to replenish it. Bands of soldiers acting as policemen searched households for political suspects and stripped them of their possessions; forced military service and ruinous taxes were imposed upon the rich. To add to the troubles of the commercial classes, he debased the silver denarius and started Rome on a disastrous policy of inflation.

Thirsting for more and more loot, the soldiers looked to adventures in the east, and Severus gave them the satisfaction of despoiling the royal Parthian city of Ctesiphon. Death finally overtook the soldier-ruler at his provincial seat of Eboracum (York), in Britain, from which he had conducted a campaign to put down an uprising of British tribes. He died in the presence of his wife, the Syrian princess Julia Domna, and of his sons Caracalla (his successor) and Geta. Some eighty years were to pass before another emperor would die peacefully in his bed.

As he was dying, Severus instructed his sons: "Be united, enrich the soldiers, and scorn the rest." He had already greatly enriched the soldiers and raised their status—arranging, for instance, for the admission of non-commissioned officers into the privileged class of equites. Coming into power in A.D. 211, Caracalla followed his father's advice and raised soldiers' pay by another fifty percent, thereby inflicting a further drain on the state. He declared openly that he was bent on basing his rule on the support not of the traditional upper and middle classes, but of the soldiery, the representatives of the plebs. Arbitrary capital levies were imposed to further undermine the patricians and merchants.

In his famous edict of A.D. 212 Caracalla granted Roman citizenship to all free persons living within the empire. But the measure, although seemingly magnanimous, was actually demagogic and in its way oppressive. Once everyone was a citizen, the hitherto cherished concept of Roman citizenship, with its rights and rewards for people of Roman or Italian birth, lost its meaning and became a mere word. As the historian Michael Rostovtzeff has remarked, Caracalla's chief purpose "was not so much to raise the lower classes, as to degrade the upper." Moreover, admission to citizenship involved the assumption of heavy taxes by all concerned. In the preamble to the law Caracalla himself remarked that the gods would look with favor on the grateful offerings by the new citizens. Certainly he himself looked with favor on this new scheme of extortion, since money was desperately needed to pay increasing bounties to the soldiers and to buy off the barbarian tribes as well. In fact, the bribes were so costly that they amounted to a sum equal to the entire military budget. There is excellent authority for this statement, for it came from Caracalla himself.

In his brief reign Caracalla amassed many titles. He was Germanicus Maximus, Parthicus, Arabicus, Alamannicus, and he had in fact led expeditions against Germans, Parthians, Arabs, and the tribe of the Alamanni, sometimes purchasing peace with money. The satirical suggestion was once made to him that he might also properly adopt the title of Geticus Maximus, for he had arranged the murder of his brother Geta. In love with grandeur, he built the largest baths in Rome and decorated them with unprecedented magnificence. He thought of himself as another Alexander the Great, destined to bring about a marriage between Rome and the East, but he ended as a travesty of Alexander. His most notorious exploit was a massacre of almost a whole generation of young citizens of Alexandria. He himself died at the hands of the Guard before he could put down the Parthians.

What was left of Roman dignity was mocked by the rule of the next emperor—a mincing, painted boy named Elagabalus. He was related to Caracalla, but had been raised in Syria as a hereditary priest of the cult of Baal. Already sexually corrupted, he found pleasures in dressing in women's clothes and posing as a prostitute; he had a fondness for walking on carpets of lilies and roses. According to the historian Herodian, who describes Elagabalus' triumphal progress through Rome, amid a rabble of eunuchs and oriental priests, the fourteen-year-old emperor wore purple silk embroidered with gold, his cheeks were stained scarlet, his eyes were artificially brightened, and pearls hung from his neck.

That a Syrian priest should be invited to occupy the highest position in the empire was not altogether surprising. The Romans were becoming weary of their ancient gods, and for centuries they had been looking toward the East in the expectation of discovering gods more powerful than their own. At the time of the Carthaginian wars they had acquired the black stone of the Phrygian Great Mother, and during the last century of the republic the cult of the Egyptian goddess Isis had flourished even when it was officially proscribed. The Great Mother promised fertility and victory, Isis promised everlasting life. Elaborate and impressive ceremonies attended the worship of these goddesses, and the hymns sung in their honor were far more colorful than the practical pleas addressed to Jupiter. The eastern mystery religions answered the need of a people thirsting for divine revelation. By the end of the first century A.D. Rome was being invaded by a host of divinities from Syria and the neighboring countries as well as by a dawning belief in Christ the Saviour.

Though the Senate showed an intense dislike for Elagabalus, the people briefly showered him with affection, and tolerated his strange ways. He summoned them to worship Baal, the unconquered Sun, and they raised no objection when in his newly erected temple of Baal on the Palatine he assembled all the sacred fetishes of the Romans—the vestal fire, the shields of Mars, the black stone of the Great Mother—insisting that the Romans should all bathe in the light of the Sun. From Carthage he imported the worship of the goddess Tanit, the heavenly mother, and celebrated the marriage of Astarte and the sun god. The *pontifex maximus*, the ancient and lofty Roman religious office, was replaced by the high priest.

The stories told about Elagabalus' pleasures exceed everything told about Nero, and sometimes they resemble the tales concerning the caliph al-Rashid centuries later. His couches were made of solid silver; his chariots were studded with jewels and gold. He would only swim in a pool perfumed with saffron or other essences; he strewed showers of roses and other flowers over his banquet hall floors and walked in them. His banquets were sheer fantasies: on one day everything served was blue in color, the next day green, and on the following day iridescent. At dinners he was partial to tongues of peacocks and nightingales, and on one occasion had the heads of six hundred ostriches brought in so that their brains could be eaten. He delighted in playing pranks on his courtiers: the cushions on which they sat were first inflated, and at a sign the air was let out. When his guests became drunk he sometimes had them shut in for the night and then let in some of his tamed lions and bears to awaken them into a state of fright. He offered a prize to the servant who could bring him one thousand pounds of spider webs. Sometimes after dark he roamed the streets incognito, slipping gold coins into prostitutes' hands with the whisper, "It is a gift from the emperor"; sometimes he appeared in public in his chariot drawn by four huge stages.

The man was evidently mad. Within a few years, Rome wearied of his outrageous presence, and he was murdered in a latrine and thrown into the Tiber. Yet he left a legacy: within a few decades the worship of the Sun became the official religion of the empire.

A respite from perversity or madness occurred when another boy emperor, Elagabalus' adopted son Alexander Severus, came to the throne in A.D. 222, at the age of thirteen, but there was no restoration of objective government. First under the thumb of his mother as regent and then of the military whose support he needed, Alexander Severus was an honest, well-intentioned, yet vacillating person in a time that cried out for manly leadership. Simple in tastes, well schooled, deeply religious in an eclectic fashion, he is said to have kept in his private shrines images of Abraham, Apollonius of Tyana, Orpheus, and Jesus, along with busts of Vergil and Cicero. The great Roman jurist Ulpian, his close friend and dinner companion, saw in him an excellent administrator of the laws. Learned in Greek philosophy and Roman poetry, he reminded some men of Marcus Aurelius. Yet he remained the prisoner of his armies, by now the outright opponents of the propertied classes, and was committed to more exactions, more requisitions, more forced service, more debasement of currency and consequent inflation, to sustain the tottering empire.

It was his misfortune to be the contemporary of Ardashir, founder of the skillful dynasty of Sassanid rulers of the Middle East who revived Persia from its long decline. Out of the disorder of the Parthian empire—the far-flung and incohesive tribal area south and southeast of the Black Sea—there emerged a vigorous neo-Persia, reminiscent of the time of Darius and Xerxes, and it promptly made war on the Syrian possessions of Rome. Alexander Severus, like Caracalla before him, attempted to model himself on Alexander the Great, "without," as he explained, "imitating him in drunkenness." But in a series of campaigns the new Alexander only demonstrated what everyone already knew: he was an excellent soldier, but he was no Alexander the Great.

His wars against the Persians were indecisive, ending in stalemate, but in order to fight them he was compelled to withdraw troops from the frontiers in Germany, and soon he was hurrying across Europe to halt a threatened German invasion. Somewhere in Germany, perhaps in Mainz, one of his soldiers entered his tent while he was sleeping. The emperor awoke and said: "Comrade, have you brought news of the enemy?" The soldier had come to steal and fearing punishment he called to his companions for help. A moment later the emperor was stabbed to death.

In the chaotic half-century following Alexander Severus' death, in A.D. 235, the distinction between a legitimate emperor and a usurper was all but to disappear. The rise and assassination of emperors of either kind became the order of the day: two reigned for only a month, three for a year, six for just two years. Alexander's successor was a rough Thracian peasant named Maximinus, of phenomenal height and physical prowess, but without other talents. Proclaimed emperor by his soldiers at Mainz, he never went through the formality of asking to be recognized by the Senate and never so much as appeared in Rome. Sometimes there were two simultaneous emperors or would-be emperors, each backed by his own military party, or by a senatorial party. There was no Augustus, no Trajan to command the loyalty of the army as a whole and keep dilution, division, and corruption in check.

Feared as they were, the soldier-emperors of this time were evidently expendable. A popular song concerning Maximinus preserved by the historian Julius Capitolinus suggests that the people were perfectly aware that emperors could be overthrown without too much expenditure of energy:

> *He who cannot be killed by one is killed by many,*
> *The elephant is a large beast, but he can be killed,*
> *The lion is strong, and he can be killed,*
> *The tiger is strong, and he can be killed,*
> *Beware of the many, if you fear not one alone.*

We are told that Maximinus was present when the song was sung on stage in Greek. He understood none of it, and when he asked why the people were cheering, he was told that the clown on the stage was merely reciting some old verses against violent men. He seemed content and relapsed into his customary uncomprehending stare. A mutiny did away with him after three years of rule.

Emperors came and disappeared so speedily that people in the farther provinces often did not know who was in power at a given time, and moreover did not care. In Gaul and Egypt, men scarcely concerned themselves with Rome. Roman order, language, and law had been imposed on them, and the somewhat questionable benefits of Roman citizenship had been extended to them, but with the decline in central leadership, local loyalties grew stronger, presaging the division of the empire into its component parts. In the provinces the Roman administrative machinery went on with decreasing reference to the incumbent in the capital, and office holders were drawn more and more from the provincial populace. The provincial armies themselves were now composed largely of local peasants or mercenaries. Emperors' agents could and often did spread political terror through even the outermost areas; but they could not be everywhere at once, and the violence of power battles in Rome sometimes contrasted strangely with the peaceful quality of life beyond the Alps or the Adriatic.

The social and political fabric of the empire was so weakened as to offer opportunities for outsiders to attack the most vulnerable points. Legions were stationed to stand guard along a European frontier, which ran from the mouth of the Rhine, across southern Germany, down the Danube to the Black Sea. In the best of times this had been a difficult line to hold intact; it could readily be breached by determined tribes. Many of the tribesmen—Goths, Alamanni, and those who were to become known as Franks—were skilled frontier fighters, with intimate knowledge of the terrain, and many, having taken service at one time or another with Rome's armies, were well acquainted with the strengths and weaknesses of the Romans.

Thus in the third decade of the third century A.D. the far-flung barriers of an ill-tended empire began to cave in. The Goths, a Germanic people who had moved southward from Sweden and had established a strong state on the Russian plains, took to harrying and raiding Roman frontiers along the Danube, in the Balkans, and in the Black Sea area as well. The Alamanni, a Suebic tribe reared in the forests and flatlands of eastern Germany, had collided with Caracalla's forces in A.D. 213, and in the 230's they were making inroads into the Rhine valley, Gaul, and Italy. The Vandals, also of Germanic origin, had moved into the Hungarian plains, where they were developing a craft of armed riding that was to make their mailed cavalry the scourge of Europe. The Franks—meaning "freemen"—were not a tribe unto themselves, but rather a combination of tribesmen of Germanic origin, growing in their threat as they massed along the Rhine. In the middle of the third century A.D. the Franks broke through the *limes*, or fortified borders, and streamed across Gaul and over the Pyrenees into Spain; they looked to Mauretania, in North Africa, as their next goal.

In this time of folk wandering and tribal assaults, the Middle East also continued on its course of disaffection from Rome. Forces of Goths sailed across the Black Sea to attack Roman outposts in Bithynia, on its southern shore, and no fleet could be mustered to stop them, so far had Rome's naval power declined.

Meanwhile, in the century's third decade, the new stir in the

eastern Parthian empire, always inimical to Rome, set its Persian people on an aggressive course that was to lead to efforts
to make common cause with the roaming Goths against Rome's
dwindling majesty. Thrusts by tall, blue-eyed, flaxen-haired
northerners and lithe, dark-complexioned easterners—men of
wholly contrasting racial and cultural backgrounds—were to
occur with growing frequency. Against this gathering threat,
following an abortive campaign against the reviving Persians by
Alexander Severus, Rome put into the field another boy
emperor, Gordian III, who was acclaimed in A.D. 238 at about the
age of thirteen. In 242 he set out for the East to subdue the Persians and fought valiantly against the Sassanid ruler Shapur I,
recovering Antioch and Carrhae. In 244 he was dead—killed at
the orders of a palace cabal led by a military official of Arab
birth who was known by the Greek name of Philippus, or
Philip.

Gordian had been a rare figure. The historian Julius Capitolinus describes him as a lighthearted, handsome, amiable
youth, versed in letters and loved by the Senate, the army, and
the people as no prince had been loved before. A Persian triumph was decreed for him, but he did not live to enjoy it. Philip
the Arab, who had reached the rank of Praetorian prefect, is
reported to have diverted supply trains from the young emperor
and intrigued with the soldiery for his downfall. This was
almost the lowest point of military Rome, an empire now split
among factions and armies, ruled by generals, boy emperors,
and usurpers, with senatorial and military classes in opposition
and disarray, its borders broken, credit undermined, corruption
rampant, and no man strong enough for the moment to hold off
dissolution and decay. Pirates swarmed across the Aegean;
tribes from the Sahara pillaged imperial cities along the North
African coast; soon Persians were to overwhelm Syria and there

to capture a Roman emperor, Valerian, leading him about in captive bonds.

Great defenders and rebuilders of Rome were still to come, and a line of emperors of east European origin was to succor it; but after the debacle of these decades, the glory of the early empire was never to be recaptured.

XI

THE LONG TWILIGHT

The fall and ruin of the world will soon take place, but it seems that nothing of the kind is to be feared as long as the city of Rome stands intact. But when the capital of the world has fallen . . . who can doubt that the end will have come for the affairs of men and for the whole world? It is that city which sustains all things.

—Lactantius, *The Divine Institutions*

The year A.D. 248 saw a great festival in Rome, celebrated with pomp, majestic rites, and games. It had been a thousand years from the time, according to tradition, that the city was founded, and the Romans gathered to honor their millennium. In that time they had accomplished unprecedented feats of growth and survival. Despite all the strife and misfortunes of the preceding century, their capital city stood at the peak of imperial grandeur, vastly enriched since the time of Caesar and Augustus with palaces, baths, gardens, monuments, theatres, thoroughfares, and the looming Colosseum. Despite political and social upheavals, many institutions had survived: the Roman Forum was still the center of daily politics, trade, and administration of law; the hereditary Senate still went through its motions of debate; temples were still thronged with adherents of the state religion. The idea of an eternal nation had deeply entered the Roman mind: on the coins of the boy emperor Gordian, minted not long before the anniversary, stood the words AETERNITAS AUGUSTI. Yet everywhere there were signs of change—and no single one was more significant, perhaps, than that the emperor who presided over the celebration was an Arab chieftain's son who had taken a Christian wife.

Rome had Romanized the world, yet it had lost much of its old identity as non-Romans swarmed in to dilute it. The capital had become the greatest melting pot of antiquity, peopled with swarthy Arabs and Syrians, olive-skinned Berbers, fair-haired Gauls, bearded Dacians from beyond the Danube, and long-haired Scythians from remote regions of southern Russia who congregated in the streets, where the emperor—an Arab like Philip or an Illyrian like his successor Decius—passed in state. Greek merchants were everywhere, and the tonsured priests of Isis, in their immaculate white robes, were seen along with Jewish followers of Christ. So many races crowded into Rome that one might have been hard put to find a Roman face in a given assembly.

As Rome became more mixed it also became more divided. Senators holding military commands sometimes sought the throne for themselves, in opposition to generals raised in the provinces. The imperial bureaucracy, increasingly militarized, became, like the armies themselves, increasingly composed of foreign elements. To strengthen their structure of rule, emperors resorted heavily to the device of requiring members of local aristocracies to act, in effect, as agents of the throne in their communities. Such leading citizens, who were known as *curiales*, were obliged to take on unpaid duties of collecting taxes and cultivating state land; and although such responsibilities could be borne by the rich, they became extremely burdensome on those who were not and who had to sell out and sink to a lower class in the event that they could not meet their obligation. The result was more hostility between classes and more uncertainty in relations between the metropolis and the provinces.

Groups of businessmen—such as shipowners and suppliers of

vital products—had been brought together into trade associations and assured of government contracts and profits in exchange for required services. But the demands of a financially and politically unstable state made these benefits increasingly questionable. In the second half of the century many men evidently wanted to leave these associations or corporations; this we know because under the soldier-emperors a process began of requiring them and their heirs to remain within and to put up their landed property as surety for their performance. Such a scheme (a prototype, it has been remarked, for the "corporative state" to be set up on the same parent soil by Mussolini) was a major departure from the older Roman encouragement of independent, private ventures.

Always there were the vast armies posted along the frontiers. They were made greater in importance both by the multiplying barbarian incursions and by their own proven ability to raise their generals to the imperial throne. The logistics of defense had demanded that the frontier armies be recruited locally; every army saw itself as a kingmaker, entitled to the *donativa* that traditionally accompanied the march on Rome and the elevation of a new ruler. The center of Rome's power lay at the mercy of the circumference. Between A.D. 235 and 260, in a time of almost constant civil wars, there were twelve emperors; by 284 another four had come to power. In the West under the emperor Gallienus, a governor of Gaul named Postumus set up a regional empire of his own, with headquarters at Augusta Treverorum, complete with a senate, a bureaucracy, and several mints; and for over a decade Gaul and to some extent Britain and Spain were ruled not from Rome, but by a usurper from the banks of the Moselle. In the East, a noble named Odenathus, of the Syrian frontier city of Palmyra, proclaimed himself an independent king, and several years later his remarkable widow Zenobia managed to seize not only Syria and most of Asia Minor but Egypt as well, where she briefly established an openly rebellious regime.

Meanwhile the rapid spread of individual conversions to Christianity was causing mounting concern in Rome. Except for brief outbursts of persecution, emperors in the second century A.D. had been inclined toward a policy of toleration: the Christians were only one of many sects worshiping their strange gods here and there in the empire and seemed to pose no danger to the state. But by the middle of the third century the new faith was making serious inroads among the upper classes no less than the lower, bringing with it the specter of wide disaffection. The refusal of Christians to join, even for form's sake, in the loyalty ceremonies of the state religion was thought damaging to public morale. The obloquy that fervid Christian converts poured upon the traditional gods of Rome—often dismissing them not only as false gods but as evil demons—seemed highly impious and a grave offense against propriety. There were many citizens in capital and countryside, shaken by continuing civil wars, mounting barbarian invasions, general disorder, and by a plague, who felt that the old gods were angered at Rome and were intent on bringing disaster down upon it. Put down the offending Christians and the curse might be lifted.

They were put down, only to increase in stature and presence by their courage under persecution. Eventually emperors would see in the Christians a creative rather than just another disruptive force in the state. But before that, strong rulers had to arise to seek to reconstitute the all but sundered empire. An Aurelian or a Diocletian was needed to prepare the way for Constantine. That Rome, with its diluted blood, its disasters, and its declining authority, was still able to provide such men was testimony to its traditions and its stamina.

Marcus Julius Philippus, or Philip the Arab as he was called, ruled from the year A.D. 244 to 249 and was a figure of brief promise in a time of decay. Rising from the post of provincial military commander, like many of his predecessors, he appears to have impressed Romans with his fine-drawn features and his bearing like that of an Arab aristocrat of the desert. (The fact of his marriage to a Christian, coupled with stories of his lack of interest in the pagan rites that marked the millennial exercises of A.D. 248, was to cause Christian commentators to argue that he was, in fact, the first Christian emperor of Rome—a claim not otherwise supported.) We know little about his mind or motives other than that he appears to have been a man who acted with firmness and dispatch amid danger. When Goths came streaming into and across the Balkans he appointed his favorite general Decius, a native of Pannonia, north of the Adriatic, to lead a Danubian army against them. It is said that the two men were friends of long standing and that Decius questioned whether he was the right man to lead the expedition, for he was popular with the army, and the frontier troops might do what they had done before: they might offer him the empire, and then, instead of fighting the Goths, they might march on Rome. Yet Philip took the risk and sent his popular general against the invaders—and soon afterward Philip himself died in battle at Verona, perhaps betrayed by Decius, who thereupon became emperor.

Coming to the throne a few months before mid-century, Decius was the first of a line of Illyrian rulers of little culture but of soldierly vigor, and under the best of them Rome's house was gradually restored to order. Though connected on his mother's side with an old Italian family, he was himself of provincial peasant background. He had a peasant's heavy, commonplace features, but his mind moved with shrewdness and clarity. In part a stranger to Rome and its traditions, he nevertheless set out to restore the older ways of the empire in the interest of its survival. He recognized the damage done by the unbridled military and felt that the civil authority must be upheld at all costs. Thus he set up a special financial office with broad civic powers, reminiscent of that of censor, and assigned it to a certain Valerian, a senator who had risen to become *senatus princeps*. Moreover, Decius was determined to compel the loyalty of all inhabitants to the state and its religion, and he took the occasion of a general sacrifice and libation to the gods in every village and city of the empire as the means of achieving this. All persons were required by decree to participate in the sacrifices and to procure from special boards of inspection certificates testifying that they had obeyed the order and that they had also made such sacrifices in the past. Those who disobeyed the order were subject to penalties leading up to that of death. Under such proscription and the use of torture the bravest of Christians still refused to forsake their convictions.

Finally, in Decius' design for order, there had to be war to the death against the Goths, those formidable invaders who were breaking down Danubian frontiers and threatening Rome's great military roads to Greece and the Near East. He himself led his legions against them, blunting their power, only to die in battle.

Before the revival that Decius sought was to come, perhaps the lowest point of Roman cohesion and prestige was reached under his successor Valerian, who found the problems confronting him all but insuperable. Barbarians on almost all the frontiers attacked simultaneously, as if by a concerted plan. Goths poured into Dacia, overran the Balkan peninsula, and plundered Roman outposts along the Black Sea's southern shore; the Alamanni appeared in force on the Po plain; in A.D. 253, the first year of Valerian's reign, Franks surged across Gaul and into Spain. So beset, the elderly emperor decided to divide rule of the empire, his son Gallienus taking charge in the West while he himself commanded the threatened East. Apart from its admission of weakness at the center, this move was an indication—more were shortly to come—of the degree to which emperors saw Rome's center of gravity moving eastward. The Persian threat was constantly growing; Palmyra was breaking away. Meanwhile the prevalence of plague in Italy was decimating the Roman population.

While making his division, though, Valerian continued to follow a policy of general attack on the Christians throughout the empire. Many had bowed to Decius' decree and paid their respects to the old Roman gods. This was not enough: they were now to be made to abjure their faith under penalty of having their goods confiscated, their places of worship shut, and their priests deported if they did not recant. The new persecutions lasted only a short time, however, for in A.D. 260, when leading an expedition against the Persian ruler Shapur I, Valerian fell into a military trap and was captured. For the first time a Roman emperor was forced to kneel in abject surrender to a foreign king. The Persians relished and exploited this humiliation, and their artists depicted him in the attitude of a man pleading for his life. "Through all his remaining years," says the historian Orosius, "Valerian was compelled to perform the menial service of helping the king to mount his horse, not in the usual way, by giving his hand, but by bending to the ground and offering his back." After so many Roman triumphs, this was exquisite retribution.

Under the rule of Valerian's son Gallienus, the fate of both the Christians and the empire itself changed for the better. In place of persecution, Christians were accorded an edict of toleration. A conservative man of intellect, who wrote poetry and liked to have philosophers around him, Gallienus felt that the best way of meeting the Christian incursion was not by making martyrs but by reinvigorating the cultural pursuits and values of pagan Rome. He befriended the thinker Plotinus, possibly an Egyptian by birth and distinctly Greek in schooling, who had

come to Rome to teach a philosophy derived distantly from
Plato's. Plotinus had gathered many followers about him as he
set forth his doctrine that the search for truth or reality behind
appearance would lead, step by step, toward a recognition of a
spiritual "One" beyond all physical things, and to communion
with that supreme force. Such a teaching, with its emphasis on
quest and mystical union, exerted great challenge in a jaded
and sundered society; it embodied perhaps something of the
same impulse that had made many Romans and provincials
turn to Christ.

At one time Gallienus lent support to a scheme of Plotinus'
to found a Platonic community on the site of a ruined
Pythagorean settlement in the Campania. Perhaps as an
instance of his desire to fuse the best of Roman and Greek traditions, he had himself elected an archon of Athens—a once-
powerful office that survived only as a local ceremonial one,
but the very name of which conjured up memories of Athenian
greatness. His interest appears to have been centered on peace
at home and abroad: Gibbon writes that Gallienus married a
daughter of one of the Germanic tribal chiefs as a means of
achieving it, and other chroniclers record that he married a
Christian woman and that he had coins struck bearing the
inscription UBIQUE PAX.

There was, however, little peace in his reign, which ended in
A.D. 268. Would-be usurpers arose on every hand to threaten his
power; he managed to put down no less than eighteen. All the
peoples along the frontiers were in revolt. Under Germanic
pressure he had to evacuate part of Gaul, but by wise concentration of forces he saved Italy from being overrun. In A.D. 267
he won a major victory over the Goths in his ancestral Illyria,
but was killed shortly thereafter by his own staff, possibly at
the instigation of one of his generals, the Illyrian Claudius, who
succeeded him.

If Gallienus had an intellectual temperament, Claudius was the pure soldier whose only aim was to reach out at the enemy's throat. He fought the Alamanni at Garda Lake and then marched into the Balkans to rout a horde of Gothic and related invaders, some three hundred twenty thousand of whom, with their women and children, had poured over the frontier, not only to conquer but to settle. He crushed them in Serbia after writing to the Senate a letter in which he described the odds against him: "If I conquer, your gratitude will be the reward of my services. If I fail, remember that I am the successor of Gallienus. The whole state is exhausted and worn to the bone. We lack javelins, spears, and shields. We shall perform greatly." Claudius, who took the title of Gothicus after his victory, spoke in accents reminiscent of the consuls of the ancient republic. Hardheaded and single-minded, he not only routed the Goths but eliminated them as a serious threat to the empire for more than a hundred years.

His successor, Aurelian, was to call himself *restitutor orbis*, meaning that he had restored the empire. But the claim could be made more properly of Claudius, who in his brief three years of rule before his tragic death by the plague in 270 had perhaps saved Rome from extinction.

Still, despite the defeat of the Goths, Rome remained vulnerable. Aurelian saw that only a determined and continuing policy of containment could stem the flood. He had to withdraw his far-flung forces to the near, or the south, side of the Danube, but on the other hand he stood off an incursion by Alamanni and others in the Po plains and recovered the lost areas of Gaul. In the East Queen Zenobia had carved out for herself an empire that extended from her capital, in Palmyra, into Egypt; Aurelian had conquered her armies and led her through the streets of Rome. Chroniclers report that there had never been such a dazzling triumphal procession in Roman

memory: the queen walked in golden chains before the triumphator's chariot, and there was also a chariot led by the
royal stags captured from the king of the Goths. Such spectacles were rare in those days when the fear of invasion had led
the Romans to build new walls around their city.

Save for Gallienus, almost all the generals who succeeded
one another on the throne were men of remarkably similar
stamp. As we see them on their coins, they might be thought of
as being brothers. There is little nobility in those heavy, determined, rather sullen faces; they were men of the camp, with
hard features and set jaws, lean and often hungry. Few of them
possessed personal magnetism; they were harsh disciplinarians
who treated their soldiers like cattle, and were in turn brutally
disposed of.

Aurelian was murdered; so was Probus, his best and most
loyal general, who came to the throne after the brief reign of an
elderly senator, Tacitus, who claimed to be descended from the
historian of that name. Probus was another Illyrian, hardy and
well built, with a talent for strategy and a quality of ruthless
determination. Yet his coins and a portrait bust show him to be
another rare exception, a man of sensitivity. He went so far as
to speak of a time when there would be no more need for soldiers. "Soon perhaps," he said, "the barbarians will be driven
back and there will be no need for an army. There will be
no more requisitions in the provinces, no demands for
compulsory payments, and the Roman people will possess unfailing revenues. There will be no camps, no
sound of trumpets, no fashioning of armaments, and the
people will be free to follow the plow and do their own work,
learn their own crafts, and sail the seas."

There were few emperors who dreamed of so idyllic a future,
but there is little doubt that he was reflecting the common
hopes and longings of many of his people. The idea of univer-

sal peace, which had haunted the Romans since the days of Numa, was revived during the last years of the third century, becoming all the more appealing the more distant it seemed to be. Probus, however, was fortunate. A brief period of peace descended on Italy during his short reign—the quietest in the later history of the empire.

Everything we know about him suggests he was a man who might have been a great emperor had he lived long enough. He treated the senators with respect, permitting them to retain the rights granted them by Augustus. He treated the soldiers without severity and preferred to see them performing useful work rather than fighting. He was on his way to Persia at the head of his army when he decided to stop at his native city of Sirmium, in the Balkans, and he set his soldiers to draining the marshes and building a canal. There, while overseeing their work, he was assaulted by some soldiers opposed to doing it, and was killed. Afterward the army built an enormous tumulus to him and carved on it an inscription testifying to its respect: "Here lies the emperor Probus, a man of probity, conqueror of all the barbarian nations, and victor over tyrants." Such a man illuminated a dark age. Of few emperors would so much be said in so few words.

Two years later in A.D. 284, there came to the throne a man who seemed to many to be a reincarnation of the great Caesars. The origins of Diocletian are obscure; all that is known is that he was a Dalmatian, and it was said that his father was a freedman bearing the Greek name Diokles. His rise, like that of his predecessors, was due to his military skills, and when he was acclaimed emperor by his troops at Nicomedia, near the Bosporus, there were perhaps few people in Rome who expected him to survive for more than a short time before a new mutiny or palace revolution overtook him in the familiar fashion. However, he accomplished the extraordinary feat of staying safely on the throne for twenty-one years and then retiring at his own volition to relax in the splendid palace he had built for himself in his Dalmatian homeland.

In this, as in all the other elements of his rule, Diocletian was a highly original person. He was the most absolute of monarchs. He surrounded himself with the aura of the representative on earth of Jupiter Optimus Maximus and required (according to the historian Aurelius Victor) that persons appearing in his presence afford him the obeisance, or *adoratio,* due to a god. On the other hand, aware of the difficulties of one-man rule of the empire, he appointed a favorite soldier-in-arms, Maximian, as co-emperor to rule in the West, while he himself ruled in the East, moving his headquarters to Nicomedia and only rarely visiting Rome.

Although virtually dividing the empire, he was no less great an administrator than an innovator. In A.D. 301 he published his edict concerning maximum prices and wages that was intended to put an end to the spiraling increase in the cost of living. At the same time he reformed the coinage and introduced a fixed relationship between the worth of the coin and its metal content. He established a new system of taxation, uniform for all the provinces and based on the value of the land, and saw to it that the tax gatherers produced correct accounts. By reorganizing the financial basis of the empire he put an end to the financial anarchy that had been sapping the energies of the people.

He did much else: he reorganized the army and the bureaucracy, abolished the secret police, dealt with revolts in Britain and Egypt, and defeated the Persians and brought the upper Tigris valley under Roman rule. Even so, there was no escaping the necessity of the empire's division. Constitutionally, when he gave his co-ruler Maximian the title of augustus in A.D. 286, he endowed him with powers equal to his own—though in practice he retained a right of veto as senior augustus. Soon he decided that not even two rulers were sufficient to deal with the complex problems of the empire, and arranged the appointment of two further men who were to serve in effect as deputy co-emperors with the title of caesar—Constantius Chlorus in the West and Galerius in the East. Both these men, vested with dignity and authority, were to conduct major military operations; and as lieutenants of their respective chiefs, they were designated eventually to succeed them—an ingenious way of solving the perennial Roman problem of succession. Together, the four men constituted what became known as the tetrarchy, an order of governance unknown before or since.

Amid these innovations Diocletian returned to another problem, namely that of the Christian presence, which he attacked in the spirit of Valerian rather than of Gallienus and with utter ruthlessness. What is known as the Great Persecution now began. Lactantius, a teacher of Latin at Nicomedia, who had become a convert to Christianity, was to recount in a tract called *De mortibus persecutorum (On the Deaths of the Persecutors)* his own version of the cause of the new assault upon believers. According to him, Diocletian was performing a sacrifice before the state gods when he observed that some of the attendants were making the sign of the cross, thereby counteracting the influence of the pagan deities and in effect canceling out the supplications and prayers offered by the emperor. In the eyes of Diocletian an act of desecration had been committed by people whom he regarded as atheists. In a state of high excitement he discussed the wanton behavior of the Christians with his deputy Galerius, and it probably was Galerius who goaded him into suppressing them.

It is more likely that Diocletian's action, far from being a fit of imperial temper, represented cold-blooded policy. Conversions had been increasing; Christian basilicas were flourishing in many cities; the imperial court itself was peopled with votaries of the new faith. A rapid series of edicts, beginning in February, A.D. 303, therefore undertook to root out the infection totally. The first ordered all copies of the Scriptures surrendered and burned and the churches destroyed; all meetings of Christians were forbidden. Next the Christians were deprived of all civil rights, including that of holding any public office. Regardless of their social rank, they could be submitted to torture after trial; Christian slaves were not to be liberated. In further edicts, setting up a progressive scale of punishments, Christian priests and then Christian laymen were to be executed unless they recanted and worshiped state gods.

In A.D. 305, a year after promulgating his last and sternest edict, and at the height of his power at the age of sixty, Diocletian abruptly abdicated and spent the rest of his days gardening the grounds of his vast palace in Dalmatia, leaving his lieutenant Galerius in full command of the empire in the East. At the same time his old and faithful friend Maximian also retired in the West, leaving his deputy Constantius Chlorus in command. Galerius, a skillful soldier, though lacking Diocletian's spacious quality of command, followed his predecessor's footsteps and also persecuted Christians with unabated vigor. Constantius, on the other hand, now the junior emperor after Maximian's retirement in the West, left them alone. He was a highly efficient ruler, who had been admired as a military leader ever since he had put down a rebellion in Britain in A.D. 296, rescuing Londinium (London) with such dispatch that a gold medallion was struck hailing him as the REDDITOR LUCIS AETERNAE—restorer of the eternal light of Rome. His extraordinary pallor won him the cognomen of Chlorus, or the "pale one." His later fame was to rest on the fact that he sired, either with his wife or with his concubine, the man who was to become known as Constantine the Great.

Diocletian had been a man with a prodigious passion for

Diocletian's plan for sound rule and orderly succession was based on dividing the realm into eastern and western portions, each ruled by an emperor or augustus, with a deputy or caesar under him who was to become his heir. The four men together formed a tetrarchy: shown above are the augusti Diocletian and Maximian, with their respective caesars, who were their sons-in-law, Constantius of the West and Galerius of the East.

building. The baths he constructed in Rome cover over thirty acres. The fortress palace he ordered for himself and hundreds of his retainers on the Dalmatian coast remains to this day a major, though ruined, monument to an emperor's leisure. Venetian conquerors embellished it, streets were to be built through it, and where the Roman emperor worshiped his gods, Christians erected their own churches out of the stone he had imported. When he retired he seems to have believed that he had built so firm an architecture of government that there would be no more civil wars, that the caesars or deputies would automatically acquire power on the deaths of the emperors, and that an ample bureaucracy would resolve all the problems confronting the peace and security of the empire. He could not have been more mistaken. When Constantius Chlorus died in the British city of Eboracum in A.D. 306, the succession in the West was thrown into disorder. The younger Constantine, distinguished like his father for his soldierly and human qualities, was promptly proclaimed emperor by the troops in Britain. Meanwhile a son of Maximian named Maxentius, who had been passed over in the naming of heirs, was living as a private citizen in Rome. There a mass of Praetorians, riding a wave of popular unrest over the capital's diminishing prestige in the imperial system and the imposition of heavy taxes, proclaimed Maxentius caesar, with rights to the throne. Both these proclamations were in effect acts of usurpation since under Diocletian's system the eastern emperor Galerius as senior augustus held the right of appointment in the West as well as in the East. Galerius had gone so far in accommodation as to recognize young Constantine as a caesar in the West, but not as augustus; to that higher rank he elevated one of his own lieutenants, Severus. But he could not brook the rival upstart Maxentius—a threat to the whole order especially since Maxentius' father, the elderly Maximian, had come out of retirement to support his son's cause. Severus was ordered to march against Maxentius, only to be captured at Ravenna. Maximian, playing a crafty game, journeyed to Gaul to make an alliance with Constantine by giving him his daughter in marriage and independently bestowing upon him the title of augustus in exchange for which the new son-in-law was to recognize Maxentius as augustus also.

In this gathering storm, with the fate of the empire at stake, Galerius called a conference of Rome's senior statesmen at Carnuntum, on the Danube, in A.D. 308. Diocletian came out of retirement to attend it, but refused the suggestion that he himself return to the helm. Maximian, on the other hand, was asked to relinquish his new bid for power, which he refused to do. With no less than six augusti now holding claims in the East and the West, Galerius tried to resolve the disorder by asking that another of his lieutenants, Licinius, a Dacian peasant who had risen to high military rank, be accepted as lawful emperor in the West. Young Constantine was urged to abandon the acclamation given him by his troops and to place himself as a caesar under the authority of Licinius. Constantine, who had kept his troops in training against Franks and Germans, bided his time.

His chance came soon. In 310 the aging Maximian seized Massilia, but Constantine's opposition is thought to have led Maximian to suicide. In the next year Galerius died. Licinius hurried to consolidate control of the western areas while another lieutenant of the late emperor Galerius, Maximinus Daza, set out to organize the East. Between them stood Maxentius, augustus at Rome. Constantine saw his opportunity.

In his twenties Constantine had served under Diocletian in Egypt and under Galerius against the Persians. In A.D. 306 he had been posted to Britain to assist his father against the Scots. Vigorous, handsome, square-jawed, with eyes remarkable for their leonine brightness, he was a commanding presence at thirty-two when his father died. He also had unusual patience and a sense of the proper moment to strike. His mind was fired with high ambitions—not only to win the West but ultimately the East as well, where Rome's greatest resources lay. Amid all the contests of empire, he soon identified Maxentius as his chief rival for mastery, and when in sure command of Gaul, prepared carefully for a march on Rome. His campaign of A.D. 312 was a masterpiece of speed and dispatch; it has been likened to Napoleon's first Italian campaign. Maxentius' numerically superior forces were destroyed little by little at Turin, at Verona, and then at the Mulvian Bridge, outside Rome, leaving the young conqueror master of the West.

Among the matters discussed at the Carnuntum conference of A.D. 308 may have been that of the religion that should now govern the state. The cult of Mithra had become a favorite of the soldiers, and there is evidence that a temple was restored by the emperors assembled on the Danube in honor of Mithra, protector of the empire (*fautoriimperii sui*). Worship of an eastern god had long been established in polytheistic Rome, and worship of a savior was not to be arrested. When Constantine took up arms against his foe Maxentius he appears to have felt the need of the protection of the strongest god of all—and for reasons that can only be surmised, he found this in the Christian god as against a pagan one. He was—at least this is how he recounted it to the historian Eusebius—overtaken by a vision in the form of a cross in the sky, and a command that he go into battle under that sign. Whatever the source of his guidance, his troops put down Maxentius with the sign of Christ's cross on their shields.

The event was to have vast consequences. Victory was now coupled with Christianity in the eyes of the western empire—a recognition highly welcomed in the far more Christianized eastern half. A merging of spiritual influences emanating from the East with the tribal vigor of the West seemed in prospect. And so it was to be. For the better part of a decade Constantine was to rule the West in an uneasy relationship with Licinius, who had become Galerius' successor in the East. When Licinius wrongheadedly resumed persecution of Christians, Constantine overthrew him in A.D. 324, and thus fulfilled his ambition: he had resolved centuries of conflict between East and West, old faiths and new, and reunited the empire under one hand.

XII

ROME BECOMES CHRISTIAN

Against the advice of the augurs, in spite of his military counsellors, unsupported by the troops of Licinius, with incredible audacity Constantine had risked everything on a single hazard—and won. How shall that success be explained? Constantine himself knew well the reason for his victory: it had been won instinctu divinitatis, *by a* virtus *which was no mere human valor, but was a mysterious force which had its origin in God . . . Victory had been promised him by the God of the Christians; he had challenged the Christian God to an Ordeal by Battle and that God had kept his pledge.*

—Lactantius, *On the Deaths of the Persecutors*

The character of Constantine, who was to leave so vast an imprint on the history of the West, remains an enigma. The brute facts of his reign, his journeys and battles and laws, are extensively recorded, and his physical appearance has been brilliantly rendered in statues and on coins; but we do not know the workings of his mind. He was to make great decisions that would change the course of history, but we can only guess why he made them. With a mysterious logic of his own he brings down the curtain on hallowed Roman traditions of antiquity, and when at last the curtain rises again, a new Rome has appeared nearly a thousand miles to the east, and an entirely new cycle of history has begun.

The two greatest achievements of Constantine were so vast in their scope that they give the impression of being carefully planned and pondered over for many years. But as Constantine

The bust of Constantine the Great, above, is thought to be originally from a statue of the emperor sitting in the manner of Jupiter. The head alone stands at eight feet tall, indicating a sense of Imperial majesty, reinforced by the unrealistically large eyes that gaze with intensity.

himself made clear, both of them came about as the result of dreams or visions. He compelled his army to adopt the sign of Christianity after he had seen a vision of a flaming cross, and he chose Byzantium as the new capital of his empire. Yet he was not by nature a visionary; he was a man of intense practicality.

The battle at the Mulvian Bridge, at which Constantine won his empire, was not one of those battles that at the time seemed to have decisive importance. Both Maxentius and Constantine were usurpers, possessing no legal or justifiable claim to the throne, and it might be expected that in the course of time both of them would have vanished before the superior forces of the imperial armies. But Constantine managed to hold on to his power. He was to claim that he won the battle and reached the throne because the Christian God had protected him; his enemies, with greater logic, might have claimed that the battle was won by default or through the malice of the god who presided over the Tiber. When Maxentius was retreating across the Mulvian Bridge with part of the army he was forced into the river and drowned, and his army was thrown into a panic. By an accident Rome fell to Constantine.

This victory over Maxentius confirmed his devotion to Christianity. But to speak of the conversion of Constantine is to misunderstand the quality of his mind. He did not immediately try to impose the Christian faith on his subjects. He continued to celebrate pagan festivals, minted coins in honor of Apollo, Hercules, Mars, and Jupiter, and even after his conversion, presented himself on coins wearing the spiked crown of *sol invictus*, the unconquered Sun. He was tolerant of all religions, and as Augustus had, he showed a special predilection for Apollo. He attached great importance to the externals of religious conduct and insisted that all services should be conducted with propriety, for he liked his religious to have clear contours and well-defined lines of command. When necessary he would himself enter as umpire and supreme religious authority, even though he had little understanding of the philosophical subtleties his bishops were arguing about. He believed that it was an emperor's right and duty to lay down all laws, even the laws of religion.

How deeply Constantine believed in the tenets of Christianity is a question that has puzzled historians, as it may very well have puzzled Constantine himself. His complex mind appears to have been capable of believing simultaneously in the Christian God and the entire pagan tradition. He acknowledged a *summus deus*, a supreme god who ordered and commanded the entire universe, but beyond this he apparently was not prepared to go, though he would pay lip service to Christ or to the unconquered Sun whom his father had worshiped. Toward the end of his life he caused to be erected, near the Colosseum, a magnificent triumphal arch in his honor, bearing an inscription testifying that all his victories were the result of the inspiration of the divine—*instinctu divinitatis*. Perhaps he was paying tribute to his own divinity or to all divinities. Certainly the ambiguous phrase does not reveal a special preference for the Christian God.

Constantine was not, after all, so deeply interested in religion; what interested him almost to the exclusion of everything else was the exploration of power, and he realized very early that toleration was itself a form of power. In a remarkable series of edicts he displayed a genuinely humane attitude toward the poor and the oppressed. He did not, of course, abolish slavery, but he made certain that slaves were given every opportunity to prove their right to freedom; a master who dealt brutally with a slave would have to answer for it; the families of slaves on an imperial estate were to be kept together even if the estate was sold. We hear of laws protecting peasants who fell into debt, and others protecting children from brutal or avaricious parents. Prisoners in jail, he decreed, must not be harshly treated, rather they must be given exercise and light; and callous jailers were to be severely punished. Condemned prisoners were not compelled to become gladiators.

The growing influence of Christianity had brought a greater emphasis on mercy and fair dealing. Sometimes the laws betray a Christian origin, as when the emperor issued an edict against the branding of criminals on the face, since the face is created "in the likeness of divine beauty," or when he abolished cruci- fixion or protested against gladiatorial displays, describing them as "bloody spectacles displeasing in a time of peace and quiet." Again, when he ordered that parents who exposed their children should be forever disbarred from claiming any rights over them, he was following the lead of the Church Fathers, who viewed the abandonment of children as a crime against God. Christian influence is evident, too, in Constantine's procla- mation of a special day in the week when factories, shops, and law courts would be closed, even though the day of rest was to be called the venerable day of the Sun. The laws of Constantine consistently demonstrate a high degree of social consciousness and decency. He was one of the few Roman emperors who seems genuinely to have desired peace and to have hated bloodshed.

Constantine's efforts to establish peace and a stable govern- ment brought changes in the administration as well as in the law. He tightened imperial control over the lives of his subjects through taxation and through the enforcement of the edicts that bound people to their work. It was almost impossible for any peasant to leave the farm on which he was born, or for any worker to obtain a job different from that of his father's. These rules were harsh, but they were designed to maintain stability in every sector of society. He invited vigorous German tribes- men to settle uncultivated lands within the empire's bound- aries, welcomed them into the army and the civil service, and encouraged their advancement into positions of responsibility.

He confiscated the treasures of pagan temples and summoned an ecumenical council of the Christian Church—the first to take place.

To increase his control over his subjects, Constantine surrounded himself with an aura of divinity. Of course, he could not, as a Christian, claim to be a god. Nevertheless his new religion gave the emperor the opportunity to announce that he was "ordained by God to oversee whatever is external to the Church"—a statement that was to have awesome consequences in the Middle Ages when emperors and popes struggled for supremacy.

Yet Constantine also established a foundation for the papacy's claims to temporal power when he gave the rights and duties of magistrates to all the bishops in his empire. Many of the bishops carefully searched their consciences before they agreed to accept the post, for Christian tradition, centuries old, looked on the state and all of its work as being corrupt. But finally, with gratitude, they assented to the change and regarded it as a sign of the new era that was dawning.

With astonishing clarity Constantine saw that the fulcrum of imperial power lay in the East and that the time had come to reinvigorate the empire by building an entirely new capital there. Already Diocletian had realized that, on strategic grounds, the empire required a capital nearer to the border where Europe met Asia. Diocletian chose Nicomedia. Constantine, however, decided against Nicomedia, and after toying with the idea of rebuilding ancient Troy, he finally chose the old Greek fishing port of Byzantium, the junction of all the roads between Asia and the West. There on May 11, 330, in the presence of high ecclesiastical officials, the city of New Rome was formally inaugurated with great pomp. Christian commentators, who carefully noted the presence of the Churchmen, appear to have glossed over the fact that the ceremony was also pagan and modeled on the legendary inauguration of Rome by Romulus.

With the founding of the new capital, old Rome lost its aura of power; it was drained of its nobility, its craftsmen, and its soldiers, who found a more prosperous outlet for their energies in Constantine's city, which was at first named New Rome, but which came to be called Constantinople after the ceremonies in 330. In its beginning New Rome was largely populated by Romans, and Latin was the language heard at court as well as in the market place. The laws were written in Latin, and so they continued to be for more than two centuries. New Rome fed on the old until it had taken all it could; and then it drank at the inexhaustible wells of Greek culture, and also became Greek.

At its founding the city had been dedicated to the Trinity and to the Virgin Mary, for Constantine's encouragement of Christianity went hand in hand with his establishment of a new capital. Both were designed to strengthen and unify the empire. Both, however, proved in the end to be divisive forces. The new capital took some of the glory away from Rome, but not all; and in the century after its foundation, the vast and unwieldy empire tended to divide more and more into eastern and western halves.

Christianity, too, failed to unify Constantine's domain. Even before he brought the new religion to dominance, the Church had been plagued with dissension, and its divisions often fell along social as well as doctrinal lines. In North Africa, one religious squabble aligned the old Berber and Punic elements in a bitter struggle against the Roman colonists. About the year 318 a more serious controversy erupted in Egypt, splitting the entire Church into factions that opposed each other in the political as well as the religious sphere.

The argument—over the nature of Christ—aroused the passions not only of theologians but of the workers and artisans of Alexandria as well, men who followed the philosophical con-

troversy with as much enthusiasm as some men devote to athletic contests. To resolve the differences between the two parties—the Arians, who claimed that Christ must have originated
after God and was not equal to Him, and their opponents, who
believed that Christ was coeternal with God—the First Ecumenical Council was called at Nicaea in 325 to settle all disputes.
There the doctrine of the Trinity was formulated. Although
greater unity was thus achieved, a few Arians refused to accept
the concept, and the Church and empire remained divided over
the question until the year 381 when the emperor Theodosius
the Great made heresy a crime.

In that same year Theodosius made paganism a crime too. It
had enjoyed a brief revival under the sponsorship of the
emperor Julian—called the Apostate—who had acceded to the
throne in the year 361. Julian had studied at the ancient university of Athens, where he developed a profound reverence for
the ideals that had inspired classical society. Some of his teachers, pagan philosophers, were attempting to combat the inroads
of Christianity by developing ethical rationalizations for the old
pagan ceremonies. Many of them were Neoplatonists, followers
of the philosopher Plotinus, who encouraged men to see all the
gods as aspects of one great God and to seek union with Him.

When Julian came to the throne he tried to establish a
pagan church throughout the empire, with bishops, priests, and
most important, ethics like those of Christianity; but paganism
was unable to compete with the vigorous new faith. A few
years after Julian's death paganism itself was moribund. The
ancient temples were abandoned or transformed into market
halls, and their estates and revenues were requisitioned by their
priests or by local magnates for their own benefit. Everywhere
citizens converted to Christianity and left behind the cults of
their ancestors. Athens and the Peloponnesus and Rome itself,
where the ancient senatorial families proudly guarded their

heritage, remained bastions of paganism; but as time went on they became more and more isolated. Most significant of all, during the reign of Gratian (375–383) the statue of Victoria, before which sacrifices had been offered since the days of Augustus, was removed from its prominent position in the Senate house in Rome.

Ironically, that happened at a time when Rome desperately needed the favor of the goddess Victoria, for the age of major barbarian invasions had begun. For centuries German tribes had been pressing relentlessly along the northern frontiers of the empire. From time to time they were massacred or driven back; when they became too strong they were appeased with generous grants of land; when they became stronger still they were permitted to enter the Roman army. In a strict sense they were not really barbarians. They had their own cultures, their own traditions in the arts, in commerce, and in warfare, and many of them were even Christians. Once they became Roman mercenaries they were in a position to defy the emperor, for they guarded the frontiers, and when rival elements were struggling for the throne these tribal mercenaries often held the balance of power.

Although the West finally succumbed to them, the East suffered the first successful incursion. Toward the end of the fourth century the most powerful of the barbarian tribes were the Goths, who had probably originated in southern Sweden and in the second century had moved into the Baltic region. They then traveled across Europe and western Asia until they came to settle peacefully in what is now Rumania, Hungary, and southern Russia. One of the Gothic tribes known as the Visigoths had settled in Transylvania. They spoke a pure and primitive Teutonic, and the majority of them embraced Arian Christianity with the passion of converts. They wore their flaxen hair long, and they dressed in skins, but their towns and cities were halfway civilized. They might have remained there indefinitely, trading with Constantinople and acting as frontier mercenaries if it had not been for the sudden, massive attack by marauding Huns from central Asia. These wild Mongolian people were to remain the scourge of Europe for centuries to come. Merciless, devoid of any sense of law, they destroyed for the sake of destruction, and they proved to be masters of the art of raiding.

About 370 a Hunnish invasion of the Gothic kingdoms forced the Visigoths to appeal to Constantinople for shelter, and they were permitted to settle south of the Danube in the region of Lower Moesia. Some eighty thousand of them crossed the Danube, only to find that the Roman officials treated them unjustly and with contempt. Goaded into action, in 378 they marched against the imperial army. In a narrow valley near Adrianople the mailed cavalry of the Goths hacked the army of the eastern emperor Valens to pieces. The emperor was pierced by an arrow and died. It was a second Cannae.

Seventeen years later, in 395, under their newly chosen warleader Alaric, whose name means "all powerful," they began to sack the empire as the Huns had ravaged their own land. Alaric struck at Thessaly, marched down the eastern coast of Greece, battered at the walls of Athens, crossed into the Peloponnesus; Corinth, Argos, and Sparta all fell before him. Nothing could stop him, and Arcadius, the eastern Roman emperor, fearing that the whole empire might fall to the Goths, tried to buy him off, rewarding him with high honors and surrendering large areas of Illyria for him to rule as an imperial viceroy. Alaric, standing between East and West, was now in a position to attack one or the other at his leisure. In 400 he decided to attack Italy and to carve out for the Visigoths a settlement on Italian soil.

Like many of his successors, he regarded Rome as the most desirable of conquests, its capture being the crown of his military career. The church historian Socrates Scholasticus tells the story of a monk who came to Alaric's royal tent and begged him to stop plundering the towns and villages of Italy. "There is something within me which every day urges me irresistibly forward," said Alaric. "It says to me, 'Go to Rome and make that city desolate.' " At last in 408, after two abortive sieges in 401 and 402, Alaric had Rome at his mercy, the city ringed by his troops and the people starving. When ambassadors came to plead for clemency he answered grimly that he would not raise the siege until they offered him all their gold, silver, movable property, and slaves. "And what will you leave us?" the ambassadors asked. "Your lives," Alaric answered, and he was as good as his word.

But in 410, one of the imperial legions broke the truce agreed to after the ransom, and Alaric moved to lay waste the city. The Visigoths sacked Rome with a quiet fury that was all the more terrible because it was so calm and methodical. There was looting, and Saint Augustine also tells of slaughter and rape and arson, but apparently the Visigoths committed far fewer atrocities than other ancient conquerors had before them. A terrified people watched the wealth of the city heaped up in the carts of the barbarians. They were only three or four days in the city, but they swept it clean. Not since the destruction of Rome by the Gauls, eight hundred years earlier, had the city known a conqueror.

Tertullian, in the second century, had believed that Rome would last as long as the world, enduring until the Day of Judgment. A special sanctity was attached to the inviolate city. But Alaric had proved that it was a city like any other, only too vulnerable. In far-off Bethlehem, Saint Jerome lamented: "The entire human race is implicated in the catastrophe. My voice is choked, and my words are broken with sobs while I write: The city now is taken that once held the world." *Capitur urbs quae totum cepit orbem*—those last words read like a funeral inscription for an empire. Saint Augustine viewed the capture of Rome with horror, but also with Christian detachment. He found some consolation in the thought that Rome—an essentially pagan city—had richly deserved its fate. "The City of God endureth for ever," he wrote, "though the greatest city on earth is fallen. . . ."

Meanwhile, other German tribes were striking at the vulnerable western provinces. For centuries, for as long as the Romans themselves had been in Gaul, Germans had been making forays into the land. But now their invasions were no longer turned back. In the year 406, marauding bands of Vandals, Alans, and Sueves marched through Gaul and devastated it. Three years later the Vandals pushed into Spain and wrested the peninsula from the Romans. Nominally Spain was still a part of the empire, but the barbarians controlled it completely, for in 411 they negotiated a treaty with the Roman emperor Honorius that put them in charge of defending the peninsula. Later in the century Britain was lost to invading Saxons and Visigoths established a kingdom in Gaul, centered about the town of Tolosa. The Vandals moved on into North Africa, and they were succeeded in Spain by the Sueves, whose earlier domain in Gaul was in turn taken over by the Franks. Province after province was claimed and reclaimed by the barbarians, and the imperial city itself had fallen; the greatness of Rome was no more.

Attila the Hun, the most ruthless of barbarian invaders, who destroyed for the joy of destruction, was persuaded partly by his own fears not to harm Rome. In 452 he destroyed the great city of Aquileia, in northern Italy; its citizens fled to the lagoons to found a new and safer town—Venice. He intended to attack Rome, but his army was racked with disease, and Alaric's death, shortly after the sack of the city by the Goths in 410, had filled the barbarians with superstitious horror. When Pope Leo I came to him to ask his leniency, therefore, Attila was ready to grant it. Attila turned back and Rome was saved. Three years later, in 455, Leo confronted Gaiseric, the Vandal, whose armies were camped outside the walls. Once again the pope was able to save Rome from destruction. Gaiseric wanted plunder, and this was given to him on condition that there would be no rape, no murder, no firing of houses, churches, and ancient palaces. For fourteen days he was permitted to strip the city of its valuables, even the precious vessels in the churches, although it was stipulated that the three most sacred basilicas were to be left unharmed. Gaiseric kept his bargain and sailed to Africa with the greatest treasure ever accumulated in Europe up to that time. For Leo it was pure victory; he had exchanged the gold tiles of the temple of Jupiter on the Capitoline and all the baubles of pagan Rome for a Christian peace.

Again and again the barbarians struck at the city in search of the loot that had escaped their predecessors. In 472 Ricimer, a Suevian, besieged and sacked Rome. He was followed four years later by Odoacer, a son of one of Attila's generals. He proclaimed himself king of Italy, independent of Romulus Augustulus, the puppet emperor of the West who had been appointed by the Roman emperor in Constantinople, and then abandoned the city of Ravenna, which could be more easily defended than Rome. The chroniclers of the time paid very little attention to Odoacer; he was merely one more of the usurpers who rose to power and vanished after stamping his features and his name on coins. Romulus was a fourteen-year-old boy. He was charming, and when Odoacer deposed him and was on the point of killing him, the usurper decided that nothing was to be gained by murdering a defenseless child. The last of the western emperors, therefore, was granted a pension by a barbarian king and ordered to spend the rest of his life with his relatives in a luxurious villa near Naples. Nothing more was ever heard of the boy, whose name combined the names of the first Roman king and the first Roman emperor.

"The western Roman empire, which started with Augustus, finished with Augustulus," wrote the chronicler Marcellinus. But in essence the western Roman empire had perished long before, dying when Constantine transferred the capital to Byzantium. After Odoacer, invading chieftains fought for power and looted and burned the city; Italy began to split into its many principalities, which were not to be reunited until the nineteenth century. But the civilizing mission of Rome did continue through the agency of the Church—especially through the monasteries, which grew in usefulness and importance during the years of the barbaric invasions when men turned in relief from war to contemplation. These monasteries preserved the manuscripts of ancient Rome and Greece, many of which have come down to us only because the monks copied them. Meanwhile, the Church grew in power and authority, for no other voice spoke so clearly in the dark ages. A few years after Romulus Augustulus vanished into obscurity, Pope Gelasius formulated the "doctrine of the two powers," which maintained that the Church should be independent of the imperial power. But when Pope Gelasius spoke, temporal power was all but gone from Rome: the empire that once had radiated from antiquity's greatest city had vanished.

What caused this breakdown of Roman power—a power that had held the world in thrall for centuries? It is tempting to search for an answer, but of course no one really knows. The great eighteenth-century historian Edward Gibbon claimed that one of the reasons was that Christianity had sapped the vigor of the Roman people. Other scholars attribute the decline and fall of the empire to the plagues, which frequently ravaged the Mediterranean world in the fourth century. Still others assert that the economy of the empire became so disorganized that its collapse was inevitable. Today's scholars are less inclined than those of the past were to explain away such a complex historical process as the empire's fall with a glib generalization. They admit quite frankly that they do not know the reasons and that they can only guess at them; and they go on to study the age's history in terms of continuity as well as in terms of change.

For although the Celtic and Roman population that inhabited Gaul, Britain, and Spain was severely tried by the atrocities of the barbarian invasions, in many ways society was not vastly different from the way it had been when imperial power was still unchallenged. True, the towns were decaying, the peasants were little more than serfs, brigandage was rife, corruption was widespread, taxes were burdensome, and the service that the taxes brought was minimal, but this had been so for a century before the sack of Rome by the Visigoths. Long after the emperor had lost all effective power in the West, most of the inhabitants—Roman and barbarian—of these lands, still considered him their overlord. The idea of Roman domination had not died and would not die until more than a thousand years later.

For the barbarians who hammered at its gates, the city of Rome itself presented problems that almost defied solution. It could be conquered easily; it could be destroyed as the Gauls had destroyed it long ago. But what were the advantages of conquering it or putting it to flames? Powerless, it was still powerful—with the power of legends and of traditions and of the knowledge of government. The ruined city was still teaching law to the world, and with law went civilization, order, the quiet pursuit of trade, the flourishing of arts. Eventually the barbarians were to one degree or another to come under the spell of Rome.

The Roman empire had had many virtues and many vices; it deployed its enormous strength for good and evil alike. Never

before had such vast regimented power been visited on the
earth; never before—and never again until modern times—had
so many lands been conquered and subjected to the commands
of a single government. Power was used wantonly and peace
came rarely. But in those intervals of peace the human spirit
flowered, magnificent buildings arose, great poems were written, and the slow march of civilization was continued. Even
those who had reason to hate that empire built up over the centuries by the Romans also were forced to find virtue in it. When
Saint Augustine wrote *De civitate dei* (*The City of God*) he cata-
logued the evils committed by Rome, and yet he offered the city
a supreme tribute: "Between the city in which it has been promised that we shall reign and the earthly city there is a great gulf
as wide as the distance between heaven and earth. Yet . . . there
is a faint shadowy resemblance between the Roman empire and
the heavenly city."

XIII

A SPACIOUS LEGACY

Alas! the lofty city! and, alas
The trebly hundred triumphs! and the day
When Brutus made the dagger's edge surpass
The Conqueror's sword in bearing fame away!
Alas, for Tully's voice, and Vergil's lay,
And Livy's pictured page!—but these shall be
Her resurrection; all beside—decay.
Alas, for Earth, for never shall we see
That brightness in her eye she bore when Rome was Free!

           —Byron, *Childe Harold's Pilgrimage*

The Roman empire perished and went on living. Long after the capital had become a small town outside the frontiers of the Byzantine empire and long after the last Roman legionary marched down the Flaminian Way, its civilization held sway in the West. The legacy of this most worldly of empires was to lie largely in the realm of ideas—in law, language, literature, government, attitudes, and styles. In innumerable ways, as century followed century, men's minds were to respond to a presence that was shorn of all the panoply of power while gradually becoming transfigured into a dominion of the spirit and of thought.

The legacy was a mixed one, inextricably compounded of Greek influence on Rome and Rome's original contributions. What we call Roman civilization was very largely a Greco-Roman civilization; but it was Rome that gave it the endurance that enabled it to survive down through the centuries. The

Romans were great borrowers, great adapters, and great trans-
mitters. In later ages men learned the Greek legends and studied
Greek philosophy through the writings of Roman authors, and
they saw Greek sculpture through the eyes of copyists working
to the Roman taste. Even in decline and defeat, Rome had the
remarkable power of assimilating other peoples. Its barbarian
invaders at first thought to stay aloof from the fallen conquerors, but they soon fell under the spell of a culture so much
richer than their own. When the Lombards swept through Italy
and intermarried with local citizens they were soon adopting
the Latin tongue in their inscriptions and incorporating some
principles of Roman law in their tribal code.

The Roman scheme of universality was shattered by the
breakup of the empire; yet the concept was to survive in a new
form—that of a Christian commonwealth in which state and
Church were united. When Constantine founded his new capital
in the ancient seaport of Byzantium he took with him the power
of the Roman name and the faith in the divine mission; and
Constantinople was "the second Rome." To the very end the
Byzantine emperors regarded themselves as Romans: not
merely as the inheritors or imitators, but as Romans in fact, and
by descent, and by renown. They employed the word *Rome* as
though there had been no sea change. Rome was eternal, but it
was also portable. These emperors, moreover, were also heads
of the Church. But since their temporal reach was limited by the
barbarian incursions and disorders in the West, there arose in
Rome—the old Rome—a line of Christian bishops who exercised
virtually independent spiritual leadership there, although they
recognized the authority of the distant emperor. Eventually
what could be called a working partnership came into being
between the presiding bishop or pope of Rome and his suzerain,
the head of state beside the Bosporus.

The Roman empire seen from the new capital at Constantinople differed in many ways from the empire of the Caesars. It was not only that Rome was uprooted and transplanted to the borders of Asia, subject to all the winds that blow across the Black Sea, from Asia Minor and Persia and the coasts of Palestine, but the orientalizing influence was now firmly established, and it was precisely this influence that Rome had combatted through all the centuries of its growth and power. The new Rome was an oriental city.

To Augustus Caesar it would have seemed the strangest of all fates that there should come into existence a city that called itself Rome, inhabited by Greeks, ruled by an emperor and by governing officials who spoke in Latin and pronounced their edicts in Latin, dedicated to a divinity born during his lifetime in Judaea, borrowing openhandedly the luxuries and sometimes the ceremonies of the Persians, once the hereditary enemies of Rome. It would have surprised him that these people and their emperors would have regarded themselves as genuine Romans, and the would have been still more surprised to discover that the new Roman empire, founded on so many fictions, would produce a tolerable and workable civilization.

As the years passed the eastern and western empires gradually drifted apart; Constantinople surrendered to the luxuries and dialectics of the East. The Byzantine emperors cultivated splendor as it had perhaps never been cultivated before. They appeared in public in jeweled garments, their gestures were minutely studied, and they almost vanished beneath the weight of their panoply. They were gods walking the earth, remote and inaccessible, moving in that breath-taking splendor that was the mark of their divinity. Their palaces were plated in gold, they sat beneath gold crowns suspended from the ceiling, and sometimes they concealed themselves behind jeweled curtains. By the time of Justinian the Byzantine court had surrendered to almost unimaginable luxury. The great palaces on the Bosporus

*A sixth-century Ravenna mosaic, above, depicts Justinian and his court;
in Byzantium, Christianity burst into flower.*

shimmered like the Christian churches with brilliant mosaics,
and the Roman emperor moved like a ghost appareled in
majesty. He was no longer merely the emperor. He was the king
of kings, the vicar of Christ, the giver of all blessings, the
divinely appointed one. The distance between the ruler and his
subjects, always great, now became so great that they seemed
to live in different worlds.

To this eastern realm Rome left a legacy of imperial organization if not order, and in the sixth century the glittering
emperor Justinian emerged in Constantinople as a man imbued
with the old Roman sense of grandeur and an impulse to revive
Rome's lost greatness. A major lawgiver, codifier of laws, and
builder of churches and palaces, he succeeded in reconquering
North Africa and parts of Italy, bringing them back into allegiance to Constantinople. But his triumphs, accompanied by

the squandering of vast sums on his palaces and fawning bureaucracy, proved to be short-lived. Later Byzantine emperors imitated his conquests, driving across Asia Minor, Syria, and Egypt, showing the panoply of their power in the deserts of the Negeb and on the borders of Persia, but about all their conquests there was an air of impermanence. The Arab invasions of the seventh century made them withdraw gradually toward the center, and thereafter the imperial pretensions grew wider as their power weakened. Finally, in 1453, after eleven centuries of grandeur, Constantinople fell to the Turks.

To the West, Rome left a legacy of quite another order; it was passed in the first instance through the Church, which inherited much of Rome's talent, character, and learning. The early Church had been the foe of the pagan Roman state; gradually it was to become the preserver and adapter of much of what had been best in it. Justinian's triumphs against the Goths in Italy only left the state in complete disorder: after 541 there were no more consuls in Rome, the Senate withered away, and only the prefect of the city, *praefectus urbis*, remained to testify to the ancient traditions of the capital.

Out of the storm of the Gothic wars there emerged one strong western power—the papacy. In the hands of Pope Gregory I, himself a former *praefectus urbis*, the office began to exert strong influence. A monkish priest who never learned Greek, though he spent many years on an embassy to Constantinople, he seemed to symbolize the ancient Roman virtues, and by the singular force of his personality he was able to bring some order to a ruined land. He believed in old wives' tales, relished mysteries, wrote a vivid and interminable commentary on the Book of Job, and pronounced himself to be the arbiter of Roman destinies.

At first he held very little power, for the papal states reached scarcely farther than Naples. But in time Italy was to become dappled with territories owing allegiance to the papacy; and the kings of Europe would find compelling reasons to accept the doctrine that all spiritual power was vested in the pope and that earthly power should receive the sanction of the spiritual. When Charlemagne permitted himself to be crowned by Pope Leo III on Christmas Day, 800, he was under no illusions that any rights had been conferred on him. Nevertheless the coronation laid the foundations for the Holy Roman Empire. For many centuries kings would struggle for possession of that crown and the title, which gave them the inheritance to an empire that had long perished. German and Norman kings would try to wrest that crown by force, seeing themselves as the divinely appointed successors of Augustus. Not until the time of Napoleon was the dream of the divine Roman empire ultimately abandoned.

What happened was that the Church had gradually acquired many qualities of the old imperial order. The Roman genius for organization, along with the Roman sense of hierarchy, had given shape to Church institutions. The Roman political imagination, which had once brought so many peoples into one orbit, had lent strength to the idea of a Church universal. Roman jurisprudence had become the basis of canon law. The Church, which had begun by being an enemy of Rome, became the chief stronghold and preserver of the ancient Roman traditions.

The Latin language—that stern, hard, and metallic language that was finally hammered into shape during the last years of the republic—continued to be spoken in western Europe, carrying with it the ideas and concepts that were to become an integral part of the culture of Italy and France, and to a lesser extent of England and Spain. There was no break. The Romance languages which grew out of ancient Latin, developed slowly and almost imperceptibly, with the result that it is quite impossible to determine when Italian, Spanish, French, Portuguese, and Rumanian came into existence. They arose not from the elegant phrases of Cicero but from the language of the camp, which tended to be happily insulting and convivial, with no pretensions to dignity. So the French word *tête*, "head" derives from the Latin *testa*, "pot," and *jambe*, "leg," derives from *gamba*, "fetlock"; *cheval* and *caballo* come not from the regular Latin *equus*, "horse," but from the horseman's *caballus*, "nag." In adapting Latin to their own use, the French showed a genius for softening a language that was essentially hard and masculine. The Latin *lux*, "light," becomes *luz* in Spanish and *luce* in Italian, and was wholly transformed by the French into the tender and feminine *lumière*. A new resilience had entered common speech; the hard outlines became blurred; the words lost the monumental, graven quality, which was the delight of Roman orators, who spoke as though they were reading inscriptions carved in stone.

The Latin of the Church was a subtle and intricate rendering of classical Latin. In that amazing fourth century when Saint Jerome and Saint Augustine were inventing new words to describe Christian ideas, ecclesiastical Latin took shape. Saint Jerome's translation of the Bible, completed at last in 405, became the accepted version of the scriptures in the West; and in Saint Augustine's prose we find Latin quivering with an excitement it never possessed before. The hymns of Ambrose, written with a quiet perfection, reflect the classical temper. And sometimes Saint Gregory the Great would find himself rebuking his priests for reading so deeply in classical authors.

Greek philosophy survived in Latin, even though knowledge of Greek had nearly disappeared in the West. Boethius, a scholar at the court of the Ostrogothic king Theodoric at Ravenna, translated Aristotle into Latin and wrote commen-

taries on Greek philosophy, music, and mathematics. Shortly
before he was executed on a charge of treason he wrote *De
Consolatione Philosophiae (On the Consolation of Philosophy)*—
a work in which he sought to recall Platonic, Stoic, and
Vergilian ideas to Christian society. King Alfred translated the
work into Anglo-Saxon.

In the Middle Ages men almost seemed to breathe in Latin.
If it was not the language of trade, it was the language of
nearly everything else. Roman themes continued to influence
the western imagination. One of the most popular medieval
romances, the *Roman de Troie*, by Benoît de Sainte-Maure,
recounts the conflict of Greeks and Trojans, evidently derived
from a Latin original. Troubadours and courtiers of love drew
widely on ancient Roman episodes of passion: Héloïse and
Abelard, the most philosophical of medieval lovers, quoted
Ovid to each other in their letters in Latin. The spirit of Vergil
hovered over the *Divine Comedy*, written in colloquial Italian.
(Even after Dante had completed the work, there were intelligent men like Dante's friend Giovanni del Virgilio who
regarded it as a waste of time to write poetry in the vernacular
and asked him to write an epic on the contemporary great conquerors in Latin, "the language common to us all." Dante
replied in a Latin poem, regretting his inability to write a Latin
epic, and offered his friend ten cantos of the *Paradiso* as proof
that there was some merit in the vernacular.)

Petrarch drew on Livy; Chaucer on Ovid at his most boister-
ous. The English playwrights Kyd, Marlowe, Jonson, and
Shakespeare drew on the brutalities of Seneca; Shakespeare
read deeply in Plutarch. The example of Plautus helped re-
establish social comedy and farce; Lucan's rodomontade passed
into Spanish epic; the oratory of Cicero was transformed into
English political prose. Rough comedy, satire, lyric poetry,
essay, oratory, drama, epic—all those forms admired by Romans

passed in adaptations to the West. The wit of Cervantes and the rhetoric of Milton both derived from Rome. The cult of antiquity never died out. Charlemagne in the ninth century ordered his scribes to copy ancient manuscripts to preserve them for posterity; the copyists succeeded so well that we can trace most of the surviving Latin manuscripts to the scribes employed in his monasteries. Carolingian palaces were adorned with sculptures, marbles, silks, textiles, and mosaics removed from Rome and Ravenna, and his court poets modeled their verses on the classics. Architects in the eighth, ninth, and tenth centuries constructed great cathedrals in the style known as Romanesque, because it was once thought to be a grotesque deformation of Roman architecture. In fact it derived straight from Rome.

Although the heritage of Rome had survived, it had done so really only at the whim of emperors and popes—by the sheerest chance. Monasteries were sacked, treasuries were emptied, old buildings were torn down to provide stones. And although the Carolingians were the first to make a conscious effort to imitate the ancient Roman forms, the scholars at the end of the fifteenth century made an even more determined effort to recover the treasures of the past. Petrarch himself discovered many lost letters of Cicero. The Florentine bibliophile Poggio Bracciolini scoured monastery libraries in search of ancient and forgotten manuscripts.

The unearthing of the Laocoön group of sculptures near the baths of Trajan in 506 revived the classical presence. So, too, did the discovery of the *Apollo Belvedere* a few years later. Both statues were promptly acquired by Pope Julius II. A passion for excavating, restoring, and imitating old sculpture arose; the young humanist, painter, and architect Raphael pleaded with Pope Leo X to halt the continuing despoliation of Roman edifices. The pope appointed the young man general superintendent or conservator of Roman antiquities, and there exists an unsigned letter, which appears to have been written by Raphael and Baldassare Castiglione, urging the pope to preserve the relics of ancient Rome:

> *Many people, Holy Father, when observing the great relics of Rome with its wonderful art, its wealth, and its ornaments, and the grandeur of the buildings, lamely judge them to be more fabulous than real. But with me it seemed, and still seems, otherwise for when I consider the many relics which are still to be seen in the ruins of Rome, and the divine gifts which dwelt in the men of ancient times, I think it not impossible that many things which seemed impossible to us seemed very easy to them. . . .*

So he wrote with fervor in a long letter that remains a classic account of a Renaissance man's devotion to antiquity. Raphael himself died too young to prevent the erosion of the city, but his influence spread throughout Italy, and soon we find the architects becoming increasingly immersed in studying Roman architecture. Palladio, Borromini, and Bramante became earnest students of the past. Bramante, the first architect of the new basilica of St. Peter's, planned to surmount it with a low dome, following the model of the Pantheon; his successor Michelangelo, more daring, undertook to raise the dome on a high support or drum—a brilliant adaptation of Roman example. When Wren was invited to rebuild St. Paul's Cathedral, in London, he wished to design it "after a good Roman manner," refusing to follow "the Gothic Rudeness of the old Design." The "good Roman manner" swept across Europe, with the result that the rather heavy, four-square forms of Roman temples were soon adapted to the needs of France and England. Although Renaissance builders adhered to a concise use of Roman motifs, the baroque designers, who followed them, rang exuberant changes on these, luxuriating in twisted columns, split pediments, and swirling volutes. The rococo fashion of the eighteenth century then carried these variations to such unbounded excess that the result was another upheaval of taste and a return to Rome in the form of the neoclassical style. Newer excavations, such as those at Pompeii, helped to influence and shape this movement, once again reviving, copying, and widely adapting the forms that had been popular during the time of the Caesars.

In the realm of civil engineering, Roman precepts and achievements survived the centuries because they were so practical and so durable. No pope or emperor thought of dismantling a Roman bridge or uprooting a Roman road; such structures outlasted the ages. Not until the introduction of the steel suspension cable and cantilever was a method found of bridging a river that improved on the old Roman masonry span. Not until the introduction of macadam as a road-surfacing material was there an appreciable improvement on the old Roman use of paving blocks. In France and Spain there are small Roman bridges still in use today; they support heavy buses and trucks, though once, two millennia ago, they supported only carts. Roman roads, with their heavy ballast, culverts, and embankments, underlie many a highway in the tourist's Italy today.

From the time of Machiavelli political historians have searched through Roman chronicles in their quest for the principles of political science. Since Roman history involved nearly every conceivable permutation and combination of forces that act on governments, students have sought to codify Roman history and to extract from it not only those principles that they desired to defend but also those that they desired to attack. Revolutionary republics would invoke the example of the

Roman republic, tyrannies would invoke the name of Caesar. To
the American and French revolutionaries all Roman history
seemed to converge on the brooding and remorseless figure of
Brutus, the champion of society that had overthrown dictatorship. They saw him as an incarnation of fury aroused to stamp
out the vestiges of authoritarian rule—the first free man. The
legend of Brutus haunted the Middle Ages; local rulers dreaded
his name, for he represented the libertarian strivings of the
spokesmen of common people.

Machiavelli believed that Rome attained its lasting place
among the nations not because it was favored by the gods or by
divine fortune, but because it practiced virtue. In his eyes and
in the eyes of many who followed him, the republic was the
embodiment of a golden age of frugality, honesty, simplicity,
and courage. Like Cincinnatus, the husbandman worked his
fields with his sword near at hand, prepared to defend the
republic to the death, quietly content with his few worldly possessions, with no desire for the blandishments of wealth. This
golden age was legendary, but the idea satisfied a human belief
that there must have been a time when tyrants were powerless
before the armed might of the people. The Renaissance philosopher Giordano Bruno commended the "magnanimity, justice,
and mercy" shown by the Romans under the republic, though the
pages of Livy testify to a remarkable absence of these virtues.

The American revolutionaries were steeped in Roman history and saw themselves as inheritors of the republican tradition. The delegations from the free American states that met in
Philadelphia in 1787 to achieve "a more perfect union"
included men of varying degrees of education; but nearly all of
them, being persons of standing and distinction in their communities, knew the classics by heart and were intimately familiar with the works of Caesar and Plutarch. The Federal
Convention debated bitterly and brilliantly the question of the

allocation of powers in the future United States, but there was never any doubt in its mind that there should be a select upper legislative house, patterned distantly on the Roman Senate, as well as a lower popular legislative house armed with the powers of the Roman assemblies.

The ultimate and most pervasive Roman legacy resides, of course, in Roman law—that vast accumulation of precepts and practices concerning the ordered relationships of man to fellow man, husband to wife, parent to child, injured to innocent, citizen to state, accused to magistrate, and finally, of state to state—on which so much of the western scheme of equality, justice, and fair dealing depends. The Romans possessed a particular gift of law—a sense of a world brought together by unbreakable bonds of rights and obligations. They thought of themselves as trustees of a legal contract, which they entered at birth and which was to be continued long after their death. Discipline, order, piety, instant obedience to commands—all these were merely different aspects of the law that guided and governed them.

The law had deep roots among the Romans, who were taught from childhood to respect it, obey it fully, and defend it with their lives. At a very early age children were taught the Twelve Tables, which were believed to have been compiled about 450 B.C. and which had been handed down little changed through the ages. Cicero in his boyhood had to learn them by heart. These laws were inscribed on wooden tablets, and the originals, or perhaps direct copies, survived well into the second century A.D. in the place reserved for them in the Forum.

The Twelve Tables were regarded with reverence, but they were not thought to possess divine sanction. In this they were fundamentally different from the Ten Commandments of the Jews. And though in earliest times Roman laws had been surrounded by an aura of mystery and had been administered by priests, there gradually emerged about the Twelve Tables a huge body of practical enactments devised and interpreted and then reinterpreted by a professional caste of laymen—the *jurispru-dentes* of Rome. Nearly a thousand years after the compilation of the Twelve Tables a supreme effort at codification appeared in the form of the *Corpus Juris Civilis* of the emperor Justinian. This monument of legal and historical study (in the course of which the Twelve Tables were restated) consisted of the *Code* in twelve books, the *Digest* in fifty, the *Institutes* in four, and a supplement of one hundred sixty new laws called the *Novels*. A Christian emperor in Byzantium gave final shape to the laws of Rome.

The three greatest gifts the Romans left to the world—their language, their traditions of republicanism, and their laws—all owed a major debt to Greece, for even the Roman language was influenced by Greek turns of phrase and ways of thought. The Greek genius for liberty and compromise sometimes took on Roman dress, and Greek philosophy entered into the mainstream of Roman thought. In law especially Greek ideas were prevalent, and when Cicero made his famous pronouncement on the nature of true law in the course of his essay *De republica*, he was following the Greek philosophers who asserted the existence of law arising from man's own soul and nature, and reigning supreme:

> *True law is right reason consonant with nature, pervading all things, constant, eternal. Its commands and prohibitions apply effectively to good men, and those influenced by them are evil. It is not lawful to alter this law, to derogate from it, or to repeal it. Nor can we possibly be absolved from this law, either by the Senate or by the Assembly. This law does not differ for Rome or for*

Athens, for the present and the future, for one unchang-
ing and eternal law shall be valid for all nations and for
all times; and so it becomes, as it were, the general mas-
ter and governor, the one God of all men, being itself its
own author, promulgator and enforcer.

As Cicero described this universal law, he was not of course describing Roman law as it was practiced in the courts. Nothing could have been more alien to the Roman spirit than the idea of an immutable code. He was saying that everyday laws should seek to approach the ideal of universal law and try justly to reflect it. This involved constant search and exploration. For all their veneration of ancient tablets, the Romans with their pragmatic sense realized that law should grow and respond to new situations and needs. "We are servants of the law in order that we may be free," Cicero remarked. This was another way of saying that self-subordination to basic principles, far from confining the human spirit, would enlarge it; and that the very respect for tradition and authority would heighten the stature of man and bring worth and responsibility to his own exercise of judgment.

Often the Romans failed to live up to this concept. Their official cult of unloved state gods often belied their critical intelligence. They produced no philosophers equal to those of Greece. Their ideals of *pietas, gravitas,* and *humanitas* were repeatedly despoiled, and in the later stages of the empire, fewer and fewer men stood up for them. Yet the idea of moral governance of men's actions never lost hold, even if Rome itself grossly violated it. The states of western Europe, all formed between A.D. 500 and 1200 under the tutelage of the Roman presence, picked and chose from it, but all remained indebted to the Roman idea of law as supreme over men and as penetrating into the remotest corners of their lives. When the framers of the United States Constitution erected what they termed "a government of laws, not men," they were in effect reasserting Rome's better self.

More lasting than Rome's victories, the vast edifice of Roman jurisprudence survives in the codes of many western nations, and the precedents and procedures established by men beside the Tiber more than two millennia ago are echoed today in the courthouses of western Europe and two Americas. The Roman genius for logic and order is with us yet. The architect poring over his drawing board, the bridgebuilder studying stresses, the attorney invoking high principles, all hark back to Roman ways; in countless ways we still live under the sign of the spacious mind of Rome.

A SELECTION OF BOOKS

Any exhaustive Roman bibliography would extend to epic length. The purpose of what follows is neither to list the works of ancient Roman authors nor to give a balanced summary of the literature about Rome subsequently produced by innumerable distinguished historians, commentators, and interpreters. All that is presented here is a group of studies, which the editors have found particularly valuable in their own pursuit of the subject.

Adkins, Leslie and Roy A. Adkins. *Handbook to Life in Ancient Rome*. New York: Oxford University Press, 1994.

Appian. *The Civil Wars*. Translated by John Carter. New York: Penguin Classics, 1996.

Birley, Anthony R. *Septimius Severus*. New York and London: Routledge, 1988.

Birley, Anthony. *Marcus Aurelius*. New Haven, Connecticut: Yale University Press, 1987.

Bonfante, Larissa. *Etruscan*. Berkeley: University of California Press, 1991.

Bunson, Matthew. *A Dictionary of the Roman Empire*. New York: Oxford University Press, 1991.

Cassius Dio, *Dio's Roman History, Vol. III (Books 36-40)*. Translated by E. F. Cary. 1916, New York: Penguin Classics, 1987.

Cassius Dio, *Dio's Roman History, Vol. IV (Books 41-45)*. Translated by E. F. Cary. 1914. New York: Penguin Classics, 1984.

Cassius Dio, *The Roman History: The Reign of Augustus*. Translated by Ian Scott-Kilvert, New York: Penguin Classics, 1987.

Casson, Lionel. *Ships and Seafaring in Ancient Times*. Arlington: Univeristy of Texas Press, 1994.

Cicero, *Selected Letters*. Translated by D. R. Shackleton Bailey, New York: Penguin Classics, 1986.

Cicero, *Selected Political Speeches*. Translated by Michael Grant, New York: Penguin Classics,1989.

Cicero, *Letters to Atticus, Vol. IV*. Translated by D. R. Shackleton Bailey, Cambridge: Harvard University Press, 1999.

Fox, Robin Lane. *Pagans and Christians*. New York: Harper & Row, 1987.

Gelzer, Matthias. *Caesar, Politician and Statesman*. Cambridge: Harvard University Press, 1968.

Grant, Michael. *A History of Rome*. New York: Charles Scribner's Sons, 1978.

Grant, Michael. *The Antonines*. New York: Routledge, 1996.

Grant, Michael. *The Etruscans*. New York: Charles Scribner's Sons, 1980.

Grant, Michael. *The Roman Emperors*. New York: Charles Scribner's Sons, 1985.

Gruen, Eich S. *The Last Generation of the Roman Republic*. Berkeley: University of California Press, 1974.

Lewis, Naphtali. *Life in Egypt under Roman Rule*. New York: Clarendon Press, 1983.

Le Bohec, Yann. *The Imperial Roman Army*. New York: Hippocrene Books, 1989.

Paterculus, Velleius. *History*. Translated by Frederick W. Shipley. 1924. Cambridge: Harvard University Press, 1998.

Pallottino, Massimo. *A History of Earliest Italy*. Ann Arbor: University of Michigan Press, 1991.

Plutarch. *Fall of the Roman Republic*. Translated by Rex Warner. 1958. New York: Penguin Classics, 1972.

Plutarch. *Makers of Rome*. Translated by Ian Scott-Kilvert, New York: Penguin Classics, 1965.

Salway, Peter, *A History of Roman Britain*. Cambridge: Oxford University Press, 1997.

Sallust. *The Jugurthine War/The Conspiracy of Catiline*. Translated by S. A. Handford, New York: Penguin Classics, 1963.

Scarre, Chris. *Chronicle of the Roman Emperors*. London: Thames and Hudson, 1995.

Scullard, H. H. *From the Gracchi to Nero*. 1988. New York: Routledge, 1996.

Spivey, Nigel. *Etruscan Art*. London: Thames & Hudson Ltd., 1997.

Syme, Ronale. *The Roman Revolution*. New York: Oxford University Press, 1956.

Veyne, Paul, ed. *A History of Private Life, Vol. I*. Cambridge: Harvard University Press, 1987.

Wacher, John. *The Roman Empire*. New York: Barnes & Noble Books, 1987.

Watson, G. R. *The Roman Soldier*. Ithaca: Cornell University Press, 1969.

AUTHOR:

ROBERT PAYNE has written many highly praised and popular books on historical topics, including *The Gold of Troy, Alexander the God, The Roman Triumph,* and *The Isles of Greece.*

CONTRIBUTORS:

RORY O'NEILL and EDEN GREIG MUIR, both professors at the Graduate School of Architecture at Columbia University, are the founders of Cybersites, Inc., a New York city-based developer of interactive online communities. They also developed *S.P.Q.R.*, a CD-ROM game set in ancient Rome, from which the computer-generated images included in this book have been selected.

BERNARD FISHER, Ph.D., Fellow, American Academy in Rome; Professor of Classics at UCLA, and VASILY RUDICH, Ph.D., a Blegen Research Fellow and Visiting Professor of Classics at Vassar College, were historical and archaeological consultants on these images. Dr. Rudich provided additional consultation on the captions.

JOHN ALTEMUELLER and SUZANNE CROSS write for the web site AncientVine.com.

www.AncientVine.com—one of the many web sites Cybersites, Inc. has developed— is an online community that encourages scholars, students, and history fans to read and write about the ancient world. The site provides a discussion board, chat rooms, historical games, recommended homepages, and articles written by members of the site.